THE THEFT
(*Il Furto*)

Italica Press
Renaissance and Modern Plays Series

Guidubaldo Bonarelli, *Phyllis of Scyros*. Edited and translated by Nicolas J. Perella.

Massimo Bontempelli, *Watching the Moon and Other Plays*. Translated, with an Introduction, by Patricia Gaborik.

Annibal Caro, *The Scruffy Scoundrels (Gli Straccioni)*. A new dual-language edition by Donald Beecher & Massimo Ciavolella.

Intronati of Siena, *The Deceived (Gl'Ingannati)*. A new dual-language edition by Donald Beecher & Massimo Ciavolella.

Luigi Pirandello, *Henry IV*. A new translation by Martha Witt and Mary Ann Frese Witt. Introduction by Mary Ann Frese Witt.

Luigi Pirandello, *Six Characters in Search of an Author*. A new translation by Martha Witt and Mary Ann Frese Witt. Introduction by Mary Ann Frese Witt.

Torquato Tasso, *Aminta*. Translated and edited by Charles Jernigan & Irene Marchegiani Jones

Francesco D'Ambra

THE THEFT
(*Il Furto*)

With *Intermedi* by
Ugolino Martelli & Francesco Corteccia

Edited and Translated by
Vanni Bramanti
Linda L. Carroll
Anthony M. Cummings
Alexander Dean

Italica Press
New York & Bristol
2025

LIBRARY OF CONGRESS CATALOGING-IN-PUBLICATION DATA

Names: Ambra, Francesco d', 1499-1558, author. | Martelli, Ugolino, 1519-1592, author. | Corteccia, Francesco, 1502-1571, author. | Bramanti, Vanni, editor, translator. | Carroll, Linda L., editor, translator. | Cummings, Anthony M., editor, translator. | Dean, Alexander, editor, translator.
Title: The theft (Il furto) / Francesco D'Ambra ; with intermedi by Ugolino Martelli & Francesco Corteccia ; edited and translated by Vanni Bramanti, Linda L. Carroll, Anthony M. Cummings, Alexander Dean.
Other titles: Furto. English
Description: New York : Italica Press, 2025. | Series: Italica Press Renaissance and modern plays | Includes bibliographical references. | Summary: "A new scholarly edition of the Italian Renaissance comedy "Il Furto" - "The Theft" - by Francesco d'Ambra, including the entr'acte madrigals by Ugolino Martelli and the musical settings of Martelli's verses by Francesco Corteccia. Includes preface and introductions on the work, the author, the composer, and performances plus notes on the music"-- Provided by publisher.
Identifiers: LCCN 2024055556 (print) | LCCN 2024055557 (ebook) | ISBN 9781599104645 (hardcover) | ISBN 9781599104652 (trade paperback) | ISBN 9781599104669 (kindle edition) | ISBN 9781599104676 (adobe pdf)
Subjects: LCSH: Italian drama (Comedy) | LCGFT: Comedy plays.
Classification: LCC PQ4562.A67 F8713 2025 (print) | LCC PQ4562.A67 (ebook) | DDC 852/.4--dc23/eng/20241212
LC record available at https://lccn.loc.gov/2024055556
LC ebook record available at https://lccn.loc.gov/2024055557

Cover art: Santo Spirito in Sassia, Antonio Tempesta, Map of Rome, Metropolitan Museum of Art, New York.

About the Contributors

Vanni Bramanti (*Dottore in Lettere*, University of Florence, and Professor Emeritus of Italian Literature at the universities of Florence and Padua) is the author of the canonical scholarly treatments of the life and work of Ugolino Martelli, the editor of many scholarly editions of period literary texts, and the author of numerous studies of the literature of the time. He is most recently the editor of *Benedetto Varchi, Lettere, 1535–1565* (Rome: Edizioni di storia e letteratura, 2008); *Lettere a Benedetto Varchi (1530–1563)* (Manziana [Rome]: Vecchiarelli, 2012); and Luigi Alamanni, *Lettere (1519–1555)* (Milan: BIT&S, 2020); as well as the author of *Uomini e Libri del cinquecento Fiorentino* (Manziana [Rome]: Vecchiarelli, 2017); and *Breve vita di Leonora di Toledo (1555–1576)* (Florence: Le Lettere, 2007). He is the recipient of the festschrift: *Varchi e Altro Rinascimento: Studi Offerti a Vanni Bramanti*, edited by Salvatore Lo Re and Franco Tomasi (Manziana [Rome]: Vecchiarelli, 2013).

Linda L. Carroll (Ph.D. Harvard University) is Professor Emerita of Italian at Tulane University. A specialist in Italian Renaissance linguistic usage and texts, she is the translator of a range of period literary works and the author of numerous studies on Italian Renaissance theatre. Her works include *Thomas Jefferson's Italian and Italian-Related Books in the History of Universal Personal Rights: An Overview* (New York: Bordighera Press, 2019) and *Commerce, Peace and the Arts in Renaissance Venice: Ruzante and the Empire at Center Stage* (London: Routledge, 2016). She is the editor and translator of Angelo Beolco (Il Ruzante), *La prima oratione* (London: Modern Humanities Research Association, 2009) and the co-editor of *Sexualities, Textualities, Art and Music in Early Modern Italy: Playing with Boundaries* (London: Routledge, 2014); Antonio Molino (Il Burchiella), *I dilettevoli madrigali a quattro voci* (Rome: Istituto Italiano per la Storia della Musica, 2014); and Michele Pesenti, *Complete Works* (Middleton, WI: A-R Editions, 2019).

Anthony M. Cummings (M.F.A., Ph.D. Princeton University) is Eugene Howard Clapp II '36, LL.D. '84, and Maud Millicent Greenwell Clapp Professor in the Humanities at Lafayette College. He is the author of *The Lion's Ear: Pope Leo X, the Renaissance Papacy, and Music* (Ann Arbor: University of Michigan Press, 2012), which is accompanied by the compact disc, *The Lion's Ear: A Tribute to Leo X, Musician among Popes*, La Morra (Brussels, Cologne, Paris:

Ramée, 2015); and *Music in Golden-Age Florence, 1250–1750: From the Priorate of the Guilds to the End of the Medici Grand Duchy* (Chicago: University of Chicago Press, 2023), which is accompanied by the 2 compact-disc set, *Music in Golden-Age Florence, 1250-1750*, Francesco Corti, La Morra, Michał Gondko and Corina Marti, co-directors, Theatro dei Cervelli, Andrés Locatelli, director (Omenga, Italy: Ramée, 2023).

ALEXANDER DEAN (Ph.D. Eastman School of Music of the University of Rochester) is the Managing Editor for Recent Researches at A-R Editions, Inc., in Middleton, Wisconsin. His research focuses on the role of plucked string instruments in the development of harmonic language in seventeenth-century Italy. He has published articles in *Recercare, Studi musicali* (with Anthony M. Cummings), and *Early Music,* and contributed with Linda L. Carroll and Anthony M. Cummings to Michele Pesenti, *Complete Works* (Middleton, WI: A-R Editions, 2019).

—⁂—

Contents

Contents

Preface

Anthony M. Cummings

This publication presents a new scholarly edition of the Italian Renaissance comedy *Il Furto* — *The Theft* — by Francesco D'Ambra with the first English translation. *The Theft* was originally performed in Florence in 1544 for the Accademia Fiorentina and for Duke Cosimo I de' Medici, duke of Florence and subsequently grand duke of Tuscany.

The Theft is the work of a gifted, accomplished, and revered period intellectual. Although performances of dramatic works in Florence often featured *intermedi* — entr'acte musical compositions — in many cases, even most, the music composed for such purposes exists only fragmentarily.[1] This play is particularly important and almost unique in the history of the Italian Renaissance theatre and the music of the Italian Renaissance, because the entr'acte entertainment materials survive in their entirety. *The Theft's intermedi* are compositionally-sophisticated musical settings of Italian madrigals. In the tradition of the chorus in the ancient Greek tragedies, they comment upon the action of the preceding act. In the "High Renaissance" mid-cinquecento, such *intermedi* were indeed understood by contemporaries as restitutions of the Greek chorus.

D'Ambra's *The Theft* is unusual in that we also possess an uncommonly rich and complete set of primary materials. Multiple period sources of the text, manuscript and printed, survive. There is also full material on the playwright D'Ambra; on the author of the texts of the entr'acte vocal music, Ugolino Martelli; and on the composer of the madrigalian musical settings of Martelli's verses, Francesco Corteccia, the

---

1. See Anthony M. Cummings, *Music in Golden-Age Florence, 1250–1750: From the Priorate of the Guilds to the End of the Medici Grand Duchy* (Chicago: University of Chicago Press, 2023), 201–3, 205 nn. 27–28, 205–9, 395 n. 39, and 396–97 nn. 47–48.

most important Florentine composer of his time. In addition, the entirety of Corteccia's musical settings of the entr'acte poetic texts survive along with illuminating information on the 1544 inaugural performances of the comedy: dates and venues, benefactors of the performances, etc.

To an almost unparalleled extent, we thus possess the principal accoutrements required to envision — and perhaps even support — a performance that recalls and embodies the performance practices of the time.

The celebrated and esteemed Italian musicologist Nino Pirrotta wrote:

> …I cannot bring myself to agree with a…respected Machiavelli scholar who, having set out to publish his…edition of *La mandragola* "restored for the first time to its integrity," felt obliged for the sake of that integrity to confine to an appendix the "*canzoni* written for the performance in Faenza."… From the strictly philological point of view (the eternal nostalgia for an Urtext!) he was quite justified in doing this, for the *canzoni* are not present in the manuscript text dated 1519 on which his edition is based, neither do they feature in any of the early printed editions nor in the more recent ones up to 1782–83. But if we are interested in *La mandragola* in all its theatrical aspects, then it is hard to dismiss what he calls a "superstructure, incidentally added,… for one performance alone."… After all, *intermedi* of some kind were always necessary, indeed as necessary as a stage setting, for the performance of a comedy…. Let us therefore restore due credit to the "*canzoni* after the acts" of *La mandragola*, for they served a precise function.[2]

We endorse the general legitimacy of Pirrotta's injunction and have actuated it here. We have provided Vanni Bramanti's scholarly editions of D'Ambra's and Martelli's original Italian texts. Professor Bramanti has compiled this edition using all the relevant primary sources and has provided a critical apparatus

2. Nino Pirrotta and Elena Povoledo, *Music and Theatre from Poliziano to Monteverdi,* trans. Karen Eales, Cambridge Studies in Music (Cambridge: Cambridge University Press, 1982), 131.

to the text and an introduction on the playwright and the play. Professor Linda L. Carroll presents the authoritative facing English annotated translation of the text. The volume also includes Alexander Dean's scholarly editions of the entr'acte music, locating it respectfully where it belongs. Also included is an introductory essay on D'Ambra and critical notes on the text by Vanni Bramanti and my introductory essay on Martelli and Corteccia and the entr'acte texts and music.

We have, I believe, assembled the ideal team of collaborators for this project. Drs. Carroll and Dean and I have collaborated on several earlier occasions, and always most enjoyably and profitably, and we three are honored to be collaborating now with Dott. Bramanti.

And now, the curtain-raising.... We hope you enjoy our "performance"![3]

—✺—

3.　I am very pleased to report that I mean my reference to our "performance" quite literally: The distinguished early-music performing ensemble Theatro dei Cervelli — Andrés Locatelli, founder and artistic director — will record the five Corteccia entr'acte madrigals for *Il Furto* for a compact disc to be entitled *Music for Medici Festivals: Verdelot, Arcadelt, Corteccia, Striggio, Ramée*, Outhere Music, forthcoming.

Acknowledgments

Anthony Cummings would like to thank Attilio Bottegal, Music Librarian, Villa I Tatti, for facilitating access to rare primary materials indispensable to completing this project.

Linda Carroll is grateful to Vanni Bramanti for generously applying his vast store of philological knowledge to the explanation of numerous complex or obscure lexical items and phrases in the text.

INTRODUCTION

VANNI BRAMANTI

Even today, little information is available on the life of Francesco D'Ambra,[1] the only son of Giovanni and Costanza da Filicaia, although there is documentation of the chief dates of his existence, which occurred between July 30, 1499[2] and January 1, 1559, the day on which he was buried in the family floor tomb in the Florentine church of Santa Croce.[3] The family's original surname was Giuntinelli, which was changed to D'Ambra after the move to Florence, which occurred around the middle of the fourteenth century. Hypotheses about the possible reasons for the change have been two: on the one hand to legitimize the family as nobility by using a surname based on their home region and on the other to

1. The only two attempts at reconstructing his biography are of little use: Emilio De Benedetti, *La vita e le opere di Francesco d'Ambra* (Florence: La Rassegna Nazionale, 1899); and Vera Lettere, *DBI*, 32 (1986), 299–302. Concerning *Il Furto*, the following studies are of note: Achille Mango, *La commedia in lingua del cinquecento* (Florence: Lerici, 1966); Franco Fido, "La scena del principe a Firenze: commedie di Francesco d'Ambra," in *Sylva: Studi in onore di Nino Borsellino*, ed. Giorgio Patrizi (Rome: Bulzoni, 2002), 261–80; Michel Plaisance, *Florence: Fêtes, spectacle et politique à l'époque de la Renaissance* (Manziana [Rome]: Vecchiarelli, 2008), 217–28.

2. Florence, Opera di Santa Maria del Fiore, Registri battesimali, 6: "Francesco et Romolo di Giovanni di ser Francesco d'Ambra, popolo di San Pier Maggiore nato a dì 30 hore 1."

3. To be precise: "Before the altar of the Confession of St. Thomas, left nave, in the center of the fourth arch." See Cristina Cheli, *Le lapidi terragne di Santa Croce dal 1500 al 1931* (Florence: Polistampa, 2012), 516–17. It should be noted that this specification challenges all of the preceding studies of D'Ambra, according to which toward the middle of the 1550s he left Florence and moved to Rome, where it is presumed that he died.

underline their affection for a place, the Val d'Ambra,[4] in which the family originated and in which they had several rural properties, which they still possessed in the sixteenth century, whose products allowed the family to live the life of well-to-do landowners. Regarding Francesco's education, no clear documentation has survived; it seems certain that he was not enrolled at the University of Pisa, the institution, along with the University of Padua, preferred by Florentine citizens seeking a university degree. As evidenced by his academic lectures,[5] he moved with ease among classical texts, which allows the conjecture that, as was the case for many of his contemporaries, he frequented the University of Florence, where he would have been able to take advantage of the Latin and Greek lessons taught by the great philologist Piero Vettori, but this hypothesis too cannot be verified because only very few documents relating to this school have survived in the archives. As is well known, Vettori regularly welcomed into his home his most talented students (Benedetto Varchi, Luca Martini, Girolamo Mei, Bartolomeo Barbadori, Francesco Spini,…), and it may be that D'Ambra as well was able to benefit from Vettori's teachings. In the lectures referred to above, dedicated to commentary on two sonnets of Petrarch (*Canzoniere*, CXXXII, CXCI), and confirming what has just been said, beyond Dante and, obviously, Petrarch, many authors are cited, from Plato to Aristotle to Epicurus and his followers, to the Stoics, to Ovid and Sextus Propertius, just to give a few examples and to emphasize D'Ambra's knowledge of ancient authors. In Florence the family home was located in via dell'Agnolo, in the quarter of San Giovanni (Gonfalon of the Key),[6] where he lived the course of his existence together with his wife Ginevra Biffoli, whom he married in 1527 and

4.   The Val d'Ambra (Ambra Valley), located in the province of Arezzo, extends south of the capital in the direction of Siena.

5.   The three unpublished lectures, given at the Accademia Fiorentina and preserved in a manuscript of the Biblioteca Apostolica Vaticana, are the object of a study by the present author to be published in the near future.

6.   ASFi, *Cittadinario,* 2, fol. 15r. Each quarter was subdivided into four parts, called "gonfalone" (banner) because each was

with whom he had in 1538 his only son, Vincenzio. As may be seen from the dates, these years belong to a fundamental period in the history of Florence, marked by the passage from the Republic of earlier days to the consolidation of the Principate, but in the pages of the various chroniclers and historians contemporary to him who dealt with this period, no trace of either Francesco or other members of his family remains aside from the fact that he, as an enrolled member of the Arte del Cambio (Bankers' and Moneychangers' Guild[7]), in 1527 was declared qualified to participate in the Great Council, the most representative body of the final three years of the Republic. Later, in 1539, he was called to become a member of the XII Buonuomini (Twelve Good Men), an institution with a lengthy history, whose mission consisted in offering assistance to the neediest. In February 1541, he was admitted to the Florentine Academy, of which, after having held various minor offices, on March 27, 1549, he found himself elected president, and whose members over the years developed an appreciation of him based on his numerous lectures. In the meanwhile, his talent for the theater had come to light with the stagings of *Il Furto* (1544) and of *I Bernardi* (The Bernardi) (1547),[8] while in 1551 he was called to join a commission whose goal was to 'reform' the Tuscan language but which did not produce concrete results. Beyond this, probably in the last decade of his life, he dedicated his efforts to a *Storia dei suoi tempi* (History of His Times) and to the translation of the *Decades rerum venetarum* (History of Venice) of Marco Antonio Sabellico, both of which were left

––––––––––

distinguished by its own banner bearing a heraldic device, in this case a pair of keys.

7.   The Arte del Cambio, the ancient corporation whose members performed the exchange of currencies, commerce in precious stones and metals, loans, and deposits of money.

8.   Another comedy of his, *La Cofanaria* (The Casketmaker), was performed posthumously on December 26, 1565, on the occasion of the wedding of the prince, Francesco de' Medici, to Joanna of Austria. See Mario Fabbri, *Il luogo teatrale a Firenze* (Milan: Electa, 1975), 95–96. The play was published in Florence by Torrentino–Pettinari in 1566.

incomplete and of which no trace has been found. The final mention of his name in the records of the Academy,[9] which are left incomplete by an unfortunate gap,[10] occurs on August 7, 1552. After this date, amidst documentary silence, the only reference remains the following sonnet by Benedetto Varchi, published in 1555[11]:

> Dear, sweet, courteous and genteel d'Ambra
> By whom the learned crowd, with which
> Florence is honored today, like a gem set in gold
> Or silk dyed deep red, is adorned with pearls and amber.
> In you, as betimes happens to straw in amber,
> Goodness becomes enclosed and shines forth that now
> Is seen of little worth and yet is of value,
> Running like the Arno and the Tiber, the Ambra.
> Except that ill fortune and evil custom
> In this wicked time, stingy and villainous,
> Turns you and draws you to other cares.
> Well could be lamented with the Tuscan lyre
> The *socco*[12] that you made beautiful
> And perhaps as high and genteel as a Roman one.

If from the first line of the sonnet one senses the profound friendship between Varchi and D'Ambra, which is confirmed by the presence of both in the Academy, in which they repeatedly held positions of responsibility, from the first tercet the Arno and the Tiber are stand-ins for D'Ambra's movement toward a new horizon, Rome to be exact, the city in which, because of "this wicked time, stingy and villainous," he will be

9.   Florence, Biblioteca Marucelliana, B. III. 52, 53, 54.

10.   The gap lasted from August 1552 to 1557.

11.   *I Sonetti di messer Benedetto Varchi,* Parte prima, (Florence: Torrentino, 1555), 148. A sonnet concerning both Varchi and D'Ambra was written in 1550 by Antonfrancesco Grazzini, called il Lasca, on the occasion of their nomionation as censors of the Academy. See Lasca, and Carlo Verzone, ed., *Rime burlesche edite e inedite* ([Hillsborough]: Lulu, 2015), 47–48.

12.   A "sock" or light, thin-soled shoe of Greek origin worn by comic actors. The sock, understood as being comedy written in the Tuscan vernacular, had been "made beautiful," almost as much as the Latin comedies of Plautus and Terence. I thank Francesco Bausi for this clarification.

required to dedicate himself "To other cares," abandoning the composing of new comedies, referred to in the abandonment of the "sock." The possibility of a move to Rome, perhaps because of the prospect of a job, remains to be considered, although this hypothesis is made uncertain if for no other reason than that of the documented financial condition of the D'Ambra family, which, beyond their house in Florence, enjoyed various properties located in their home region, as can be seen in the record of their tax assessment.[13] No evidence was produced even by a search for verification in the voluminous correspondence of the two Florentine ambassadors resident in Rome in this period (Averardo Serristori and Bongianni Gianfigliazzi): not only were the anti-Medici exiles kept under assiduous surveillance but even those who did not belong to this faction were the objects of the unavoidable attention of the embassy's collaborators, the reason for which the absolute silence around the topic of D'Ambra's Roman sojourn cannot fail to raise a number of questions, together with the fact that even his return to Florence is shrouded in mystery, except for the day of the consignment of his remains to the pavement of the Church of Santa Croce, mentioned above. Further complicating things, given that his death does not appear in the two registers of deaths preserved in the State Archive, Florence,[14] is the possibility that he died in Rome and that his body was transported to Florence for burial, a thesis that is difficult to support in particular because it refers to a private individual and contrasts with the customs of the time.

Beyond the interest in the comedy itself, additional reasons justifying the present edition deserve attention. Its first printing dates to 1560, more or less a year after D'Ambra's demise, and all of the numerous editions published subsequently rely on

13. ASFi, *Decima Repubblicana,* 31, Campione del quartiere di San Giovanni. Gonfalone Chiavi 1498–1534, fol. 662 r. and ASFi, *Decima Granducale,* 3647, register 7, fols. 171r–171bis.

14. Raffaele Ciasca, *L'Arte dei Medici e Speziali nella Storia e nel Commercio Fiorentino dal Secolo XII al XV* (Florence: Olschki, 1927), 251; and ASFi, *Ufficiali poi Magistrato della Grascia,* 191.

it,[15] while the principal characteristic of the text contained in this volume is owing to the fact that for the first time it sets forth the reading of a manuscript, the only one known to date,[16] that preserves it, a manuscript that to all effects can be considered an autograph. And this is thanks to the discovery of another manuscript,[17] which contains D'Ambra's subsequent comedy, *I Bernardi* (The Bernardi), whose final folio the author signed in his own hand and that is written in a hand that in a close examination appears to fully correspond to the hand of V. The staging of *I Bernardi* occurred between the end of 1548 and the beginning of 1549 in the large hall (today, the Salone of the Five Hundred) of the Palazzo della Signoria.[18] On this occasion, the notary Domenico Gorini ordered several of his colleagues to copy the text of the comedy, probably making a number of copies to be distributed to the actors.[19] It is therefore possible that a similar operation existed for *Il Furto* as well, this time paid for by the members of the Academy and not by Duke Cosimo de' Medici, as happened for the comedy cited above. As will be seen in more detail below, *Il Furto* was staged in Florence in November of 1544 three times; according to Frosino Lapini,[20] the editor of the first edition of the comedy, the author, "resolved to get some of his friends to participate, who took it beyond his nest to various locations in Italy, where they were applauded for staging it

15. See further details in the Textual Note, p. xxvii below. In further references, this edition will be indicated by the letter S.

16. Venice, Biblioteca Nazionale Marciana, It. IX, 126. Subsequently it will be referred to with the letter V. It is described in the catalogue of the exhibit Fabbri, *Il luogo teatrale*, p. 83.

17. Florence, Biblioteca Riccardiana, 2970/3.

18. Fabbri, *Il luogo teatrale*, 94. Printed: Florence: Sermartelli, 1564.

19. Veronica Vestri, and Eliana Carrara, *Prima e dopo Vasari: Celebrazioni, programmi e apparati effimeri nella Firenze dei Medici* (Pisa: ETS, 2020), 90–91n. I thank Eliana Carrara and Veronica Vestri, who edited the biographical notes, for this reference.

20. A Florentine priest and man of letters, he was also a respected preceptor of many young people of his city (Giuseppe Girimonto Greco, *DBI*, 63: 721–24).

numerous times at public expense with great favor and with no small satisfaction to the spectators."[21] Unfortunately, with the exception of the Florentine performances, at least to date, there are no details of this "great favor" elicited on the stages of the various cities of the peninsula. However, it is certain that *Il Furto* had a respectable number of printed editions over the course of the sixteenth century, seven in Florence and Venice together before the end of the century (see the Textual Note below), not many fewer than the comedies of a much more popular author such as Antonfrancesco Grazzini (Il Lasca), his friend and a fellow member of the Florentine Academy. Once it was printed, the comedy found attentive readers and actors north of the Alps, as may be discerned from the following. In 1563, the young Johann Georg Werdenstein, a future musician and bibliophile, during a period of study at the University of Siena, had occasion to read *Il Furto*, as is documented in a note that he made on the frontispiece of S, a volume that later would become part of his great library.[22] Having become interested in the subject, the attentive student did not stop at his usual habit of simple possession but scattered marginal notes throughout the text, both to underline topics (*landsknechts* [German mercenary soldiers who fought in Italy], *women's maladies, the modus operandi of cheaters, envy*) and to complete or correct certain passages with details that could make one think of the presence of a manuscript, as yet undiscovered, that was connected to the tradition of V. A few years later, a *canovaccio*, or commedia dell'arte sketch, was derived from D'Ambra's comedy and titled *Li Furti* (The Thefts),[23] while *Il Furto* circulated in Spain, where copies of various editions of D'Ambra's three comedies have been located, "and to be specific, in a collection as important

21. S, p. III.

22. A member of an aristocatic family, Werdenstein was a canon, organist, and choir master of the cathedral of Augsburg and Eichstatt. In 1592, approximately nine thousand volumes of his extraordinary library were sold to William V, duke of Bavaria, then donated to the Bayerische Staatsbibliotek of Munich, which still holds a copy of the comedy annotated by him.

23. Fabbri, *Il luogo teatrale*, 83.

as the one put together by the count of Condomar between the sixteenth and seventeenth centuries."[24] Later on, although absent from the first two editions of the *Vocabolario della Crusca* (1612, 1623), in 1691, *Il Furto,* together with *I Bernardi* and the *Cofanaria,* made its entrance with a great number of citations into the third edition in three volumes, a work to which, in its "Veronese" version,[25] between 1823 and 1824, Alessandro Manzoni would refer as he looked to the 1827 printing of his novel with particular attention to the texts of Tuscan comics of the sixteenth century, in whose pages he would find linguistic material suited to creating the speech of characters of the popular classes, such that "when it is Agnese, Perpetua, Lucia, Renzo, Don Abbondio, or Griso, Manzoni found himself needing to explore experimental avenues."[26] The family library was certainly not lacking in resources for him to do this, from *Teatro comico fiorentino* (Florence: n.p., 1750) that contained in its fifth volume D'Ambra's three comedies, to the above-cited "Veronese Crusca," such that, as has been demonstrated in the study just cited, numerous turns of phrase of *Il Furto* contributed to legitimize the language of the characters of novels that were destined to become immortal.[27]

At this point, regarding the circumstances that gave rise to the staging of the comedy, it is important to recall that

24. Maria del Valle Ojeda Calvo, "Un ejemplo de la fortuna europea de Francesco d'Ambra: Los enredos de Martín, compuesta por Cepeda," in *Filologia e critica nella modernità letteraria: Studi in onore di Renzo Cremante,* ed. Andrea Battistini, Arnaldo Bruni, and Irene Romera Pintor (Bologna: Clueb, 2012), 13.

25. Published between 1806 and 1811 by Father Antonio Cesari.

26. Fundamental to this section is Sabina Ghirardi, "La ricerca di una lingua 'viva' e 'vera' per il romanzo: I notabilia manzoniani al *Furto* di Francesco d'Ambra," *Annali Manzoniani,* 3rd series, no. 1 (2018): 92–115. An earlier reference to this question was made by Franco Pignatti, *Ludi esegetici* (Manziana [Rome]: Vecchiarelli, 2005), 117n.

27. The phrasings adopted by Manzoni from D'Ambra's three comedies are in Alessandro Manzoni, *Scritti linguistici inediti,* 2, eds. Antonio Stella and Maurizio Vitale (Milan: Centro di Studi manzoniani, 2000), 426–27.

on June 9, 1544, during a meeting of several members of the Academy, the following decision was made: "Gathered together by order of the the Honorable President[28] in a sufficient number the Academy and the magistrates in the home of Messer Bartolomeo Bartolini, His Lordship (Cosimo Bartoli, president of the Academy) who had in mind to have a new comedy staged under the name of the Academy, inviting and seeking out for this purpose all those who favored his undertaking."[29] From some references contained in the text (which will be detailed in the notes), the composition of the comedy probably occurred in 1542 or in the first months of the following year, and therefore it was already completed when the president of the Academy made his request. It is not known if there were other comedies under consideration; as it happens, it was Ugolino Martelli,[30] author of the *intermedi*, who proposed *Il Furto*,[31] and following that nominated the 'festaioli', the members appointed to organize and finance the staging.[32] As recorded in the *Acts* of the Academy cited above, the first performance was held on November 9, 1544 in the Sala del Papa (Papal Room) of the Florentine monastery of

28. Niccolò Martelli, merchant and poet, founder of the Accademia degli Humidi, later changed by Duke Cosimo to the Florentine Academy (Elisabetta Stumpo, *DBI,* 71, 2008, 61–64).

29. M, fol. 18v. The Academy's initiative of staging theatrical texts did not end with *Il Furto*. In fact in 1551, it was the turn of Antonfrancesco Grazzini's *La gelosia* (Jealousy), and in 1567, of Lionardo Salviati's *Il Granchio* (The Crab).

30. A man of letters, student of Piero Vettori, later in the service of Cardinal Lorenzo Strozzi in France and eventually bishop of Glandèves. See Vanni Bramanti, *Uomini e libri del cinquecento fiorentino* (Manziana [Rome]: Vecchiarelli, 2017), 95–145.

31. M, fol. 21v.

32. Their names are Agnolo Guicciardini, Gismondo Martelli, Pagolantonio Mannelli, Lorenzo Antinori, Averardo Sacchetti, Antonio Cambini, Lorenzo Spinelli, Francesco Miniati, Francesco de'Medici, Giovanni Cavalcanti, Alessandro Pucci. Director: Piero Fabrini (M, fol. 21v). According to the catalogue entry in Fabbri, *Il luogo teatrale,* 83, the actors were members of the Compagnia di San Bernardino e Santa Caterina, with which D'Ambra too seems to have been affiliated.

Santa Maria Novella, with a repeat performance for women only in the same room on November 11, and a third one on November 15 at the Medici villa of Castello in the presence of Duke Cosimo.[33] Despite some unruliness at the beginning of the evening that he mentions, the good outcome of the performance is evident in a letter written the next day by Pierfrancesco Riccio, tutor and chief of staff of the duke, to Ugolino Grifoni, a doctor at the Ospedale di Altopascio [Hospice of Altopascio] and ducal secretary:

> Your Lordship will tell my Doctor Andrea [Pasquali][34] that the comedy yesterday evening opened as his Lordship knows and was acted by that Bigio most divinely, to the surprise of those who called out and criticized such a comedy, saying 'What is this?', 'What is he saying?' and in the end it was concluded that it was a caprice of Bigio's, an extemporaneous recital.[35] The number of spectators was very great, the comedy opened to the catcalls of the attendees, but then they listened to it appreciatively and in my view the majority of them were satisfied with it. The comedy is lovely, full of complications, and it was well acted and the vocal musical accompaniments were divine. To sum it up, the author merits commendation and must be viewed as worthy. For myself, I am more than satisfied.[36]

In moving to an examination of the prologue of the comedy, which is written in prose and according to the canonical five acts for a total of forty-three scenes and respects the equally canonical unities (place: Campo de' fiori; time: one day),[37] a preliminary observation should be made: Il Furto and

33. M, fol. 21v.

34. The personal physician to Duke Cosimo.

35. The audience was probably irritated by the unusual content of the prologue, emphasized by Bigio's performance. Nothing is currently known about this actor.

36. ASFi, *Mediceo del Principato,* 1169, fols. 508v–509r (Florence, November 10, 1543).

37. The unities were not always respected in sixteenth-century comedy.

its prologue were written and staged in the period before interventions were made in texts in conformity with the dictates of the Counter Reformation with their moralizing and edifying purpose.[38] In the second half of the century, things went differently, proof of which is found in Il Furto itself, in which, both in S and in all of the subsequent sixteenth-century printings, the prologue is missing. A propos of this, the following citation is sufficient:

> But leaving this aside, I must on behalf of the author inform you that this is the city of Rome, which if you [the spectators] at first don't recognize it, don't be surprised, because, having been more than two hundred years at the discretion of priests, which is of a kind that the whole world knows, it has changed and taken on a form that is completely different from the one that its first inhabitants by means of their qualities gave it.

This declaration was destined to disappear from S, together with others alluding to the wrongdoings of the Roman government, of which the following example will suffice for all: "Pope Devil," that is Pope Paul III.[39] The initial sentence of the text gives rise to several questions: "A new comedy comes today before you, most illustrious and most excellent prince and most noble spectators," according to which Duke Cosimo was present at the performance of the comedy, except that on that day (November 9, 1544) the duke could not have been in the Papal Room because for a good part of the months of October and November he was sojourning at his villa in Castello together with his family and the court, as attested in a reading of the letters addressed to him in that period.[40]

38. Donatella Riposio, *Nova comedia v'appresento: Il prologo nella commedia del cinquecento* (Turin: Tirrenia Stampatori, 1989), 70.

39. Other examples will be given in the comment to the text. The prologues of D'Ambra's other two comedies, *I Bernardi* and *Cofanaria,* will be more circumspect. It could be added that this aggression toward the contemporary pope might have been received favorably by Duke Cosimo, whose political program was opposed by Paul III.

40. ASFi, *Mediceo del Principato, 369.*

This means that the first performance was given before the members of the Academy, the second for the women, and the third in the presence of the ducal family and courtiers, thus the thought arises that the prologue, at the opening of which the duke is directly addressed, was delivered publicly on the occasion of the third performance, given that it would have been rather inappropriate to address the highest Florentine authority in his absence.

By then rather distant in time from the prologues of what had been presented as the "new" comedy[41] that dealt with entirely different historical circumstances, when comedies were "found for the use and delight of the spectators,"[42] the prologue of *Il Furto*, rather brief and simple, aside from the fiercely anticlerical comment cited above, proceeds with the necessary specification of the place of the action ("this is the city of Rome"),[43] underlining the allusions to multiple languages that appear in the text, from Neapolitan to Spanish, with it remaining the case, however, that the speech of the majority of the characters is permeated with a Florentine flavor.[44] It should be noted as well that in his prologue, D'Ambra does not give a lengthy plot summary, preferring to follow the Terentian model of entrusting it to two of the protagonists of the comedy, the elderly Cornelio, whose name is already a forewarning, and the young Mario,[45]

41. For example, Ariosto *(Suppositi)*, Bibbiena *(Calandria)*, Machiavelli *(Mandragola, Clizia)*.

42. Machiavelli, prologue of *Clizia*.

43. In addition, there are references to specific locations in Rome. Similar toponomastic information is in Bibbiena, *Calandria*, Plot Summary: "the city that you see here is Rome"; Aretino, *Cortegiana*, Prologue: "You see St. Peter's Palace, the Square, the Guardhouse, the Tavern of the Hare, the Moon, The Spring, St. Catherine, and everything."

44. This flavor, typical of the spoken language in Florence, will be extensively normalized in S. (See the Textual Note, below).

45. A propos of prologues, setting aside many recent contributions, it is appropriate to recall the excellent essay of Alessandro Ronconi, "Prologhi 'plautini' e prologhi 'terenziani' nella commedia italiana del '500," in *Il teatro classico italiano nel cinquecento* (Rome: Accademia

who, with their respective servants (Norchia and Gualcina), will be the protagonists of the first and third scenes, in which they will make known their love, Mario for Cammilla and Cornelio[46] for the same young woman, even if in the case of the elderly doctor it is a question less of love than of seeking a "companion" for his old age, possibly with a "little troublemaker" (a child) around the house. An additional victim of the same lovesick suffering is the young Gismondo, in love with Aurelia, a girl kidnapped by pirates, who is part of the warp and woof of the comedy without ever appearing on stage. Unraveling the knot of all these loves will require the intervention of Zingaro (Gypsy), a rogue from Spoleto, a rather close relative of Ligurio of the *Mandragola* ("a hanger-on who is the plaything of spite")[47] and of other more or less similar scoundrels. This, in its general outline, together with further complications, is the plot summary that the author has confined to the first scenes of the comedy and delegated to the exchanges of a few of the characters.

---

dei Lincei, 1971), 197–214; as well as Franca Angelini, "Vecchio e nuovo: i prologhi," in *Letteratura italiana*, 6 (Turin: Einaudi, 1986), 77–84; and Antonio Stäuble, "Tipologie dei prologhi nelle commedie del cinquecento," *Lettere italiane*, 63 (2011): 5–34.

46. Of elderly men who are in love with, or to be more accurate, desire a young girl, sixteenth-century comedy, like its Latin archtypes, is full. In Machiavelli's *Clizia*, one of the protagonists is Nicomaco ("an old man all full of love"), who is quite different from Cornelio, aware of the mistake that he has made and ready to accept the proposal of his wife Sofronia: "here is the thing now: if you will get back on track, and be that Nicomaco that you were a year ago, all of us will do the same and the thing will not be noised about and when it will be found out, [you can say that] it is normal to err and to correct oneself." It is known that *Clizia* was performed on January 13, 1525, in the home of Jacopo Falconetti, called il Fornaciaio. D'Ambra, who was then 26, could have been present at the performance, and at the preceding one of *La Mandragola*, or he might have seen a repeat performance. Obviously this is only a tantalyzing conjecture, while it is certain that he read the printed texts of the two comedies.

47. There will be other references in the comedy to *La Mandragola*.

In addition to "love," other themes, not by chance ones that recur in a good part of sixteenth-century comedy, define the plot of *Il Furto*, starting from economic motives: it is not immaterial that a theft is understood as the loss of a good whose recovery seems to justify all means. Prominent among the servants is Madame Appollonia, whose consistent good sense is joined with a magic formula (the "spell") thanks to which the besotted Mario would be compelled to resolve his problems with his beloved ("if she will not come for love, she will come by force").

A comment must be added about the customary artifices of the theater of the time, the references to place names, cross-dressing, and the consequent confusion of identities, the lightning-bolt recognitions of identity, ending with a character (the Spaniard Don Diego) whose sudden appearance clears up the entire business. All of this framed by a few references to fundamental events of those decades: the Sack of Rome of May 1527 in the course of which the tragic episode of Cornelio's family takes place, the violent death of his wife and the disappearance of his little girl, and the ill-fated expedition of Charles V against Algiers in 1541, dates that, as indicated in the notes, permit us to clarify the period (late 1542–early 1543), in which in all probability D'Ambra wrote his comedy.

As has been noted, Duke Cosimo de' Medici enjoyed theater, probably for reasons that went beyond the appeal of the texts and the performances of them. One reason for his enjoyment can be glimpsed in the fact that all three of the comedies are based on a principle of authority: if the characters cannot manage to resolve things among themselves, there is nothing left to do except turn to a higher authority, as in *Il Furto*, in which someone who had suffered a wrong, whether real or imagined, threatened to report it to the imprisoning authorities, to the governor, or even to the pope. As has been noted,[48] the presence in the plot of the comedy of a Spanish gentleman was probably appreciated by the duke and his wife, Eleonora of Toledo, given that precisely in that

48. Nicoletta Lepri, *Le feste medicee del 1565–1566* (Vicchio: LoGisma, 2017), 208.

period of time a good number of Spanish were converging upon Florence, at court and in the troops defending the duchy. In conclusion, beyond the happy ending, with the young people happy because they had succeeded in achieving their emotional aspirations, what remains is the portrait of a world dominated by the self-interest of individuals, repeatedly termed "honorable men" but in reality bearers of a dominating preference for money and for all that one can acquire with money.

TEXTUAL NOTE

As has been noted above, the present edition of *Il Furto*, in addition to re-introducing the original madrigals and the music of the *intermedi,* is the first to date to be based on the transcription of the sole autograph manuscript of the comedy, enriched with marginal annotations composed of a kind of director's notes, which lead one to think that V might have been one of the scripts distributed to the actors as part of the preparation for the performance.

MANUSCRIPT

V = Venice — Biblioteca Nazionale Marciana, It. IX, 126 (provenance: Nani[49]), fols. [I–II] 1–63, [I′–II′]. Numeration in pencil 1–63 in the upper right-hand margin, 222 x 147 mm.[50]

EDITIONS

S = Florence, Giunti. 1560, 8°. All later editions were based upon this one. Prefaced to the text a dedicatory letter "To the Reader" by Frosino Lapini, always included in the later editions. From this letter it is learned that the comedy was

---

49. Giacomo Nani (1725–1797) was one of the commanders of the Venetian fleet, later a senator and author of works of political theory. A passionate collector of manuscripts and printed books, the majority of which now belong to the Marciana.

50. Described by Jacopo Morelli (1745–1819), custodian and later director of the Marciana in *I codici manoscritti volgari della libreria Naniana* (Venice: Zatta, 1779), 130–32. The prologue of the comedy is published here for the first time.

composed "at the request of his very close and singular friend Antonio del Giocondo,"[51] who shared it "as if they were all one thing with those whom he had met and theirs and who were very dear friends of the author" and who would then make it available "first to the members of the Florentine Academy, who with great enthusiasm had sought it from him." It is evident that these statements must mean the existence of a number of manuscripts, until Giocondo allowed himself to "be persuaded to give them up and allow it to be seen, which prior to this he had never allowed anyone with whom he consulted." The edition produced appears to not be without blemish, lacking, with respect to V, the headings of many scenes and with the complete loss of some scenes in the fifth act, to the point that a note at the end of the book states: "Because the printer, after having received permission, began his work using a copy that was not very faithful, several mistakes were made up to the fourth Act, which, when it was compared with the author's copy, were discovered and corrected and, to reduce the damage to the printer, fixed up in the best way that could be managed. The question marks and the periods are left to the discretion of the reader."[52] Six editions followed over the course of the century:

Venice, Rampazetto, 1561, 12°.

Florence, Giunti, 1561, 8°.

Florence, Sermartelli — Eredi Bernardo Giunti. 1564, 8°. "Newly corrected and reprinted with the greatest diligence." With variants, in comparison with S, that indicate a text close to V.

Venice, Sessa, 1567, 12°.

Venice, Bonibelli, 1596, 8°.

---

51. At the time *camarlingo del Fisco* (keeper of the Fisc), as he signs himself in a letter to Duke Cosimo de' Medici (ASFi, *Mediceo del Principato*, 477, fol. 672r at the date of March 22, 1559). The *camarlingo* or *camarlengo* was a type of administrator of ducal revenues.

52. S, fol. 43r.

Venice, Rampazetto, 1596, 12°.

The four Venetian editions, printed in the space of 35 years, raise the issue of possible performances in the lagunar city, a hypothesis, however, for which there is no documentation. No edition appeared over the course of the seventeenth century, while three editions appear in the three centuries that followed:

Teatro comico fiorentino, 5 (Florence: n.p., 1750), 2–122. Together with *I Bernardi* and *La Cofanaria*. On the frontispiece: "Copied from the first very rare edition of 1561.[53] With the V.L. of the two cited by the Crusca, Florence, 1564, Venice, 1567."

Il teatro classico del secolo XVI, n. 7 (Trieste: Lloyd Austriaco, 1858), 5–38. The prologue is published for the second time. The volume includes also *La Cofanaria* and *I Bernardi*.

Commedie del cinquecento, 2, ed. Aldo Borlenghi (Milan: Rizzoli, 1959), 9–115. In this edition as well, the only one for the twentieth century, the prologue is included.

At this point is is appropriate to indicate some of the correctors' interventions in S, all of them oriented toward the banalization-modernization of the linguistic particularities of D'Ambra, to which the version preserved in V are witness, as in the following examples, starting with the verb forms: uccisono > uccisero, servimo > servimmo, mancono > mancano, troverrei > troverei, debbo > debba, faccendo > facendo, parturire > partorire, fussi > fosse, advenire > avvenire, hauta > avuta. The same may be said for the nouns and adjectives: picciolo > piccolo, giovinetta > giovanetta, voluntà > volontà, istrumenti > strumenti, longha > lunga, adiuto > aiuto, inbasciata > ambasciata, dua > due, sua > suoi, tua > tuoi, and similarly for the articles: el > il, li > gli. This is an operation that tends precisely to suppress the originality of the language of *Il Furto,* that in the day-to-day speech of V had found a kind

53. In actuality the second edition.

of colloquial tone, in some passages even slangy, that was well suited to an entertainment genre like comedy.

The present edition is the transcription of the text as preserved in V, respecting the manuscript's reading while applying the following criteria:

- The use of capital and small letters has been made uniform.

- The punctuation has been modernized with discretion.

- The *u* has been distinguished from the *v*.

- The variation between single and double consonants has been preserved.

- The Latinizing spelling of clusters (such as *-ti-*) has been preserved.

- Abbreviations have been expanded.

- The few conjectural interventions have been enclosed within square brackets; the equally rare losses caused by damage to the paper or the presence of stains are shown by the symbol [***].

—⚬—

Introduzione

Vanni Bramanti

A tutt'oggi non sono molte le notizie sulla vita di Francesco D'Ambra[1], unico figlio di Giovanni e Costanza da Filicaia, anche se note e verificate restano le date cardine della sua esistenza, compresa tra il 30 luglio 1499[2] e il primo gennaio 1559, giorno in cui fu sepolto nella tomba terragna di famiglia situata nella chiesa fiorentina di Santa Croce[3]. In origine il cognome della famiglia era Giuntinelli, cambiato in D'Ambra dopo il trasferimento a Firenze, avvenuto intorno alla metà del Trecento. Si può ipotizzare che le ragioni di questa modifica siano state due, la prima legata ad una sorta di legittimazione nobiliare riconducibile alla località di provenienza, l'altra per sottolineare l'affezione nei confronti di un luogo, appunto

1. Di scarsa utilità gli unici due tentativi di ricostruzione biografica: De Benedetti, Emilio. *La vita e le opere di Francesco d'Ambra*, Firenze, La Rassegna Nazionale, 1899 e Lettere, Vera, *DBI*, 32 (1986), 299–302. Per quanto riguarda *Il Furto*, si ricordano i seguenti contributi: Mango, Achille. *La commedia in lingua del Cinquecento*, Firenze, Lerici, 1966; Fido, Franco. "*La scena del principe a Firenze: commedie di Francesco d'Ambra.*" *Sylva. Studi in onore di Nino Borsellino*, a cura di Giorgio Patrizi, Roma, Bulzoni, 2002, 261–280; Plaisance, Michel. *Florence. Fêtes, spectacle et politique à l'époque de la Renaissance*, Manziana (Roma), Vecchiarelli, 2008, 217–228.

2. Firenze, Opera di Santa Maria del Fiore, *Registri battesimali*, 6: «Francesco et Romolo di Giovanni di ser Francesco d'Ambra, popolo di San Pier Maggiore nato a dì 30 hore 1».

3. Per l'esattezza «Davanti all'altare della Confessione di San Tommaso, navata sinistra, al centro della quarta campata » (Cheli, Cristina. *Le lapidi terragne di Santa Croce dal 1500 al 1931*, Firenze, Polistampa, 2012, 516–517). Da notare che questa precisazione mette in discussione tutti gli studi precedenti dedicati ad Ambra, secondo i quali, verso la metà degli anni Cinquanta, avrebbe lasciato Firenze per trasferirsi a Roma, dove sarebbe poi deceduto.

la Val d'Ambra[4], dal quale provenivano e nel quale avevano alcune proprietà fondiarie, per altro ancora in essere nel secolo sedicesimo, i cui ricavi consentivano alla famiglia una vita agiata da possidenti. Per quanto concerne l'educazione di Francesco al momento non sussistono riferimenti certi: di sicuro non frequentò lo Studio di Pisa, istituzione privilegiata, insieme a quello di Padova, dai cittadini fiorentini che intendevano laurearsi. Come attestato dalle sue lezioni accademiche[5], si muoveva a suo agio tra i classici, per cui si può congetturare che, come era accaduto per molti dei suoi contemporanei, abbia frequentato lo Studio fiorentino, dove avrebbe potuto usufruire dell'insegnamento di latino e greco impartito da Piero Vettori, ma anche questa ipotesi non risulta verificabile, dal momento che scarsissimi documenti relativi a questa scuola sono sopravvissuti negli archivi. Vettori, è noto, era solito accogliere nella sua abitazione i suoi allievi più talentuosi (Benedetto Varchi, Luca Martini, Girolamo Mei, Bartolomeo Barbadori, Francesco Spini…), può darsi che anche Ambra abbia potuto beneficiare degli insegnamenti del grande filologo. Nelle lezioni di cui sopra, consacrate al commento di due sonetti petrarcheschi (*Canzoniere*, CXXXII, CXCI), a conferma di quanto appena detto, oltre Dante e, ovviamente, Petrarca, molteplici sono le citazioni da Platone, Aristotele, Epicuro e i suoi seguaci, dagli stoici, da Ovidio e Properzio, tanto per fare qualche esempio e ribadire la sua conoscenza degli autori dell'antichità. A Firenze la residenza di famiglia era situata in via dell'Agnolo, nel quartiere di San Giovanni (gonfalone chiave)[6], dove visse nel corso della sua esistenza insieme alla moglie Ginevra Biffoli, sposata nel 1527, dalla quale ebbe nel 1538 il suo unico figlio, Vincenzio. Come si vede dalle date, gli anni ricordati appartengono ad un periodo fondamentale per la storia di Firenze, segnato

4.   La Val d'Ambra, in provincia di Arezzo, si estende a sud del capoluogo, sulla direttrice di Siena.

5.   Le tre lezioni inedite, tenute all'Accademia Fiorentina e conservate presso la Biblioteca Apostolica Vaticana saranno oggetto di uno studio di prossima pubblicazione da parte di chi scrive.

6.   ASFi, *Cittadinario*, 2, c. 15r.

dal passaggio dell'antica Repubblica al consolidarsi del Principato, ma nelle pagine dei vari cronisti e storici a lui coevi che si occuparono di questa vicenda non è restata traccia né di Francesco, né di altri della sua famiglia, a parte il fatto che questi, immatricolato nell'Arte del Cambio[7], nello stesso 1527 venne dichiarato abile a partecipare al Consiglio Grande, organo maggiormente rappresentativo dell'ultimo triennio repubblicano. Successivamente, nel 1539 fu chiamato a far parte dei XII Buonomini, una secolare istituzione, la cui missione consisteva nel prestare aiuto alle persone più disagiate. Nel febbraio 1541, fu ammesso all'Accademia fiorentina, dove, una volta ricoperte varie cariche minori, il 27 marzo del 1549 si ritrovò eletto a capo («console») del medesimo consesso, all'interno de quale, nel corso degli anni, ebbe modo di farsi apprezzare in occasione delle sue numerose lezioni. Nel frattempo era venuta alla luce la sua vocazione per il teatro con le rappresentazioni de *Il Furto* (1544) e de *I Bernardi* (1547)[8], mentre nel 1551 venne chiamato a far parte di una commissione che avrebbe dovuto «riformare» la lingua toscana, tuttavia senza concreti risultati. Oltre a tutto questo, probabilmente nell'ultimo decennio della sua vita, si dedicò ad una *Storia dei suoi tempi* e alla traduzione delle *Decades rerum venetarum* di Marco Antonio Sabellico, opere rimaste incompiute e delle quali non è emersa traccia alcuna. Infine, nei verbali dell'Accademia[9], inficiati da una inopportuna lacuna[10], l'ultima volta che compare il suo nome risale al 7 agosto 1552. Dopo questa data, nel silenzio dei documenti,

7.   Antica corporazione i cui membri si dedicavano al cambio delle valute, al commercio di pietre e metalli preziosi, ai prestiti e depositi di denaro.

8.   Un'altra sua commedia, *La Cofanaria,* fu messa in scena postuma il 26 dicembre 1565, in occasione delle nozze del principe Francesco de'Medici con Giovanna d'Austria (*Il luogo teatrale a Firenze*, Milano, Electa, 1975, 95–96). A stampa, Firenze, Torrentino–Pettinari, 1566.

9.   Firenze, Biblioteca Marucelliana, B. III. 52, 53, 54.

10.   Lacuna estesa dall'agosto 1552 al 1557.

l'unico indizio resta il seguente «sonetto di Benedetto Varchi, edito nel 1555[11]:

> Caro, dolce, cortese e gentile Ambra
> Per cui la dotta schiera, onde s'honora
> Hoggi Fiorenza, qual gemma s'indora
> O seta inostra, ogn'hor s'imperla e inambra
> In voi come talhor festuca in ambra.
> Bontà si chiude e fuor traluce, c'hora
> Poco si stima e valeriasi ancora,
> Correre al par d'Arno e del Tebro l'Ambra.
> Se non che rea fortuna e uso vile
> D'esto secol malvagio, avaro e fello,
> Ad altre cure vi rivolge e tira.
> Ben può dolersi colla tosca lira
> Il socco che per voi veniva bello
> E quanto il roman forse alto e gentile.

Se dal primo verso del sonetto si può cogliere il senso della profonda amicizia tra Varchi e Ambra, confermata dalla presenza di entrambi in Accademia, dove più volte ricoprirono posizioni di notevole responsabilità, a partire dalla prima terzina, l'Arno e il Tevere stanno a significare il passaggio di Ambra verso un nuovo orizzonte, appunto Roma, città nella quale, a causa del «secol malvagio, avaro e fello», dovrà dedicarsi «Ad altre cure», tralasciando la scrittura di nuove commedie, sintetizzata nell'abbandono del «socco»[12]. Resta aperto il problema del trasferimento a Roma, forse causato da un eventuale impegno di lavoro, ipotesi, questa, quanto mai labile, non fosse altro per l'accertata condizione economica della famiglia D'Ambra, che, oltre alla casa di Firenze, godeva

---

11. *I Sonetti di messer Benedetto Varchi*, Parte prima, Firenze, Torrentino, 1555, 148. Un sonetto diretto ad entrambi (Varchi e Ambra) fu scritto nel 1550 da Antonfrancesco Grazzini, detto il Lasca, in occasione della loro nomina a censori dell'Accademia (*Rime burlesche edite e inedite*, a cura di Danilo Romei–mastro Stoppino, Firenze, Lulu, 2015, 47–48).

12. Il *socco* era una calzatura piana e leggera, di ascendenza greca, indossata dagli attori delle commedie. Il socco, inteso come la commedia toscana volgare, era «venuto bello», quasi come le commedie latine di Plauto e Terenzio. Ringrazio Francesco Bausi per la precisazione.

di diverse proprietà situate nella zona di provenienza, come si può vedere dalla nota delle imposte a suo carico[13]. Anche una verifica nei voluminosi carteggi dei due ambasciatori fiorentini residenti a Roma in questo periodo (Averardo Serristori e Bongianni Gianfigliazzi) non ha condotto ad alcun risultato: non solo i fuoruscciti antimedicei erano controllati assiduamente, ma pure chi non apparteneva a questa fazione non sfuggiva all'attenzione dei collaboratori dell'ambasciata, ragion per cui l'assoluto silenzio intorno al soggiorno romano di Ambra non può non suscitare più di una perplessità, insieme al fatto che anche il suo ritorno a Firenze è ammantato nel mistero, a parte il giorno già ricordato della deposizione della sua salma nel pavimento della chiesa di Santa Croce. A complicare le cose, dal momento che il suo decesso non compare nei due registri di morti conservati presso ASFi[14], si potrebbe anche pensare che sia deceduto a Roma e trasportato a Firenze per l'inumazione, tesi difficilmente sostenibile, in particolar modo riferita ad una persona privata ed in contrasto con le consuetudini del tempo.

Al di là dell'interesse in sé della commedia, sarà bene soffermarsi su ulteriori motivi che giustificano la presente edizione, la cui prima stampa risale al 1560, più o meno un anno dopo la scomparsa di Ambra, sulla quale si fondarono tutte le numerose edizioni pubblicate nel corso del tempo[15], mentre la caratteristica principale del testo consegnato a questo volume è data dal fatto che per la prima volta viene proposta la lezione di un manoscritto, l'unico a tutt'oggi, che la tramanda[16], un manoscritto che a tutti gli effetti può essere considerato autografo. E questo grazie alla scoperta di un altro

13. ASFi, *Decima Repubblicana*, 31, Campione del quartiere di San Giovanni. Gonfalone Chiavi 1498–1534, c. 662 r. e ASFi, *Decima Granducale*, 3647, registro 7, cc. 171r–171bis.

14. *Arte dei Medici e Speziali* 251 e ASFi, *Ufficiali poi Magistrato della Grascia*, 191.

15. Altri dettagli nella *Nota al testo*. Da qui in avanti questa edizione sarà indicata con la lettera S.

16. Venezia, Biblioteca Marciana, It. IX, 126. Segnalato nel catalogo della mostra *Il luogo teatrale a Firenze*, cit., 83. Da qui il manoscritto sarà citato con la lettera V.

codice[17], dove viene conservata la successiva commedia di Ambra, *I Bernardi*, firmato nella sua ultima carta dalla mano dell'autore e redatto con una grafia che, dopo un attento esame, appare del tutto simile a quella di V. La rappresentazione de *I Bernardi* avvenne tra la fine del 1548 e l'inizio del 1549 nella sala grande (oggi, salone dei Cinquecento) del Palazzo della Signoria[18]. In questa occasione il notaio Domenico Gorini ordinò ad alcuni colleghi di copiare il testo della commedia, verosimilmente in più copie da distribuire agli attori[19]. È pertanto possibile che una simile operazione sia stata fatta anche per *Il Furto*, questa volta a spese dei compagni di Accademia e non del duca Cosimo de'Medici come per la commedia citata in precedenza. Come vedremo meglio più avanti *Il Furto*, nel novembre 1544, venne rappresentato per tre volte a Firenze, stando poi a Frosino Lapini[20], curatore della prima edizione della commedia, l'autore «[…] si risolse a farne parte ad alcuni suoi amici, i quali fuori del suo nido portandola in più luoghi dell'Italia celebratissimi recitare la viddero con publica spesa et favor grande e satisfazione degli Spettatori non piccola»[21]. Purtroppo, a parte le recite fiorentine, almeno fino ad ora non sono emersi indizi di questo «favor grande» riscosso sui palcoscenici delle varie città della penisola, tuttavia è certo che *Il Furto* abbia avuto un ragguardevole numero di edizioni a stampa nel corso del Cinquecento, sette, tra Firenze e Venezia fino allo scadere del secolo (Cfr. *Nota al testo*), poco meno di quelle delle commedie di un autore ben più popolare come Antonfrancesco Grazzini detto il Lasca, suo amico e compagno nell'Accademia

17. Firenze, Biblioteca Riccardiana, 2970/3.

18. *Il luogo teatrale a Firenze*, cit, 94. A stampa, Firenze, Sermartelli, 1564.

19. Carrara, Eliana. *Prima e dopo Vasari. Celebrazioni, programmi e apparati effimeri nella Firenze dei Medici*, Pisa, ETS, 2020, 90–91n. Ringrazio per la segnalazione Eliana Carrara e Veronica Vestri, redattrice delle schede biografiche.

20. Sacerdote e letterato fiorentino, fu anche un apprezzato precettore di molti giovani della sua città (Girimonto Greco, Giuseppe, *DBI*, 63, 721–724)

21. S, p. III.

fiorentina. Anche oltralpe la commedia, una volta stampata, trovò lettori attenti e partecipi, come risulta dai casi seguenti. Nel 1563 il giovane Johann Georg Werdenstein, futuro musicista e bibliofilo, durante un soggiorno di studio presso l'università di Siena, ebbe modo di leggere *Il Furto*, come testimoniato da una sua nota sul frontespizio di S, un volume che successivamente avrebbe fatto parte della sua grande biblioteca[22]. Interessato all'argomento, il solerte studente non si limitò all'abituale formula di possesso, bensì disseminò il testo di postille marginali, sia di messa in rilievo di argomenti (*Lanzi, malattia delle donne, costumi delli barri, Invidia …*), sia ad integrazione–correzione di vari passi, con interventi che potrebbero far pensare alla presenza di un manoscritto a tutt'oggi sconosciuto, comunque legato alla tradizione di V. Pochi anni più tardi dalla commedia di Ambra fu tratto un 'canovaccio' ad uso dei comici dell'Arte, con il titolo *Li Furti*[23], mentre *Il Furto* circolava in Spagna, dove sono state reperite varie edizioni delle tre commedie di Ambra «[…] y concretamente, en una colleccion tan importante como la formada por el conde de Condomar entre los siglos XVI y XVII»[24]. Più avanti nel tempo, assente nelle prime due edizioni del Vocabolario della Crusca (1612, 1623), nel 1691 *Il Furto*, insieme a *I Bernardi* e alla *Cofanaria* fece il suo ingresso nella terza edizione in tre volumi con moltissime occorrenze, opera alla quale, nella sua versione «veronese»[25], tra il 1823 e il '24, ricorse Alessandro Manzoni in vista della stampa

---

22. Di famiglia aristocratica, Werdenstein fu canonico, organista e maestro del coro delle cattedrali di Augsburg e Eichstatt. Nel 1592 circa novemila volumi della sua straordinaria biblioteca vennero venduti a Guglielmo V, duca di Baviera, poi conferiti alla Bayerische Staatsbibliotek di Monaco, dove a tutt'oggi è conservata la copia della commedia da lui postillata.

23. *Il luogo teatrale a Firenze*, cit., 83.

24. Del Valle Ojeda Calvo, Maria. *Un ejemplo de la fortuna europea de Francesco d'Ambra. Los enredos de Martin, compuesta por Cépeda, Filologia e critica nella modernità letteraria, Studi in onore di Renzo Cremante,* a cura di Andrea Battistini, Arnaldo Bruni, Irene Romera Pintor, Bologna, Clueb, 2012, 13.

25. Redatta tra il 1806 e il 1811 da padre Antonio Cesari.

«ventisettana» del suo romanzo, con particolare attenzione ai testi dei comici toscani del Cinquecento, nelle pagine dei quali avrebbe trovato alcuni materiali linguistici adatti per connotare la parlata dei personaggi appartenenti al popolo, così che «[…] quando a parlare sono Agnese, Perpetua, Lucia, Renzo, don Abbondio o il Griso, Manzoni si vide costretto a percorrere vie sperimentali»[26]. Per fare questo nella biblioteca di famiglia non mancavano certo gli strumenti, dal *Teatro comico fiorentino* (Firenze, 1750), all'interno del quale il quinto volume comprendeva le tre commedie di Ambra, alla citata «Crusca veronese», così che, come dimostrato nello studio appenata ricordato, numerosi modi di dire del *Furto* contribuirono a legittimare il linguaggio di personaggi romanzeschi destinati a diventare immortali[27].

A questo punto, in merito alla genesi della rappresentazione della commedia, mette conto ricordare che in data 9 giugno 1544, nel corso di una riunione di alcuni membri dell'Accademia fu deciso quanto segue: «Ragunata per ordine del magnifico consolo[28] in sufficiente numero l'Academia et i magistrati in casa di messer Bartolomeo Bartolini, manifestò Sua Signoria (Cosimo Bartoli, console della Accademia) che haveva in animo di far recitare una nuova commedia sotto il nome dell'Accademia, invitando e ricercando ciascuno a tal fine della sua opera e favore»[29]. Da alcuni riferimenti

26. Per questa parte risulta fondamentale Ghirardi, Sabina. "La ricerca di una lingua 'viva' e 'vera' per il romanzo. I notabilia manzoniani al Furto di Francesco d'Ambra", *Annali Manzoniani*, terza serie, n. 1, 2018: 92–115. In precedenza alla questione aveva fatto cenno Pignatti, Franco, *Ludi esegetici*. Manziana (Roma), Vecchiarelli, 2005, 117n.

27. Gli spogli manzoniani delle tre commedie di Ambra sono in Manzoni, Alessandro. *Scritti linguistici inediti*, II, a cura di Antonio Stella e Maurizio Vitale, Milano, Centro di Studi manzoniani, 2000, 426–427.

28. Niccolò Martelli, mercante e poeta, fondatore dell'Accademia degli Humidi, poi trasformata dal duca Cosimo in Accademia fiorentina (Stumpo, Elisabetta. *DBI*, 71, 2008, 61–64).

29. Firenze, Biblioteca Marucelliana, B. III. 52, c. 18v. L'iniziativa accademica di mettere in scena testi teatrali non si esaurì con *Il Furto*,

contenuti nel testo (segnalati più avanti nelle note) la stesura della commedia dovrebbe risalire al 1542 o ai primi mesi dell'anno successivo e quindi già pronta quando il console dell'Accademia fece la sua richiesta. Non è dato sapere se ci furono altre commedie in lizza, fatto sta che fu Ugolino Martelli[30], autore degli intermedi, a proporre «*Il Furto*»[31], insieme alla conseguente nomina dei «festaioli», cioè coloro che erano investiti del compito di organizzare e sovvenzionare la rappresentazione[32]. Come ricordato dagli *Atti* accademici citati, la prima recita si tenne il giorno 9 novembre 1544 nella Sala del Papa del convento fiorentino di Santa Maria Novella, con una replica nello stesso spazio riservata alle donne l'11 ed una terza il 15 presso la villa medicea di Castello alla presenza del duca Cosimo[33]. A dispetto di qualche intemperanza registratasi in apertura della serata, il buon esito della stessa traspariva in una lettera scritta il giorno successivo alla recita da Pierfrancesco Riccio, precettore e maggiordomo del duca a Ugolino Grigoni, maestro dell'Ospedale di Altopascio: «[…] Vostra Signoria dirà al mio maestro Andrea <Pasquali>[34] che la comedia iersera hebbe quel principio che Sua Signoria sa

---

tanto è vero che nel 1551 fu la volta de *La gelosia* di Antonfrancesco Grazzini e nel 1567 de *Il Granchio* di Lionardo Salviati.

30. Letterato, allievo di Piero Vettori, poi al servizio del cardinale Lorenzo Strozzi in Francia ed infine vescovo di Glandèves (Bramanti, Vanni *Uomini e libri del Cinquecento fiorentino*, Manziana (Roma), Vecchiarelli, 2017, 95–145).

31. Firenze, Biblioteca Marucelliana, cit., c. 21v.

32. Questi i nomi: Agnolo Guicciardini, Gismondo Martelli, Pagolantonio Mannelli, Lorenzo Antinori, Averardo Sacchetti, Antonio Cambini, Lorenzo Spinelli, Francesco Miniati, Francesco de'Medici, Giovanni Cavalcanti, Alessandro Pucci. Proveditore: Piero Fabrini (Firenze, Biblioteca Marucelliana, cit., c. 21v.). Secondo la relativa scheda in *Il luogo teatrale a Firenze*, cit., 83, gli attori sarebbero stati alcuni membri della Compagnia di San Bernardino e Santa Caterina, alla quale anche Ambra sembra fosse affiliato.

33. Firenze, Biblioteca Marucelliana, B. III. 52, c. 21v.

34. Medico personale del duca Cosimo e membro dell'Accademia Fiorentina.

et recitato da quel Bigio divinissimamente, con meraviglia di chi gridava et diceva a tal comedia, dicendo che cosa è questa, che dice colui e finalmente fu concluso che fusse capriccio di quel Bigio, così ex tempore[35]. Il numero delli spectatori fu grandissimo, nel principio della comedia fu con strepito de' popoli, di poi hebbe grata audientia et, secondo me, satisfece della maggior parte. La comedia è vaga, piena di nodi et fu ben recitata et le musiche di voci furono divine. In somma l'auctore merita commendatione et deve essere conosciuto da per bene. Io, per me, sono restato più che sodisfatto»[36]. Dunque, un successo, per altro destinato a non restare effimero, dal momento che, quasi sei anni dopo, lo stesso maggiordomo Riccio consigliava al suo duca di rimettere in scena la commedia: «Siamo dietro a trovare una comedia piacevole et per ancora non vedo cosa secondo questi gusti et pur se ne sono vedute parecchie. All'Eccellenza Vostra non piacerebbe forse pigliarne una delle vecchie, che sono belle, et quella del *Furto* di Francesco D'Ambra non fu veduta se non una volta nella sala del Papa et secondo me può stare al paragone. Userassi diligentia per trovarne una bella, se la ci sarà, che vorrei pure havesse a sodisfare»[37]. In calce alla stessa lettera, un rescritto del duca Cosimo veniva a troncare sul nascere l'ipotesi del suo maggiordomo: «La comedia trovisi. Una, non più et sia manco bella, pur che sia nuova»[38].

Passando all'esame del *Prologo* della commedia, in prosa e articolata nei canonici cinque atti per complessive 43 scene, con il rispetto delle altrettanto canoniche unità

35. Probabilmente il pubblico restò contrariato per l'anomalo contenuto del *Prologo*, enfatizzato dalla recitazione del Bigio. Su questo attore al momento non sono pervenute notizie.

36. ASdF, *Mediceo del Principato*, 1169, cc. 508v–509r (Firenze, 10 novembre 1544).

37. ASdF, *Mediceo del Principato*, 613, cc. 118v–119r (Firenze, 27 settembre 1550).

38. Si ricorda che nel Palazzo della Signoria, ormai dimora della famiglia ducale, nel 1550 fu rappresentata *La gioia* di Giovanni da Pistoia e nel corso del carnevale del 1551, nella sala del Papa, *La gelosia*, di Antonfrancesco Grazzini detto il Lasca.

(luogo: Campo di fiori; tempo: un giorno)[39] andrà fatta un'osservazione preliminare: *Il Furto* e il suo prologo furono scritti e rappresentati prima che i dettami della Controriforma intervenissero sui testi in chiave moraleggiante ed edificatoria[40]. Dopo metà secolo le cose andarono diversamente, prova ne sia proprio *Il Furto*, dove, tanto in S che in tutte le cinquecentine successive, il prologo risulta mancante. A questo proposito, basterà riportare quanto segue: «Ma lassato questo da canto, vi debbo per parte dell'autore advertire che questa è la città di Roma, la quale se voi <gli spettatori> così alla prima non riconoscesti, non vi maravigliate, per ciò che essendo ella stata più di dugento anni a discretione di preti, la quale di che sorte sia lo sa tutto il mondo se l'ha mutato et forma diversa in tutto da quella che i suoi primi habitatori per mezzo della vertù gli dierono». Affermazione, questa, destinata a scomparire in S, insieme ad altre in cui si alludeva alle malefatte del governo romano, un esempio su tutti «Pappa Diavolo», cioè Paolo III Farnese[41]. Qualche perplessità nasce dalla frase iniziale del testo: «Viene questo giorno alla presentia vostra, illustrissimo et eccelentissimo Principe et voi altri nobilissimi spectatori una commedia nuova», stando alla quale il duca Cosimo sarebbe stato presente alla rappresentazione della commedia, se non che in quel giorno (9 novembre 1544) il duca non poteva trovarsi nella sala del Papa dal momento che per buona parte dei mesi di ottobre e di novembre stava soggiornando nella sua villa di Castello, in compagnia della famiglia e della corte, come risulta dall'esame delle lettere a lui indirizzate in quel torno di tempo[42]. Ciò significa che la prima recita della commedia si era svolta alla presenza degli accademici, la

39. L'unità di azione non veniva sempre rispettata nella commedia cinquecentesca.

40. Riposio, Donatella. *Nova comedia v'appresento. Il prologo nella commedia del Cinquecento*, Torino, Tirrenia Stampatori, 1989, 70.

41. Altri esempi nel commento al testo. Molto più circostanziati saranno i prologhi delle altre due commedie di Ambra, *I Bernardi* e la *Cofanaria*. Si potrebbe aggiungere che questa aggressività nei confronti del Papa in carica, poteva essere accolta con favore dal duca Cosimo, la cui linea politica era avversata da Paolo III.

42. ASFi, *Mediceo del Principato*, 369.

seconda delle donne e la terza al cospetto della famiglia ducale e dei cortigiani, così che viene fatto di pensare che il prologo, all'inizio del quale il duca veniva direttamente chiamato in causa, sia stato reso pubblico in occasione della terza replica, visto che sarebbe stato abbastanza inopportuno rivolgersi alla massima autorità fiorentina in absentia.

Ormai abbastanza lontani nel tempo i prologhi di quella che si era presentata come la commedia «nova»[43], referente di tutt'altre congiunture storiche, quando le commedie venivano «[…] trovate per giovare e dilettare alli spettatori»[44], il *Prologo* de *Il Furto*, abbastanza breve e piano, a parte la feroce battuta anticlericale già ricordata, procede con la necessaria localizzazione della vicenda («questa è la città di Roma»)[45], sottolineando gli accenni di plurilinguismo che non mancano nel testo, dal napoletano allo spagnolo, ferma restando la sostanziale patina fiorentineggiante che permea il parlato della maggior parte dei personaggi[46]. Resta da notare che, nel suo *Prologo*, Ambra non si dilunga sull'*Argomento*, preferendo, sulla scorta di Terenzio, affidarlo a due protagonisti della commedia, l'anziano Cornelio, il cui nome è già un presagio, e il giovane Mario[47], che con i rispettivi servitori (Norchia

43. Ad esempio, Ariosto (*Suppositi*), Bibbiena (*Calandria*), Machiavelli *(Mandragola, Clizia)*.

44. Niccolò Machiavelli, *Prologo* della *Clizia*.

45. Non mancano, inoltre, i riferimenti ad alcuni specifici luoghi di Roma. Identica indicazione toponomastica in Bibbiena, *Calandria, Argumento:* «[…] la terra che vedete qui è Roma»; Aretino, *Cortigiana, Prologo:* «Vedete Palazzo San Piero, la Piazza, la Guardia, l'Osteria de la Lepre, la Luna, La Fonte, Santa Caterina e ogni cosa».

46. Questa patina, tipica di una lingua parlata a Firenze, viene abbondantemente normalizzata in S (cfr. *Nota al testo*).

47. A proposito dei prologhi, a prescindere da molti recenti contributi, è opportuno riesumare l'eccellente saggio di Ronconi Alessandro. *"Prologhi «plautini» e prologhi «terenziani» nella commedia italiana del '500." Il teatro classico italiano nel Cinquecento*, Roma, Accademia dei Lincei, 1971, 197–214, insieme a Angelini, Franca, *"Vecchio e nuovo: i prologhi." Letteratura italiana*, VI, Torino, Einaudi, 1986, 77–84 e Stäuble, Antonio. *"Tipologie dei prologhi nelle commedie del Cinquecento, "Lettere italiane»*, LXIII (2011): 5–34.

e Gualcina), saranno i protagonisti della prima e della terza scena, dove renderanno pubblico il loro amore, Mario per Camilla, e Cornelio[48] per la stessa giovane donna, anche se nel caso dell'anziano medico più che d'amore si trattava di cercare una qualche «compagnia» per la sua vecchiaia, magari con un «rabacchino (un bambino) in giro per casa. Inoltre, anche lui preda delle stesse sofferenze amorose, il giovane Gismondo, innamorato di Aurelia, una fanciulla già rapita dei pirati, presente nel tessuto della commedia senza mai apparire al proscenio. Per sciogliere il groviglio di tutti questi amori sarà necessario l'intervento dello Zingaro, un ribaldo spoletino, non lontano parente del Ligurio della *Mandragola* («un parassito di malizia il cucco»)[49] e di altri malfattori più o meno simili. Questo, nelle sue linee generali, insieme con altre ulteriori complicazioni, l'*Argomento* che l'autore ha confinato nelle prime scene della commedia e delegato alle battute di alcuni dei personaggi. Oltre all'«amore», altri temi, non a caso ricorrenti in buona parte delle commedie cinquecentesche, connotano la trama de *Il Furto*, a cominciare dalla ragione economica: non per nulla un furto viene inteso come la perdita di un bene, per recuperare il quale ogni mezzo sembra legittimo. Tra i servitori figura monna Appollonia, il

48. Di anziani innamorati, o meglio che concupiscono una fanciulla, pullula la commedia cinquecentesca, insieme ai suoi archetipi latini. Nella *Clizia* di Machiavelli, uno dei protagonisti è Nicomaco («un vecchio tutto pieno d'amore»), ben diverso da Cornelio, consapevole dell'errore commesso e pronto ad accettare quanto gli propone sua moglie Sofronia: «[…] ora la cosa è qui, se tu vorrai ritornare al segno, et essere quel Nicomaco che tu eri da un anno indietro, tutti noi vi torneremo e la cosa non si risaprà et quando la si risapessi, egli è usanza errare et emendarsi». La *Clizia*, come è noto fu rappresentata il 13 gennaio 1525, in casa di Jacopo Falconetti, detto il Fornaciaio. Ambra, che allora aveva 26 anni, avrebbe potuto essere stato presente alla recita della commedia, come a quella precedente della *Mandragola* o che abbia visto una delle repliche. Ovviamente questa altro non è che una suggestiva congettura, mentre è certo che abbia letto i testi a stampa delle due commedie.

49. Non mancheranno nella commedia altri riferimenti alla *Mandragola*.

cui corrente buon senso si coniuga con una formula magica
(l'«incanto») grazie alla quale l'innamorato Mario sarebbe
irrimediabilmente sollecitato a risolvere i suoi problemi con
la donna amata («[...] se non vorrà venire per amore e' verrà
per forza»). Da aggiungere i soliti artifici della scena teatrale
del tempo, come i richiami toponomastici, i travestimenti e
i conseguenti scambi di persona, le fulminee agnizioni, per
finire con un personaggio (lo spagnolo don Diego) la cui
improvvisa comparsa chiarisce l'intera vicenda. Il tutto nel
quadro di alcuni riferimenti ad eventi capitali di quei decenni:
il Sacco di Roma del maggio 1527 nel corso del quale si
consumò la tragica vicenda della famiglia di Cornelio, la
morte violenta della moglie e la scomparsa della sua bambina,
e la sfortunata spedizione di Carlo V contro Algeri del 1541,
date queste, come indicato nelle note di commento, che ci
permettono di individuare il periodo (fine 1542–inizio 1543),
in cui con ogni probabilità Ambra scrisse la sua commedia.
Come già notato, questo teatro risultò gradito al duca
Cosimo de' Medici, probabilmente, al di là della piacevolezza
dei testi e delle relative rappresentazioni. Una delle ragioni di
questo gradimento si può intravedere nel dato di fatto che
in tutte e tre le commedie è presente un sorta di principio di
autorevolezza: se i personaggi non sono capaci di risolvere le
cose tra di loro, allora non c'è altro da fare se non rivolgersi ad
un'autorità superiore, come ne *Il Furto*, dove chi aveva subito
un torto, reale o supposto, minacciava di ricorrere al bargello,
al Governatore e, addirittura, al papa. Come già è stato
notato[50] anche la presenza nella trama della commedia di un
gentiluomo spagnolo fu molto probabilmente apprezzata dal
duca e dalla sua consorte, Eleonora di Toledo, che proprio
in quel giro di anni stavano calamitando a Firenze un buon
numero di spagnoli, sia alla corte, sia nelle truppe a difesa del
ducato. In conclusione, al di là del lieto fine, con i giovani felici
per essere riusciti a soddisfare le loro aspirazioni sentimentali,
quello che rimane è il ritratto di un mondo dominato dagli
interessi dei singoli, a ripetizione evocati come «huomini da
bene», ma che in realtà erano portatori di un'inclinazione

50. Nicoletta Lepri, *Le feste medicee del 1565–1566*, Vicchio,
LoGisma, 2017, 208.

dominante, quella per il denaro e per quanto con il denaro
si può avere.

—〰—

The Translation of the Comedy

Linda L. Carroll

In *Il Furto,* D'Ambra's sophisticated use of the nascent Italian language based on the works of the Tuscan Three Crowns — Dante, Petrarch, and Boccaccio — demonstrates his pride in it and in being a native speaker of it. Through the play's range of characters, he explores the many registers of spoken Tuscan, which I have striven to convey meaningfully in the translation: colloquial repartee, criminal jargon, merchants' specialized vocabulary, the learned forms of courtly speech. In the prologue, he praises Tuscan's beauty and sweetness, warning that those qualities will be missing in the speech of the Roman characters, unfamiliar with its fine points. He notes that because their city attracted peoples from many places and often possessing little culture, Romans do not have a language of their own.

D'Ambra concludes his linguistic discussion with the proclamation that the speakers will be understood by all, reflecting that Tuscan had achieved the status of peninsular standard, at least among elites, by the mid-sixteenth century. It was promoted as a form of cultural hegemony by the Medici, especially Pope Leo X and Pope Clement VII who, interrupted only by the brief rule of Adrian VI, headed the Church from 1513 to 1534. A single language understood throughout the peninsula also offered many material advantages. It especially benefited Italy's growing publishing industry in allowing economies of scale; more copies of a work could be sold in a market extending to the entire peninsula than in one limited to a single region. Important aid to the spread of Tuscan was given by Pietro Bembo, a Venetian patrician who became secretary to Leo X. He wrote a guide to the use of Tuscan, the *Prose della volgar lingua* (Prose in the Vernacular Tongue) and composed his own literary texts in it rather than Venetian.

Standardization was still a work in progress, however, and some of the linguistic forms and spelling norms in use in D'Ambra's time did not last. The transition leaves traces in the text in such details as imperfect subjunctive forms *-ssino* and *-ssono* for the third person plural and *-ssi* for the third person singular; the first person plural future in *-en/o (potren')*; use of initial *h-* in imperfect forms of the verb *avere*; loss of *-v-* in the indicative imperfect ending *(havea)*; varying irregular past participles; conjunctive subject pronouns *(fin che la gli venga nelle mani)*; the placing of conjunctive object pronouns at the end of conjugated verbs *(vorrannocisi)*; agreement of the final vowel of the past participle with following direct object noun *(Un vecchio…ha presa per donna)*; *-a* as plural ending reflecting the Latin neuter plural *(mia consorti, amendua)*. Some phraseology may reflect popular use, such as postposition of helping verb for emphasis *(perduto havea = aveva perduto)*; the substitution of the imperfect subjunctive with the conditional *(interverrebbe)*. A number of graphic uses continue the earlier tradition such as *-ti- (-z-), in magino (immagino)*.

The differences between the manuscript and the print versions of the madrigals' lyrics generally result from free variants of spellings and linguistic forms not yet standardized and the elimination of final vowels to bring the syllable count into conformity with the musical notes.

Some of the semantic content of the play and the madrigals reflects the Italian tradition connecting comedies with Carnival and weddings, which were often performed at Carnival time. Erotic double entendres abound, especially in the prologue, as appropriate to the season in which the usual strictures were loosened and as an aid to the new couple in producing offspring.

D'Ambra also demonstrates his up-to-the-minute knowledge of developments in theater by including a few details derived from the comic texts and practices of Venice and Padua. The characters maestro Cornelio and Gualcina show features reflecting the nascent commedia dell'arte being developed in Venice. Several puns and exclamations

seem to refer to the works of Ruzante, who was *famosissimo* (very famous) at the time, e.g. Cornelio/corniolo ("cornel," an exceptionally hard wood; Ruzante, *Prima oratione*); *lingua* ("tongue," both "language" and "bodily organ"; Ruzante, numerous comedies); *canchero* ("pox"). They could have been transmitted to him by Ugolino Martelli, who from 1537 to 1542 studied in Padua, where he belonged to the Accademia degli Infiammati to which Ruzante also belonged.

The Composer and His *Intermedi* for *Il Furto*

Anthony M. Cummings

Francesco Corteccia — the composer who set Ugolino Martelli's texts for the *intermedi* (entr'acte visual and musical entertainment)[1] for the 1544 performances of Francesco D'Ambra's *Il Furto* — was easily the most important Florentine composer of the early- to mid-cinquecento. Much has been written about Corteccia; much could be written here. I shall confine myself to the most relevant matters: the composer's biography, his theatrical and festival uses of music, and the music for *Il Furto*.

The principal pertinent elements of the composer's biography can be presented concisely in tabular form. Deferred for the moment are references to the festive occasions for which he composed music.[2]

1. On the practice and tradition of theatrical *intermedi*, see my *Music in Golden-Age Florence, 1250–1750: From the Priorate of the Guilds to the End of the Medici Grand Duchy* (Chicago: University of Chicago Press, 2023), 160–64, 169–70, 193–94, 203–09, 211–16, 219–21, 239, 253–58, 294, and 311–14. Rather than the term "intermezzo," which, for a musicologist, has a very different and specific meaning, we use the term "intermedio" (plural: "intermedii" or "intermedi"; Latin: "intermedium"), which conforms to standard sixteenth-century usage.

2. My principal source is a foundational article by Mario Fabbri, "La vita e l'ignota opera-prima di Francesco Corteccia, Musicista italiano del Rinascimento," *Chigiana* 22, n.s. 2 (1965): 188, 191–98, and 201–2. The sections dedicated to the composer's biography in Bianca Maria Antolini's "Corteccia, Francesco," *DBI* 29 appear to be little other than a synopsis of Fabbri's article. I also made extensive use of my own *Music in Golden-Age Florence* and others' writings, as noted in the relevant specific context.

27 JULY 1502:

Born "Mercholedj adj 27 d.[etto]" and baptized the same
day as "Pierfranc[esc]o et rom[o]lo di bernardo di Tomaso[3]
/ ...d[i] po[polo] santo p[aol].° N[at].° adì 27 de[tto] h[ore]
13½"]

22 AUGUST 1515–22:

Admitted 22 August 1515 to service as a singer at the church
of S. Giovanni Battista, the Baptistery of Florence, together
with seven other *Cherici del Coro* ["Clerk–Choristers"], which
suggests that Corteccia was simultaneously enrolled at the
Collegio Eugeniano, the Cathedral school of grammar and
chant.[4] Having thus been directed toward the priesthood
by his parents, Corteccia was to remain among the Clerk–
Choristers until 1522.

CA. 1515–CA. 1520:

According to Corteccia's own account, "[Bernardo]
Pisanello [*sic; recte:* "Pisano"[5]] [was] my first master in
composing and acquiring a conversance with music."
Concurrently, Corteccia can easily have had training in
organ performance — and likely did — with Bartolomeo

3.   And of Bartolomea ("Bacci") Cristofora(?) Corteccia.

4.   Frank A. D'Accone, "Corteccia, Francesco," *GMO,* accessed 23
October 2017. On Pope Eugenius IV's establishment of the Collegio
Eugeniano, see Cummings, *Music in Golden-Age Florence,* 79 and n. 22.

5.   On the use of the diminutive in reference to the important
early- to mid-cinquecento Florentine composer Bernardo Pisano —
sometimes "Pisanello," sometimes "Bernardino" — see Anthony M.
Cummings, *MS Florence, Biblioteca Nazionale Centrale, Magl. XIX,
164–167,* Royal Musical Association Monographs 15 (Aldershot,
Hants: Ashgate Publishing Limited, 2006), 72 and accompanying
notes; on Pisano more generally, see Cummings, *MS Florence,*
ix, 2–3, 7, 42, 45, 49–50, 53, 56, 60, 62–72, 79–82, and 122;
and references in the index to "Pisano (Pisanello), Bernardo," in
Anthony M. Cummings, *The Maecenas and the Madrigalist: Patrons,
Patronage, and the Origins of the Italian Madrigal,* Memoirs of
the American Philosophical Society 253 (Philadelphia: American
Philosophical Society, 2004)."

degl'Organi, organist at the Baptistery and Cathedral of Florence from 1509–39.

CA. 1522 TO CA. 1526:

Decisive years for Corteccia's preparation for the priesthood, during which he likely was simultaneously completing both his humanistic studies at the Collegio Eugeniano and his musical training.

1526–27:

The approximate date when Corteccia took his vows as priest, which can be deduced from the date when he was appointed chaplain at the baptistery (see the following entry), an appointment that at that time required that one have had the status of priest for at least one semester.

22 OCTOBER 1527:

Appointed "chaplain in the Church and Oratorio of San Giovanni Battista."

1531:

Appointed chaplain (5 March) and organist (7 June) at the Church of S. Lorenzo, the Medici family parish church, where he lived for the rest of his life and also held such administrative positions as chapter secretary, archivist, and chamberlain.[6]

1532:

Resigned post as organist at S. Lorenzo.

CA. 1535–CA. 1539:

Likely served as organist at the Baptistery of Florence.

MARCH 1540:

The consuls of the Arte dei Mercantanti di Calimala (the Merchants' Guild, administratively responsible for the baptistery since the duecento) resolved as follows:

> [d]esirous…of…[bringing] satisfaction to our most
> illustrious and excellent prince and lord, Duke

6.   D'Accone, "Corteccia," *GMO.*

Cosimo de' Medici, who…in emulation[7] of his most illustrious ancestors…desires that the many talented people in this field who are at present in his city be recognized,… [it has been decided]…that all the herewith inscribed singers…be appointed to the chapel,… Master of the chapel messer Francesco di Bernardo Corteccia,…[*et al.*].[8]

1547:

Styled "Chapelmaster of the Most Illustrious & Most Excellent Duke Cosimo De['] Medici[,] Second Duke of Florence."[9]

25 January 1550:

Unanimously elected "supernumerary canon of San Lorenzo." The number of canonicates at S. Lorenzo then being fixed, an election ordinarily took place only upon the death or departure of one of the members of the chapter.

7. For an earlier period encomium of the Medici as patrons of music — e.g., Lorenzo the Magnificent — see Cummings, *Music in Golden-Age Florence*, 88.

8. Fabbri, "La vita," reports that Corteccia was simultaneously named chapelmaster at the Medici court, an assertion echoed by Antolini, "Corteccia," *DBI*. But see Cummings, *Music in Golden-Age Florence,* 151 n. 32 and 263 n. 1; and D'Accone, "Corteccia, Francesco," *GMO*.

9. He is so styled as Cosimo's chapelmaster in at least one contemporary source — e.g., Francesco Corteccia, *Libro primo de madriali* [sic] *a quatro voci di Francesco Corteccia Maestro di Cappella dello illustrissimo et eccellentissimo Duca Cosimo de Medici Duca Secondo di Firenze. Con l'aggiunta d'alcuni madriali novamente fatti per la comedia di Furto* (Venice: Antonio Gardano, 1547) — but I regard this as an honorific. Formally and officially, Corteccia was an appointee of the cathedral and baptistery, not of a musical establishment at the Medici Court. Of course, styling him as Cosimo's chapelmaster when he was in fact chapelmaster of the principal public ecclesiastical institutions suggests an identity — a oneness of family and city: of the Medici family and the city of Florence — a oneness that Cosimo was keen to assert. My friend Professor Philippe Canguilhem argues differently in his forthcoming book on musical patronage in Cosimo's Florence, which promises to be an extremely important study.

The conditions necessary for an appointment as regular canon therefore as yet unrealized in 1550, the status of "supernumerary" canon was conferred honorifically upon Corteccia, testimony to the esteem in which he was held.

1554:

Recognized with a benefice and an appointment as priest–rector ("pievano") at the Pieve di Sta. Maria a Micciano, near Anghiari in the diocese of Arezzo.

1563:

A regular canonicate having become vacant, Corteccia was invested with the post, after having served as supernumerary canon since 1550.

†7 June 1571

****

To judge from the number of festive Medicean occasions for which Corteccia composed important secular music, he clearly was much in favor with Duke (later Grand Duke) Cosimo I de' Medici. The composer's status as priest, *pievano,* chaplain, and canon certainly did not exclude him from composing for very different kinds of venues and occasions. Here I present, again in tabular form, the documentary evidence for such secular musical activity, some of it attested by extant compositions, some of it not, alas. I defer discussion of the documentation relating to the 1544 performances of *Il Furto.*

1539:

For the wedding festivities for Duke Cosimo and Eleonora of Toledo, daughter of the Spanish viceroy of Naples:[10]

10. Cummings, *Music in Golden-Age Florence,* 202–3, and the bibliographic citations in the notes. See also Antolini, "Corteccia," *DBI.*

Ingredere, a Latin sacred "occasional"[11] motet, sung to instrumental accompaniment during Eleonora's ceremonial entry to Florence (extant);[12]

Sacr'et santo Himeneo, a secular polyphonic vocal composition for the first of the banquets at Palazzo Medici (extant);

Madrigals serving as *intermedi* for a performance of Antonio Landi's comedy *Il commodo* (all extant):

1. *Vatten'almo riposo*
2. *Guardan'almo pastore*
3. *Chi ne l'a tolt'oime*
4. *O begl'anni del'oro*
5. *Hor chi mai canterà*
6. *Vientene almo riposo*
7. *Bacco bacco e u o e*

CARNIVAL, 1541:

For carnival in 1541, Niccolò Martelli composed a *Canzona delle Fante,* staged by members of patrician families. The music was composed by Francesco Corteccia[13]:

11. By an occasional motet is meant a composition whose Latin sacred text is not taken from the established liturgy of the Church but is newly-composed for a specific "occasion" and is appropriate to no other.

12. For another, excellent example of a Latin occasional motet by Corteccia, also extant — for the ceremonial entry to Florence of Archbishop Antonio Alberti in 1569 — see Cummings, *Music in Golden-Age Florence,* 187–89, and the bibliographic citations in the accompanying notes. The motet is featured on the compact disc *Music in Golden-Age Florence, 1250–1750,* Francesco Corti, La Morra, Michał Gondko and Corina Marti, co-directors, "Il Theatro dei Cervelli," Andrés Locatelli, director, 2 CDs, Ramée (Brussels and Paris: Outhere Music, 2024).

13. This information is contained in records of the Accademia degli Umidi. See Florence, Biblioteca nazionale centrale, MS II IV 1, *Libro Capitoli, Compositioni, et Leggi della Accademia degli Humydi di Firenze creata l'anno del S.re MDXL,* fols. 63v–64v, as reported on in Philippe Canguilhem's excellent article "La cappella fiorentina e il duca Cosimo Primo," in *Cappelle musicali fra corte, stato e chiesa nell'Italia del Rinascimento: Atti del Convegno internazionale, Camaiore, 21–23 ottobre 2005,* ed. Franco Piperno,

> On Saturday of carnival, the song of the above
> said *canzona* went on. Messer Francesco Corteccia,
> master of the chapel of His Excellency, did the music
> ["fece le note"]. The concept, the music, [and] the
> words satisfied greatly, and it won favor.... It went
> on until midnight with more than 200 torches.

CARNIVAL, 1546:

> [T]he most illustr[ious] Don Francesco (firstborn of
> his Most Excellent Lord [*i.e.*, Duke Cosimo]) sent
> forth the triumph,... the *canzone* well sung in the
> public venues.

Later that carnival season, "a most beautiful comedy by Vittorio de' Pucci, titled *The Astrologer*, was performed for the ducal banquet, with *intermedi* of heavenly music," among which may have been Corteccia's *Mascherata d'astrologi* (extant), from his *Secondo Libro de' Madrigali* (1547).[14]

1565:

> [Lost] music[15] for the *intermedi* for [n.b.!] Francesco
> D'Ambra's comedy *La Cofanaria*, performed on the occasion
> of the wedding of Prince Francesco and Giovanna d'Austria:

> The concept and texts of the *intermedi* were by Messer
> Giovanni Battista Cini, and they were conducted
> under his care, as was the comedy [itself] and
> everything else pertaining to it. Messer Alessandro
> Striggio did the music of the first, second, and fifth

Gabriella Biagi Ravenni, and Andrea Chegai, Historiae Musicae Cultores 108 (Florence: Leo S. Olschki, 2007), 237 and 243. See also Michel Plaisance, "Une première affirmation de la politique culturelle de Côme Ier: La transformation de l'Académie des «Humidi» en Académie Florentine (1540–1542)," in *Les écrivains et le pouvoir en Italie à l'époque de la renaissance*, ed. André Rochon (Paris: Université de la Sorbonne nouvelle, 1973), 419–20.

14. Cummings, *Music in Golden-Age Florence*, 205, and the bibliographic citations in the notes.

15. In addition to Cummings, *Music for Golden-Age Florence*, see also Antolini, "Corteccia," *DBI*; and Nino Pirrotta, "Corteccia, Francesco," in *Enciclopedia dello spettacolo* 3 (Rome: Casa editrice Le Maschere, 1956), col. 1531–32.

intermedi. That of the third, fourth, and final one was done by the master of the chapel[16] of their most illustrious excellencies: Messer Francesco Corteccia.

1568:

[Lost] music for the festivities for the christening of Eleonora di Principe Francesco di Duca Cosimo I de' Medici[17]:

> [O]n the 2nd…of…February [1568],… the Most Illustrious Lord Duke…sent out a Masque from his ducal Palazzo Pitti…. The theme was of Hunters…. They had…sixteen musicians, some of whom were singing, some playing…. The song was authored by a young gentleman of our city on commission of the Most Illustrious Lord Duke, in the style that our ancients utilized to compose *canzoni à ballo*…. [T]he sixteen musicians…were divided thus…: The music was *à* 6, composed by the Excellent *M[æstro]* Francesco Corteccia, that is, all the voices doubled from the tenor on down, and the voices were accompanied and concerted by two trombones, two crumhorns, [and] two *cornetti,* all of which together were making the sweetest harmony. The *canzone* was divided in two,… one for the day and the other for the night…: "*Canzone* for the day. *Noi siam[o] Donne Cacciatori…. Canzone* for the night. *Cacciator[i] Donne scorriamo.*"… At night, great numbers of torches were lighted by the said Masqueraders, accompanied by a good many in masks,… and they sang an endless number of *canzoni t*o the noblest and most beautiful ladies of the city.

We come to Corteccia's madrigals for Ugolino Martelli's *intermedi* for Francesco D'Ambra's *Il Furto.*[18] Two of the

16. On this title, see above, xl–xli.

17. See Anthony M. Cummings, "Music for Medici Festivals: Some Additional Works Recovered," *Musica Disciplina* 56 (2011): 275–334; and Antolini, "Corteccia," *DBI.* For another theatrical event in which Corteccia played a role, though not a fully and clearly articulated one, see Cummings, *Music in Golden-Age Florence,* 192.

18. The relevant sources, primary and secondary, will be cited in what follows. The most important of these is Mario Fabbri's series of contributions to Mario Fabbri, with Elvira Garbero Zorzi and Anna

1544 performances took place in the *sede* — the headquarters — of the Accademia fiorentina: the Sala del Papa off of the Chiostro Grande in the Church of Sta. Maria Novella. Both D'Ambra and Corteccia were members of the Accademia,[19] and Ugolino Martelli — the author of the texts for the madrigalian *intermedi* — also took part in the life of the Accademia between May 1542 and January 1548,[20] during precisely the period when *Il Furto* was performed. It is not difficult to imagine how the collaboration among the three academicians came about.

Ugolino Martellli was not the only member of his family who was a gifted and accomplished *letterato*. Our Ugolino (di Luigi di Luigi di Ugolino Martelli) was the second cousin of the distinguished poet and playwright Ludovico di Lorenzo di Niccolò di Ugolino Martelli,[21] who evidently shared his cousin's status as author of madrigalian texts serving as theatrical *intermedi*. The renowned early madrigalist Philippe Verdelot composed a madrigal on a text that appears as a chorus in Ludovico's tragedy *Tullia*. More interesting still is that Ludovico may have been the Luigi Martelli who was a member of the Company of the Cazzuola, which staged performances of Cardinal Bernardo Dovizi da Bibbiena's renowned comedy *La Calandria,* Ludovico Ariosto's *I suppositi,* and Niccolò Machiavelli's *La Clizia* and *La mandragola.* Ludovico (Luigi?) Martelli was associated with Cazzuola member Giovani Gaddi and Cardinal Ippolito de'

Maria Petrioli Tofani, eds., *Il luogo teatrale a Firenze. Brunelleschi, Vasari, Buontalenti, Parigi. Firenze. Palazzo Medici Riccardi. Museo Mediceo. 31 maggio / 31 ottobre 1975* (Milan: Electa Editrice, 1975), 83–84.

19. Cummings, *Music in Golden-Age Florence,* 167; on the history, evolution, and activities of the Accademia more generally, see also 166–70.

20. Vanni Bramanti, "Ritratto di Ugolino Martelli (1519–1592)," *Schede umanistiche* 2 (1999): 1–49 at 24.

21. Alessandra Civai, *Dipinti e sculture in casa Martelli: Storia di una collezione patrizia fiorentina dal quattrocento all'ottocento* (Florence: Opus Libri, 1990), 120. For this reference, I am indebted to Vanni Bramanti.

Medici, illegitimate son of Cazzuola member Giuliano di Lorenzo de' Medici "il Magnifico." In addition, Ludovico's madrigalian verse — like his second cousin Ugolino's — was set to music by a distinguished Florentine early madrigalist, Francesco de Layolle.[22] The larger Martelli family evidently had considerable experience in composing madrigalian verse and staging performances of comedies with *intermedi*.

In contradistinction to the normal contemporary practices of the Accademia, which — unlike its earlier, inaugural iteration, the Umidi — apparently did not wish to encourage new literary initiatives, it thus undertook to support performances at its *sede*.[23] (Indeed, before 1544, the Accademia had even been inoperative for a time.[24])

The first performance at the Sala del Papa was on 9 November 1544,[25] the second — "for the women" — on 11 November.[26] The *Atti dell'Accademia Fiorentina* for the years 1540–52 provide precious information about the two

22. On this material, see Cummings, *The Maecenas,* 99, 103, and 249 nn. 19–20. On Verdelot's and Layolle's associations with another early-cinquecento sodality, one quite different in character from the Cazzuola, however — the famous group that met in the garden of the Rucellai — see Cummings, *The Maecenas,* ch.1; and Anthony M. Cummings, "Musical References in Brucioli's *Dialogi* and Their Classical and Medieval Antecedents," *Journal of the History of Ideas* 71, 2 (April 2010): 181–85.

23. Cummings, "Musical References," 25.

24. Fabbri, *Il luogo teatrale,* 83.

25. M, fol. 21v.

26. "Alii XI del medesimo [November 1544] si recitò la detta commedia la seconda volta nel medesimo luogo aile donne [On the 11th of the same (month) the said comedy was performed the second time, for the women, in the same venue]." M, cc. 21v. Fabbri, *Il luogo teatrale,* 83, reports that the performers were members of the Confraternità di S. Bernardino e Sta. Caterina, on what basis I do not know. However, such performing personnel would have made the 1544 performances precisely like those of later sacred dramas, performed by members of confraternities and featuring *intermedi sacri e morali.* See Cummings, *Music in Golden-Age Florence,* 193–97, and the accompanying notes and musical example.

performances and the norms observed by the academicians in mounting such a production:

> On the 9th day of November [1544], in the Sala del Papa — [the] venue assigned to the service of the Accademia — the comedy already put forth by former consul Messer Ugolino Martelli and authored by Francesco D'Ambra, entitled *Il Furto,* was publicly performed, for which effect *festaiuoli* had been privately organized by the Consul, who [i.e., the *festaiuoli*] arranged for the expenses for which there was need with an administrative functionary who had custody of everything, the names of whom [i.e., the festaiuoli] are...

and there follow the names of several of the academicians.[27]

According to one period "reporter," the comedy was performed "with sumptuous apparatus,... full of magnificent pomp of the richest costuming, and adorned with beautiful *intermedi.*"[28]

The production was reprised for Duke Cosimo at the Medici villa in Castello on 15 November.[29] The duke set some specific conditions for the performance, which are informative and illuminating for musicologists (and others) interested in cinquecento Florentine musico-theatrical performance practice:

> His Excellency wants the comedy...recited here [at Castello] on Saturday next at the 17th hour and consequently he'll order all the actors to be here by the 15th hour.... In addition, he would like [the] music of viols [did they reinforce the singers' parts, *colla parte,* or play independently of the theatrical presentation?].

27. Fabbri, *luogo teatrale,* 83; M, cc. 21v–22r.

28. Fabbri, *Il luogo teatrale,* 83–84. Michel Plaisance, "La politique culturelle de Cosme Ier et le fêtes annuelle a Florence, 1541–1550," in *Les fêtes de la Renaissance* 3 (Paris: Centre national de la recherche scientifique, 1975), 146–47. Plaisance states that the comedy was again performed on 9 June that year, but I am uncertain as to what the basis is for that statement.

29. Bramanti, "Ritratto," 25 and n. 97; M, fols. 21v–22r; Antolini, "Corteccia," *DBI.*

And Corteccia likewise should be here with all those
young singers.[30]

Martelli's *intermedio* texts are transmitted independently
in manuscript,[31] but not in the 1560 printed edition — the
Urtext — of the comedy.[32]

Corteccia's madrigalian musical settings of Martelli's
intermedio texts were published in 1547.[33] As Professor Carroll
observed, there are differences between the versions of the
texts in Florence, Biblioteca Nazionale Centrale, Panciatichi,
164, fols. 243r–246v — *Madrigali di Messer. Vgolino Martelli
/ sopra la Commedia di Francesco Danbra [sic]* — and the 1547
music print, most of which are likely attributable to the need
to elide contiguous vowels in the texts in the music print to
align the syllables of the text properly with the notes that set
them to music. There was no need for such elisions in the
text when it circulated in an exclusively "literary" version
independent of the musical setting.

30. Frank A. D'Accone, ed., *Music of the Florentine Renaissance 8*
(Neuhausen–Stuttgart: American Institute of Musicology, 1981),
xii; Canguilhem, "La cappella Fiorentina," 234–35; James Haar,
"The Florentine Madrigal, 1540–60," in *Music in Renaissance Cities
and Courts: Studies in Honor of Lewis Lockwood*, ed. Anthony M.
Cumming and Jessie Ann Owens (Warren, MI: Harmonie Park
Press, 1997), 148 and n. 52.

31. Florence, Biblioteca Nazionale Centrale, Panciatichi, 164, fols.
243r–246v — *Madrigali di Ms. Vgolino Martelli / sopra la Commedia
di Francesco Danbra [sic]* — which contains the poetry of several
cinquecento authors (Benedetto Varchi, et al.), various instances of
which were destined for theatrical performances, with or without
musical elements. The section of the manuscript that reports the
Madrigali bears the title *Rime di Diversi*. Fabbri, *Il luogo teatrale,*
83–84.

32. *Il Furto: Comedia di M. Francesco d'Ambra cittadino, e
Accademico Fiorentino nuouamente data in luce* (Florence: Giunti,
1560). There is a manuscript exemplar of the comedy in Venice:
Biblioteca Nazionale Marciana, ms. It. IX 126 (=6482). Here,
too, in the prologue on fol. 61v, is a notice that the comedy was
performed in the presence of Duke Cosimo; see Fabbri, *Il Luogo
teatrale,* 83.

33. Corteccia, *Libro Primo,* 34–37.

Indeed, the 1547 music print may have a certain canonical status in the entirety of Corteccia's *oeuvre,* as it is a reprint of an earlier issue of the print (1544) that did not contain the madrigals for *Il Furto,* which in 1547 were published as an *aggiunta* (addition) to the earlier issue, as is stated on the title page. Corteccia himself may have had a direct role in the 1547 reprint, and he would presumably have been scrupulously attentive to such matters as the unambiguous, accurate underlaying of the text to the music. In any event, someone — whether Corteccia or someone else — exercised a strong, knowing editorial hand.

We thought it important to print the texts as they also appear in Biblioteca Nazionale Centrale, Florence, Panciatichi, 164, 243r–246v, so that any interested reader can make comparisons and isolate the differences between the two versions of the texts. The manuscript versions of the texts appear before the musical presentation of each madrigal in the edition.

As theatrical *intermedi,* Corteccia's 1547 madrigals are unusual, indeed, almost unique. The music for the 1539 wedding festivities for Cosimo I and Eleonora was published more-or-less in its entirety. The music for the 1589 *intermedi* for Girolamo Bargagli's comedy, *La pellegrina,* performed on the occasion of the wedding festivities for Grand Duke Ferdinando I and Grand Duchess Cristina, was published in its entirety. However, the extant festival music from the intervening half-century remains only fragmentarily with the sole exception being Corteccia's 1544 madrigals. There are: a) only two *intermedio* madrigals remaining from 1565/66; b) a fragmentary explanatory song for a procession of floats and two *intermedio* madrigals (one fragmentary) for 1568; c) one explanatory song for a procession of floats, five *intermedio* madrigals (all fragmentary), and one instance of the realistic use of music for the performance of a comedy in 1569; and d) three explanatory songs for a procession of floats for 1579, two of which are fragmentary. Our edition thus uniquely makes available the complete material for a festive theatrical event from that half-century: the complete original text of

the parent comedy; the texts of the *intermedi,* which are transmitted independently of their musical settings; and Corteccia's musical settings. One can undertake a reading — or, indeed, a performance — of all the theatrical elements, as reclaimed here and integrated into their intended, original organic whole.[34]

Relative to the stylistic features of Corteccia's contributions to the 1539 festivities, those of his 1544 madrigals represent a momentary reversion to the style of Philippe Verdelot's *intermedio* madrigals for performances of Machiavelli's comedies in the mid-1520s — *La Clizia* and *La Mandragola* (*The Mandrake Root*)[35] — and Jacques Arcadelt's, presumably for a 1536 performance of Lorenzino di Pierfrancesco de' Medici's comedy *L'Aridosia.*[36] The 1544 madrigals were seemingly performed entirely by voices[37] and characterized by a prevalently-chordal setting of the text.[38] In 1539, on the other hand, in an apparent search for sonic variety, Corteccia had sought and attained such an attractive variety through his diverse choices as to instrumental color and the disposition of the performing resources, vocal and instrumental. Through

34. See Cummings, *Music in Golden-Age Florence,* chap. 14; Anthony M. Cummings, "Music for Medici Festivals: Some Additional Works Recovered," *Musica Disciplina* 56 (2011): 275–334; and Anthony M. Cummings, "On the Testimony of Fragments (or, Alessandro Striggio the Elder and the Genesis of the *Genere Concitato*)," *Studi musicali* 4, n.s. 1 (2013): 39–60.

35. Cummings, *Maecenas and the Madrigalist,* 25–26 and 106–07 and the accompanying notes.

36. Anthony M. Cummings, *The Politicized Muse: Music for Medici Festivals, 1512–1537,* Princeton Essays on the Arts (Princeton, NJ: Princeton University Press, 1992), 155–57 and the accompanying notes.

37. But see above for Duke Cosimo's call for a consort of viols for one of the 1544 performances. What was their role? Did they double, *colla parte,* and thus reinforce and add sonic color to the vocal lines of the madrigals?

38. Antolini, "Corteccia," *DBI;* and Cummings, *Music in Golden-Age Florence,* 205.

such means he expressed the distinctive mood and character of each text.[39]

Moreover, in 1539's *Il Commodo*, the *intermedi* were performed scenically.[40] On the contrary, the five 1544 *intermedi* — sung before the prologue and after acts I through IV — featured no choreographed movement, no dancing, no stage combat, no stage set, no instrumental *sinfonie*. However, the singers were evidently in full view and may even have been costumed. The text of the first *intermedio* — *Udendo ragionar che qui si denno,* which makes reference to "il Furto [the Theft]" — seems to indicate the visible presence of a chorus (or masquerade) of *zingari* (Romani).[41]

And like the *canzona* before the prologue of Machiavelli's *La Clizia,* one of Martelli's *intermedi* for *Il Furto* — *Quanto sia dolce voglia,* sung after act I — is directed to the audience. But although the madrigals after acts I through IV relate generally to the themes of the play and events in it, the first three do not refer directly to any of the characters, and, indeed, the second and third make no explicit reference to the play itself.

In several of the 1539 *intermedi* (1, 3, and 6), a solo-song — seemingly in fully-developed vocal polyphony — is performed. But in reality it is a polyphonic composition of which the singer performed the superius line, while the other lines are entrusted to an instrument or instruments. In one case (*intermedio* 4), the singer accompanied himself, performing the instrumental part on a *violone.*[42] However, the 1544 madrigals are, as suggested, fully vocal in their scoring.

What are the explanations for Verdelot, Arcadelt, and Corteccia's simpler style? In response to the musical experiences and tastes of the Florentine intellectual and cultural figures for whom the earliest madrigalists composed, as well as the

---

39. Cummings, *Music in Golden-Age Florence,* 205. Also on the musical style of the 1539 *intermedio* madrigals, especially as contrasted with those for *Il Furto,* see some predictably sensitive observations in Pirrotta, "Corteccia."

40. Pirrotta, "Corteccia."

41. Cummings, *Music in Golden-Age Florence,* 169–70.

42. Pirrotta, "Corteccia."

need for a musical style that made the text intelligible and thus effectively served the purpose of providing revealing interpretive commentary on the action of the parent comedy, Verdelot, Arcadelt, Corteccia, and other madrigalists of the 1520s, 1530s, and 1540s opted for a relatively simple, homorhythmic setting of the text. Although the product of such practical considerations, the homorhythmic design was also appropriate to the modest musical abilities of some of the consumers of the new genre, many of whom were amateurs. As a member of the Accademic Fiorentina, Corteccia may also have been responding to a debate in the Accademia about the efficacy of polyphonic, polyrhythmic vocal settings of text.[43] Of course, the performing resources available for the Verdelot madrigals in the 1520s and the Corteccia madrigals in 1544 were more modest than those for the more lavish Corteccia madrigals in 1539, which may also have permitted the contrasting styles of the compositions produced for those different occasions

But unlike Verdelot's setting of some of Machiavelli's *intermedio* texts, in Corteccia's 1544 madrigals there is no recycling of the same music for parallel moments in the poetic structure: All the madrigals for *Il Furto* are "through-composed."[44]

In 1544, Corteccia resorted to a greater variety of rhythmic values than is ordinarily found in madrigals from this moment in the history of the genre, which affords changes of pace from one phrase to the next. This, too, permits the words to be more fully intelligible, in a manner responsive to their natural accents. His madrigals are examples of the *"note nere"* phenomenon, where the notes' rhythmic values are shorter: In contrast to the half notes usual in many earlier madrigals, here quarter and eighth notes — thus "black" notes — figure prominently.[45]

43. In the foregoing paragraph, I am borrowing extensively from my *Music in Golden-Age Florence,* 165 and 167–70.

44. Cummings, *Music in Golden-Age Florence,* 165 and 167–70.

45. Cummings, *Music in Golden-Age Florence,* 165 and 167–70.

Corteccia's 1544 madrigals can thus display the faster note values, nervous, "choppy" rhythms, and abrupt textural changes characteristic of the style of *"note-nere"* madrigals of the early 1540s. Black-note madrigals make up the bulk of Corteccia's theatrical pieces for the *intermedi*.[46]

In this edition, we have placed the five *intermedio* texts, their English translations, and their musical settings "where they belong" — i.e., before the prologue and between the acts — and thus restored them to their rightful sequential place among the various dramaturgical elements of the comedy that made for so singular and memorable a series of performances in 1544. In Greek chorus-like fashion, they comment on the action of the parent comedy and provide informative interpretations. In the sixteenth century, these *intermedi* were indeed understood as restitutions of the choruses of the ancient Greek tragedies and comedies,[47] an expression of the Renaissance era's respectful reclamation of whatever could be effectively and legitimately reclaimed of the classical world.

—⚏—

46. D'Accone, "Corteccia," *GMO.*
47. Cummings, *Music in Golden-Age Florence,* 163 and 347.

Abbreviations

ASdF	Florence, State Archive.
ASFi	Florence, State Archive.
DBI	*Dizionario biografico degli italiani.* (Rome, Istituto dell'Enciclopedia italiana, 1960–).
ES	*Enciclopedia dello spettacolo* (Rome: Casa editrice le Maschere, 1956).
GMO	Grove Music Online, https://www.oxfordmusiconline.com/grovemusic.
M	Florence, Biblioteca Marucelliana, B.III.52.
S	*Il Furto* (Florence: Giunti, 1560).
V	Venice, Biblioteca Nazionale Marciana, ms. It. IX, 126.

Plot Summary

Act I

The elderly Doctor Cornelio, whose wife was killed in the recent wars, believes that his daughter and son were killed in them too. To have another child, he arranges to marry Cammilla, a young woman living with his neighbor, Madam Gostanza.

Gismondo is in love with Aurelia, captured by a Corsican corsair. He tries to ransom her using expensive silk cloth "borrowed" from his merchant brother Lottieri. The corsair will turn the girl over only for a larger ransom and only to her father. Gismondo asks his friend Mario for help, who asks his servant Gualcina, who recruits his friend, the con man Gypsy, to pose as Aurelia's father.

Mario is in love with Cammilla. To keep Doctor Cornelio from marrying her, he plans to elope. To induce Gismondo to help him, he plans to obtain from his father the money for Aurelia's ransom.

Act II

Gualcina convinces Gypsy to help. Mario joins them, promising money, and they hatch their plot.

Cammilla plots with Miss Appollonia, Madam Gostanza's maid, to get word to Mario to rescue her. She reveals that they have promised themselves to each other, which constituted a valid marriage. Appollonia recounts that Cammilla was separated from her family during the war and entrusted to Madam Gostanza.

Act III

Mario and Gualcina discuss how Aurelia convinced the pirate that Gypsy was her father.

Lucio, Mario's father, decides to play a joke on his son and tells him that he has arranged for him to marry Virginia, who had been married to Doctor Cornelio's son. Mario despairs, but Gualcina tells him to remove Cammilla from Madam Gostanza's home before Doctor Cornelio gets there, delaying his arrival with a medical mission.

Rinuccio complains that the con artist Wolf tricked him and that the payment was stolen from him.

To get Doctor Cornelio out of the way, Gismondo convinces him to assist an unmarried girl who is pregnant. Pretending to take him to her, he locks him in Lottieri's warehouse.

Act IV

Mario and Gualcina, disguised as cooks, help Cammilla escape from Madam Appollonia's home.

Guicciardo tells Lottieri that he is looking for his long-lost daughter, and Lottieri offers to help.

Wolf brags about how he stole Rinuccio's payment of cloth. He tries to sell it to Lottieri, who recognizes the silk as his own goods. Wolf says he got it from Rinuccio, who got it from Guicciardo as ransom for his daughter. Guicciardo denies it but wants to know about the daughter. It eventually comes out that he is the true father and that Gypsy faked his identity. Gypsy tries to convince the others that he is the true father by claiming that Guicciardo was robbed by his servant Gypsy and sees him everywhere. Guicciardo finally establishes his identity, and Gypsy flees.

Act V

Gismondo reveals that he has convinced Guicciardo to let him marry Aurelia after he has been forgiven by Doctor Cornelio.

Valerio arrives and identifies Cammilla as his sister.

Lucio informs Doctor Cornelio that Cammilla is his daughter Lucrezia, that his son Valerio is alive, and that Valerio has given Lucrezia to Mario as his wife. Doctor Cornelio pardons Gismondo, who in turn causes Gypsy to be pardoned.

—⁂—

IL FURTO

EDITED BY Vanni Bramanti

THE THEFT

TRANSLATED BY LINDA L. CARROLL

Personaggi[1]

Messer Cornelio, medico vecchio

Norchia, suo famiglio

Mario, giovane [figlio di Lucio, promesso di Virginia de'
Massimi, ma innamorato di Cammilla]

Gualcina, suo famiglio

Zingaro, soldato

Monna Apollonia, fante [di Madonna Ghostanza]

Cammilla, fanciulla in casa [di Madonna Ghostanza]

Rinuccio, còrso

Messer Lucio [padre di Mario]

Gismondo [fratello di Lottieri]

Guicciardo [Gualandi, pisano, padre di Aurelia]

Lottieri Castrucci, lucchese [mercante]

Fabio [fratello di Virginia de' Massimi]

Valerio, figliuolo del medico

Vantaggio [ragazzo]

Don Diego, marrano

Un servitore di don Diego

Madonna Ghostanza [vedova napoletana, in casa della quale
vive Cammilla]

Lupo [baro][2]

1. I personaggi sono riportati nell'ordine voluto dall'autore,
insieme a qualche chiarimento, in parentesi quadre, necessario al
fine di una migliore comprensione dello sviluppo dell'azione.
2. Imbroglione, malfattore.

Characters[1]

Signor Cornelio, an elderly doctor[2]

Norchia, his servant

Mario, a young man, Lucio's son, promised to Virginia de' Massimi, the presumed widow of Valerio, but in love with Cammilla

Gualcina, Mario's servant

Gypsy, a soldier

Miss Apollonia, Madam Gostanza's maid

Cammilla, a young girl living in Madam Gostanza's home

Rinuccio, a Corsican/corsair

Signor Lucio, Mario's father

Gismondo, Lottieri's brother

Guicciardo, a Pisan

Lottieri Castrucci, a merchant from Lucca

Fabio, Virginia de' Massimi's brother

Valerio, Doctor Cornelio's son

Vantaggio, a young servant

Don Diego, a *converso*[3]

A servant of Don Diego

Madam Gostanza, a Neapolitan widow

Wolf, a trickster

1. The characters are presented in the order in which the author presents them.

2. In the Italian original, this character is sometimes referred to with his title and sometimes without; in the translation, the title is used consistently.

3. A Jewish convert to Christianity.

Viene questo giorno alla presentia vostra, illustrissimo et eccellentissimo Principe,[1] et voi altri nobilissimi spectatori una nuova commedia, la quale, già più mesi sono partitasi dal proprio padre, che da lui poco prezzata, da voi nobilissimi giovini della nostra fioritissima Accademia fu cortesemente riscevuta. Et quantunque in tutto ella non fusse tale che la meritasse honore alcuno da loro, non di meno con somma liberalità, ne fu fatto publico spectacolo. Della qual cosa l'auctore d' essa molto si duole, come quello che manifestamente cognosce che questo gli ha recato non piccola fatica, per ciò che veduto egli, mercè della diligentia di quegli addornarla et abellirla,[2] esser advenuto di lei il contrario di quello ch' ei si immaginava, et è forzato di nuovo a farne un'altra. Ma tornando alla presente, è il nome di quella Il Furto, *né vi apporti maraviglia questo nome infame, che, ben che egli nel primo incontro apparisca infame et dalla maggior parte dannato, ben si possono non di meno trovare di furto, che non solamente non sono da esser biasimati, ma ancora da quelli stessi che rubbati sono, grandemente honorati et desiderati. Et questi sono quelli che dalle bellissime et gratiosissime donne con i loro accorti et honesti sguardi ogni giorno si commettano. Per ciò che quale è quello che sentendosi in tal modo essere da donna involato[3] non la honori, non la coli[4] et in tutti e' modi a lui possibili non la celebri? Et di questo solo exempio vuole l' auctore che vi contentiate. Et quando pure alcuno di voi, nobilissimi auditori, ci fusse che, volendo stare in su la forza et rigorosità della voce, per ogni modo lo dannasse, dice egli che per questo non gli deve questo nostro* Furto *essere del tutto molesto, per ciò che né a lui molesto torremo cosa alcuna et renderemolo per lo innanzi di tenere ben guardato il suo molto ben considerare dove egli lo mette, acciò che male non gliene incolga che egli se l' habbia a perdere. Ma lassato questo da canto, vi debbo per*

---

1.   Cosimo de' Medici, duca di Firenze.

2.   I giovani accademici (i "festaiuoli") che avevano contribuito alla messa in scena del *Furto*.

3.   Metaforicamente, rapito.

4.   Non ne abbia cura, dal latino *colere*.

Prologue

Today will come before you, most illustrious and excellent Prince[1] and you, most noble spectators, a new comedy which left its father some months ago because he did not appreciated it enough. Yet it was received courteously by you, most noble youths of our flourishing Academy. And even though it was not at all worthy of being honored by them, nonetheless with great generosity, they have staged a public performance of it. The author is most aggrieved by that as one who clearly understands that it cost them no small effort, because he has seen that through their diligence in adorning and embellishing it,[2] it has become quite the opposite of what he imagined. And so, he must start over and make another one. But returning to the present one, its name is *The Theft.* And you should not wonder at the ill repute of the name because, although at first it appears criminal and condemned by most people, it is nonetheless true that one can find thefts that not only are not decried but are even greatly honored and desired by the very victims of the theft. And these are the ones that women, very beautiful and graceful, commit every day with their penetrating and chaste glances. Because who is he who, perceiving himself to be carried away[3] thus by a woman, fails to honor her, to care for her, and in all possible ways to celebrate her? And the author wishes you to be satisfied with this single example. And if it happened that one of you, most noble spectators, focusing on the strength and rigor of the term "theft," condemned it, he says that this should not cause our *Theft* to bother him at all, because we will not take anything from the person who is bothered, and we will remind him beforehand to keep under close watch everything that he values and where he put it, so that he will not take it badly if he happens to lose it.

1.   Cosimo de' Medici, duke of Florence, documented as present at the third staging of the comedy.
2.   The young members of the academy (the 'festival sponsors') who had contributed to the staging of *The Theft.*
3.   Metaphorically, kidnapped or captured.

parte dell'autore advertire che questa è la città di Roma, la quale se voi così alla prima non riconoscesti, non vi maravigliate, per ciò che essendo ella stata più di dugento anni a discretione di preti, la quale di che sorte sia lo sa tutto il mondo, non è gran fatto se l'ha mutato et forma diversa in tutto da quella che i suoi primi habitatori per mezzo della vertù gli dierono. Essendo adunque qua Roma, non fia imputato, vi priego, all' autore se quelli che parleranno non osservassino così a punto la dolcezza et leggiadria della lingua, per ciò che li habitatori d'essa, come sapete, non sono thoscani, se ben vi sono vicini, oltre che ella, (mercè de' suoi buon portamenti), [ha] mistiata la lingua sua con tante barbare nationi, che non solamente ha perduta la sua bella et pregiata di prima, ma a tale è venuta che non ha lingua che si possa dire propria sua. Doletevi adunque seco insieme et con benigne orecchie ascoltate quello che ellino vi diranno, perché per parte sua vi prometto che e' parleranno in modo che da tutti agevolmente saranno intesi. Potrebbe forse uno spagniuolo, che al fine della favola vedrete comparire alla presentia vostra, non essere da qualch' uno di voi così a pieno inteso, pure si sforzerà, essendo altra volta stato in Italia, mistiare di una maniera la lingua sua con la vostra, che molto bene, se non tutte le voci, intenderete el concetto suo. L'argumento non vi faccio io altrimente, per ciò che io non fui mai tanto presuntuoso che io volessi tor l'arte sua ad alcuno. Et però da maestro[5] Cornelio che qui abita, preparatevi a risceverlo, che già s'è messo in ordine per farvelo, al quale, per esser l'arte sua, penso che meglio gli s'adverrà che a nessun altro. Ma se per esser egli vecchio non vi sodisfacessi a pieno, verrà doppo di lui un giovine che a tutto quello che egli havessi mancato soplirà. Ma che gente son queste che di qua vengono, zingare per certo, oh, ve'[6] che cosa è questa, ell' harano sentito ragionar di furti

5.   Questo era il titolo con il quale venivano chiamati i medici.
6.   Vedi.

But leaving this aside, I must inform you on the author's behalf that this is the city of Rome, and if at first you don't recognize it, don't be surprised because with the city having been for more than two hundred years under the guidance of priests — and everyone knows what that means — it is not a big deal if it has changed and is in a completely different form from the one it was given by the talents of its first inhabitants.

This being Rome, please do not blame the author if the speakers do not observe in its fine points the sweetness and loveliness of the language, because the city's inhabitants, as you know, are not Tuscan, even though they are close to it. And in addition the city — thanks to its good behavior — has mixed its tongue with so many barbarous nations that not only has it lost the beautiful and prized form it had before, but it has been so reduced that it doesn't have a tongue that could be called its own.

Take your complaints to them, therefore, and with benign ears listen to what they will tell you, because on their behalf I promise you that they will speak in such a way as to be easily understood by all. Perhaps a Spaniard, who at the end of the tale you will see appear before you, might not be fully understood by some of you, however he will try his best, after being earlier to Italy, to mix his tongue with yours in such a way that you will understand his meaning very well, even if not all of the words.[4] I will not tell you more about the content of the play because I have never been so presumptuous as to want to steal anyone else's profession. And therefore prepare to receive it from Doctor[5] Cornelio, who lives here and who has already prepared himself to give it to you, and I believe that, because it is his profession, it is more appropriate for him to do it than for anyone else. But in case, since he is old, he does not fully satisfy you, he will be followed by a young man who will make up for everything that he was lacking.

But who are these people who are coming this way, gypsy women for sure. Oh, look. What is this? They must have heard talk

4. This pun on *tongue* as language and as physical organ is developed in the prologues of Ruzante's *Moscheta, Fiorina,* and *Piovana.*

5. The Italian text has *maestro,* the title used for medical doctors.

et vorrannocisi trovare ancora elleno. State adunque advertiti, accioché, in mentre che voi credessi stare a veder rubare altrui, non fussi rubati voi et parlando con voi uditele et insiememente tenete loro diligente cura alle mane, perché le son ladre per natura.

El fine

about a theft and wanted to be here too. Therefore, be forewarned, so that while you believe that you are watching other people being stolen from, you don't get stolen from yourselves and while they are speaking to you, listen to them and at the same time pay close attention to their hands, because these women are thieves by nature.

The End

MADRIGALE AL PRIMO ATTO

Udendo ragionar che qui si denno[7]
atti soavi e cari
di furto presentare, ond' altri impari
con gran diletto assai prudenza et senno,
noi ch'a tal gioco non havremmo pari,
zingare d'alta pruova,
cui di sempre furar diletta et giova,
qui venghian per giovare cosa sì nuova.

Stanza seconda[8]

Et dirvi in tanto che non è sempre il furto
cosa malvagia et ria
devesi riputar ch'en tutto sia,
perché di lui gran ben tal hora è surto.
Ruba il seme la terra et rubò pria
questa il vivace humore,
ruban le ninfe a i loro amanti il core,
onde ne sorge il dolce ben d'Amore.

7. Devono.

8. Questa seconda stanza è assente nell'edizione a stampa dei Madrigali di Corteccia.

Madrigal before the First Act

Hearing voices that discuss
gentle and loving acts of theft
that will be presented here, so that others may learn
with great delight and much prudence and wisdom,
we who are peerless at this game,
much-tested gypsy women,
who have always had delight and profit
from picking pockets,
we come here now to serve this new thing.

Second Stanza[6]

And to tell you, in the meanwhile, that theft
should not always
be held to be an entirely evil and terrible thing,
because sometimes from it a great good has arisen.
The seed steals from the earth, which earlier
had stolen the vivifying humor.
Nymphs steal the hearts of their beloveds,
which gives rise to the sweet benefit of Love.

6. This second stanza is missing from the printed edition of
Francesco Corteccia's madrigals for the *intermedi* of the comedy.

Francesco Corteccia

de - nz'et sen - no, noi ch'a tal gio - co non hav-re -
de - nz'et sen - no, noi ch'a tal gio - co non hav-re - mo
de - nz'et sen - no, noi ch'a tal gio - co non hav-re -
sai pru - de - nz'et sen - no, noi ch'a tal gio - co non hav-re -
- mo pa - ri. Zin - ga - re d'al - ta pro - va, cui
pa - ri. Zin - ga - re d'al - ta pro - va, cui
mo pa - ri. Zin - ga - re d'al - ta pro - va, cui
mo pa - ri. Zin - ga - re d'al - ta pro - va,
di sem - pre fu - rar di - let - t'et gio - va,
di sem - pre fu - rar di - let - t'et gio -
di sem - pre fu - rar di - let - t'et gio -
cui di sem - pre fu - rar di - let - t'et gio -

Francesco Corteccia

ATTO PRIMO

SCENA PRIMA

Maestro Cornelio vecchio et Norchia famiglio

MAESTRO CORNELIO: *Fate voi altri che questa casa sia spazzata et rassettata tutta da capo a piè et non cercate altro et tu Norchia ne vien fuor meco che io ho bisogno favellarti.*

NORCHIA: *Volete voi che io selli la mula?*

MAESTRO CORNELIO: *No, no, lascia stare la mula per stamane, essendo festa, anderò solamente alle cure più importante.[1]*

NORCHIA: *Eccomi.*

MAESTRO CORNELIO: *Io penso, Norchia, che tu ti sia molto maravigliato che non mi essendo io possuto mai rallegrare da quattro anni in qua che Valerio,[2] mio figliuolo, che Dio gli faccia pace se gli è morto, si partì da casa, da hier sera in qua mi sia dimostro tanto allegro et tanto contento.*

NORCHIA: *Certo, sì, et se io vi ho a dire il vero mi inmaginavo che voi havessi qualche buona novella di lui, perché, come voi mi avete più volte detto, la sua morte non si è mai saputa di certo.*

MAESTRO CORNELIO: *Ohimé, gli è ben vero che non si è ancora udito chi dica di haverlo veduto morto, non di meno essendo male capitati tanti in quel naufragio et non ci essendo nuove di lui in sì lungo tempo, si po' metter per fatto. Ma io non vo'*

---

1. La presente battuta e la precedente di Norchia mancano in S, fol. 1r.

2. Come si vedrà più avanti, Valerio era partito per la cosiddetta «impresa di Algeri» nell'ottobre 1541 guidata da Carlo V. La spedizione si risolse in un fallimento, causato anche dalle avverse condizioni atmosferiche, con un terribile naufragio avvenuto il giorno 24. Quello che era rimasto della flotta imperiale rientrò in Spagna, a Cartagena, ai primi di dicembre.

Act One

Scene One

Doctor Cornelio, an old man, and Norchia his servant

DOCTOR CORNELIO: You all — see that the house is swept and put in order from top to bottom, and don't try anything else. And you, Norchia, come outside with me because I need to talk to you.

NORCHIA: Do you want me to saddle the mule?

DOCTOR CORNELIO: No, no, forget the mule this morning. Because it's a holiday, I'll only take care of the most important things.[1]

NORCHIA: At your service.

DOCTOR CORNELIO: I think, Norchia, that you're quite surprised, given that I haven't been able to be happy in the four years since my son Valerio — God grant him peace if he has died — left this house,[2] that since yesterday evening I have been so cheerful and content.

NORCHIA: That's right. And to tell you the truth, I imagined that you had some good news about him, because you've always told me that there has never been a confirmation of his death.

DOCTOR CORNELIO: Ah, yes, it's quite true that no one has yet heard anyone say that they have seen him dead, nonetheless with so many having come to a bad end in that shipwreck and there having been no news of him in such a long time, it can be taken as a done deed. But I don't want to mix bitter

1. Doctor Cornelio's line of speech and the preceding one by Norchia are missing from source S (fol. 1r).

2. As will be seen later, Valerio left for what was termed "the invasion of Algeria" in October 1541. Led by Charles V, the expedition ended in failure, in part because of a terrible shipwreck on October 24 resulting from adverse weather conditions. The remnants of the imperial fleet returned to the port of Cartagena in Spain early in December.

mescolar l'aloe col mele.[3] Io mi sono rallegrato, per tornare al proposito nostro, per altro, il che voglio che tu sappia, a fine che anche tu ti rallegri et faccia festa, quel tanto che io ti dirò.

NORCHIA: *Mi rallegro per certo, perché essendo vostra famiglia[4] ogni mio bene et male depende da voi et sono per ubbidirvi a quanto voi mi comandate.*

MAESTRO CORNELIO: *Nota addunque. Ritrovandomi io, come tu vedi, senza figliuoli et havendo pure, la Dio grazia, ragionevoli facultade, ho giudicato che sarebbe non picciolo herrore il mio se io non facessi ogn'opra di lasciare di me un rampollo che resti herede de' mia beni, onde mi sono resoluto, ancora che io sia di questa età, a ripigliar moglie et hier sera, col nome di Dio, conchiusi il parentado et ho tolto una figliuola, ma che dico io, figliuola no, ma allevata da una vedova da bene napolitana che sta in su questa piazza. Et la fanciulla, secondo che dicono, è romana et di nobile sangue, benché e' sua parenti non si sono ancora trovati. El suo nome è Cammilla.*

NORCHIA: *È ella quella bella giovine che sta in sul canto della piazza?*

MAESTRO CORNELIO: *È essa, che te ne pare?*

NORCHIA: *In buona fe' che voi havete conperato bene et buon prò vi faccia.*

MAESTRO CORNELIO: *A questo modo harò io pure in casa chi mi farà qualche amorevolezza et harò altro governo che di fante. Et se bene ella è giovinetta, perché in vero quanto all'età mia potria essere mia figliuola, come io ti dissi nel principio, io non l'ho fatto per altro che per acquistare figliuoli, al che, secondo ne insegnano i nostri doctori, sono più atte quelle di tenera età*

3.   Mescolare l'amarissima aloe con il miele.
4.   Essendo al servizio della famiglia del medico.

aloes with honey.[3] I've cheered up, to return to the topic at hand, for another reason, which I want you to know so that you too will be cheered and will celebrate at what I tell you.

NORCHIA: I certainly will be cheered. Because I'm part of your household, my entire good and ill depend on you, and I'm ready to obey your every command.

DOCTOR CORNELIO: Note this then. As you see, I have no children but, by the grace of God, I am of reasonable means and therefore I've decided that it would be no small mistake on my part if I did not do everything that I could to leave offspring who would inherit all my goods. I therefore have resolved, despite my age, to marry again, and yesterday evening, in the name of God, I concluded the agreement with the family[4] and chose a girl — what am I saying, not a girl — raised by a respectable Neapolitan widow who lives in this square. And the young thing, they say, is Roman and of noble blood, although her family has not yet been located. Her name is Cammilla.

NORCHIA: That lovely young woman who lives at the corner of the square?

DOCTOR CORNELIO: The same. What do you think of her?

NORCHIA: Upon my faith, you've struck quite a bargain and may it do you good.

DOCTOR CORNELIO: In this way, I'll have someone in my house who will treat me with loving kindness and someone to care for me other than a servant. And even though she's very young — because in truth with respect to my age, she could be my daughter — as I told you at the beginning, I'm only doing this to have children and this, according to what the experts say, young women do more easily than

3.   To mix the very bitter (aloes) with the sweet.

4.   Prior to a marriage, the male heads of the two families drew up a contractual agreement concerning the bride's dowry and other practical matters. Here Cornelio does so for himself; shortly thereafter he does so for his son.

che le soprastate,[5] che se ha a fare supplimento col tenerla bene et col farli vezzi.[6]

NORCHIA: *A toccare dove fa mestiero, a far vezzi alla moglie penso io che sì gli averrà male.*

MAESTRO CORNELIO: *Come di'?*

NORCHIA: *Che delle cose giovani non si fece mai male et poi, essendo voi nell'arte vostra eccellentissimo, meritteresti biasimo non sapendo voi conoscere i buoni bocchoni.*

MAESTRO CORNELIO: *Et quest'è la cagione della mia allegrezza, che io spero mediante questo partito, non havendo nel paxato mai hauto bene, al manco nella mia vecchiezza riposarmi al quanto. Et perché un ragionamento tira l'altro, io vo' che tu sappia quale sia stata la vita mia con tutte le mie fortune, a cagione che tu mi possa scusare appo quelli che mi riprehendessono.*

NORCHIA: *Farollo, benché io penso che da ogn' uno più presto ne habbiate ad essere commendato.*

MAESTRO CORNELIO: *Tornai da studio che io havevo 24 anni, non mi trovando al mondo se non questa casa et una vigniuola, per il che, messo il collo sotto, feci tanto che in pochi anni ragunai tanto havere che io potevo, venendo in famiglia, acconciamente nutrirla. Onde, per fare quello che si aspetta a fare a ogni huomo ragionevole, presi donna[7] et ne acquistai dui figliuoli, Valerio, che tu conoscesti, et una femmina che sarebbe hora dell'essere, fa' conto, di questa mia donna. Et quando io pensava di riposarmi ci venne addosso la passata di Borbone,[8] di che ne seguì il sacco di questa ciptà, dove io, con tutti li altri, con perdita d'ogni mio mobile fui prigione e capitai alle mani de' lanzi,[9] co' quali, oltr' all'essere il più del tempo ebri, non si poteva havere commertio alchuno di parlare.*

---

5.   Mature, avanti con l'età

6.   Carezze, amorevolezze.

7.   Moglie.

8.   Carlo III di Borbone, comandante delle truppe imperiali che il 6 maggio 1527 iniziarono il sacco di Roma.

9.   Lanzichenecchi.

those who have been around for a while, whom you have to encourage with good treatment and by spoiling them.

Norchia: *(aside) Based on my expertise, I would say that the matter of spoiling wives will go badly for him.*

Doctor Cornelio: What are you saying?

Norchia: In choosing young things, you never go wrong and with your being most excellent in your art, you would be criticized if you did not recognize a yummy morsel.

Doctor Cornelio: This is why I'm so happy, because I hope that with this move, I, who have not had much good in the past, at least in my old age will be able to rest a little. And because one explanation draws another one, I want you to know what my life has been like with all of its ups and downs so that you can excuse my actions with those who might upbraid me.

Norchia: And I will, even though I think that you'll sooner be praised by everyone.

Doctor Cornelio: I finished my studies when I was twenty-four, and all my worldly goods consisted of this house and a small vineyard. And so I put my nose to the grindstone and worked so hard that in a few years I accumulated enough that I could support a family properly if I had one. And so, doing what was expected of every reasonable man, I took a wife and had two children, Valerio, whom you know, and a little girl who, calculating her age, would now be about as old as the new woman in my life. And just when I thought I could rest, the duke of Bourbon[5] came down on us in Rome and the sacking of this city followed, such that I, like everyone else, lost all my worldly goods and fell into the hands of the German soldiers,[6] who most of the time were drunk and with whom it was impossible to have a conversation.

5. Charles III, duke of Bourbon, commander of the imperial troops that on May 6, 1527 sacked Rome.
6. The Italian is *lanzi,* which refers to the *landsknechts,* German mercenary soldiers employed principally by the Holy Roman Emperor.

NORCHIA: *É vero, e' pare proprio che bestemmino quando parlano.*

MAESTRO CORNELIO *Hora ascolta. Io un giorno, come volle Dio, hauta la occasione o che gli andassono a fare la rassegna o ad altro, essendo rimaso a guardia di non so che ragazzi con loro donne, col mio figliuolo che haveva 12 anni mi fuggì da loro.*

NORCHIA: *Oh, bene.*

MAESTRO CORNELIO: *Questi cani, vedutomi essere partito, furono da tanta rabbia[10] sospinti che gli uccisono la mia povera donna.*

NORCHIA: *Ohimè, che mi dite voi.*

MAESTRO CORNELIO: *Et gittoronla in fiume et non contenti a questo presono la mia figliuola di 3 anni et ne dovettono fare il simile.*

NORCHIA: *Oh, traditori micidiali, s'io gli havessi fra' denti!*

CORNELIO: *Poi che la cosa fu quietata et che e' malvagi se ne portavono la roba et ci lasciarono solamente vergogna, io con una mia povera gabbanella[11] insieme col mio figliuolo me ne tornai a casa, riputandomi a grande sorte che quello al manco era salvo.*

NORCHIA: *Fu grande per certo, che un figliuolo tale valeva più che quanto thesora ha il mondo.*

CORNELIO: *Io in breve recuperai altrotanto di quello che perduto havea et parendomi essere tornato in buon termine detti moglie al mio figliuolo una bella fanciulla, di bon parentado, con dote più che ragionevole.[12]*

NORCHIA: *Certo gli homini sono la palla della fortuna, hora in alto gli fa balzare, hora per terra gli getta.*

CORNELIO: *Finalmente non potendo Valerio manchare a certi amici di corte, andò in loro compagnia alla maladetta impresa di Algieri. Et da che si partì, che sono circa a quattordici*

---

10. Palese errore in V,4r: «santa rabbia».

11. Corta e semplice veste.

12. Cornelio aveva fatto un contratto per un matrimonio da realizzare più avanti nel tempo.

NORCHIA: That's true, and it really seems that when they speak, they swear.

DOCTOR CORNELIO: Now listen to this. One day, as God willed it, I had the chance, when they were away for a review or something, and only some boys with their women were guarding I don't know what, I escaped with my twelve-year-old son.

NORCHIA: Oh, good!

DOCTOR CORNELIO: Those dogs, when they saw that I had left, grew so enraged that they killed my wife.

NORCHIA: Oh, dear! What are you telling me?

DOCTOR CORNELIO: And they threw her in the river. And this wasn't enough for them, so they also grabbed my three-year-old daughter to do the same to her.

NORCHIA: Homicidal maniacs! If I could get my teeth into them!

DOCTOR CORNELIO: After things quieted down and the bad guys took off with everything, leaving only shame to us, I took my threadbare jacket and my son and went home, seeing myself as very lucky that at least that had been saved.

NORCHIA: And that was certainly great because such a son is worth more than all the treasure in the world.

DOCTOR CORNELIO: In a short time, I made back what I had lost, and seeing that I was in good shape again, I gave my son a wife, a lovely girl from a good family with a more than reasonable dowry.[7]

NORCHIA: Certainly fortune treats men like a ball, tossing them high in the air and then throwing them to the ground.

DOCTOR CORNELIO: In the end, Valerio could not put off certain friends at court any longer and departed with their company on the cursed invasion of Algeria. And since he

---

7.   Cornelio, as was customary, arranged the dowry by contract with an authoritative male relative of the bride prior to the actual marriage.

mesi,[13] non ho mai inteso nulla di lui, se non che, essendo pericolati molti, habbian fatto iuditio che ancora egli sia perito et in su questa presuntione publicamente si dice che gli è morto. Et Fabio, fratello della nuora mia, se l'ha ritirata in casa. Hammi fatto sborsare fino a un quattrino[14] della dote, che mi sono cavato di mano me"[15] che 4 milia ducati contanti, che cercano di rimaritarla.

NORCHIA: *Voi havete ragione a stare male contento.*

CORNELIO: *Tu hai inteso et però per ristorarmi un poco ho io cerco di havere chi mi governi bene, con vedermi, se fia possibile, un rabacchino[16] per casa che sia il trastullo della mia vecchiezza.*

NORCHIA: *Dio ve ne dia la gratia.*

CORNELIO: *Hor quel che io vo' da te è questo. Io penso stasera a ogni modo d'andare alla donna, per il che, mentre che io testè andrò a certe mie cure, voglio che tu vadi a casa di Scipione et di Cammillo, mia consorti,[17] et dica loro il tutto del parentado et come io mi sono lasciato ire in dotarla sino alla somma di 500 fiorini et che io vorrei che amendua o uno di loro almeno mi facessi compagnia. Et fatto questa mia inbasciata, fa d'essere a Santo Spirito,[18] dove io capiterò doppo le mia faccende.*

NORCHIA: *Tanto sarà fatto, volete altro?*

CORNELIO: *Non altro, fa' quel che io t'ho detto.*

---

13. Come ricordato, *Il Furto* fu rappresentato per la prima volta il 9 novembre 1544. Pertanto, fermo restando i «quattordici mesi» qui citati, si può arguire che Francesco d'Ambra abbia scritto la sua commedia tra il 1542 e il 1543.

14. Moneta di minimo valore.

15. Più di.

16. Fanciullino.

17. Compagni.

18. La chiesa di Santo Spirito in Sassia, nel rione Borgo.

left, which was about fourteen months ago,[8] I've heard nothing of him, so, given that many of them were in great danger, people have come to the conclusion that he has already perished and on this assumption it is said publicly that he's dead. And Fabio, my daughter-in-law's brother, has taken her back to his home. He has made me pay back every last penny of her dowry, which took better than four thousand ducats out of my hands, because they are looking to remarry her.

NORCHIA: You've reason to be unhappy.

DOCTOR CORNELIO: You understand. And so to feel a little better, I'm looking for someone who will take good care of me and if possible, to see a little troublemaker around the house who'll be the delight of my old age.

NORCHIA: May God grant you that.

DOCTOR CORNELIO: Now what I want from you is this: I'm thinking that this evening, in one way or another, I'm going to the young woman's home. So, while I'm quickly taking care of some things, I want you to go to my associates, Scipione and Cammillo, and tell them everything about the agreement with her family and that I've gone so far as to provide her with a dowry of up to five hundred florins and that I'd like for both of them, or one of them at least, to accompany me. And once you've finished acting as my ambassador, get to the church of the Holy Spirit,[9] where I'll be after I've finished my errands.

NORCHIA: I'll take care of it. Anything else?

DOCTOR CORNELIO: Nothing else, just do as I've told you.

8. As stated above, the play was staged for the first time on November 9, 1544. For this reason, accepting the "fourteen months" referred to here, it may be argued that Francesco D'Ambra wrote the comedy between 1542 and 1543.

9. The church of the Holy Spirit in Sassia, in the Borgo neighborhood.

Atto primo

SCENA SECONDA

Norchia solo

NORCHIA: *Io ti so dire che questa vale un fiorino![19] Un vecchio di 60 anni ha presa per donna una giovine che a pena ne ha 18, parti che gl'habbia hauto voglia di fichi fiori.[20] Maestro Cornelio, maestro Cornelio, io ho paura che i fatti non corrispondino al nome. Una fanciulla vorrà altro che ricette o lattovari[21] et in vero le gioveranno poco, excepto che per le veste et per le collane, che ben vestita serà ella, ma se altro li mancherà, suo danno. Ma dove i' son mandato?*

SCENA TERZA

Mario giovane et Gualcina famiglio

MARIO: *Io non ti ho ancor detto, Gualcina, quel che io vo' da te, perché, a dirte il vero, ancora che io sia stato teco, io ho hauto l'animo sempre qui in torno. Dove poi che interamente sono arrivato te lo dirò al presente.*

GUALCINA: *Et io penso che voi harete hora maggiore difficultà, perché se prima havevate occupato l'animo, ora alla presentia della dama harete occupato l'animo et il corpo, ma io mi inmagino a punto quello che voi volete, che io vi dia aiuto o consiglio in questo vostro amore.*

MARIO: *Che tu m' haiuti et consigli voglio per ogni modo, perché se mai io ne hebbi bisogno hora ne ho necessità, ma pure, in verità, altro è quello che io ti vo' dire et in quello che io mi voglio servire di te.*

GUALCINA: *Eccomi paratissimo.*

---

19. Una situazione particolare. Il fiorino era un'antica moneta d'oro.

20. Cose stravaganti.

21. Medicamenti.

Act One

Scene Two

Norchia alone

NORCHIA: I can tell you, this is worth a florin.[10] An old guy who is sixty is marrying a girl who is barely eighteen. Does it seem to you that he wants to eat strawberries in January?[11] Doctor Cornelio, Doctor Cornelio, I'm afraid that the facts do not correspond with your name.[12] A girl will want more than prescriptions and medications, and in truth, these will not do her much good except to pay for her clothes and necklaces, so she will be well dressed but if he is lacking other things, too bad for her. But where am I being sent?

Scene Three

Mario, a youth, and Gualcina, his servant

MARIO: I have not yet told you, Gualcina, what I want from you because, to tell you the truth, since I have been with you my mind has been on things here. What I have committed entirely to, I will tell you shortly.

GUALCINA: And I think that you will have greater difficulty now because while before your soul was taken up with things, now with the woman present, both your soul and your body will be taken up. But I can imagine exactly what you want from me, help and advice about this love of yours.

MARIO: I definitely want your help and advice because if I needed it before, it is a necessity to me now, but in fact what I want to tell you is something else, and this is the thing that I want your services for.

GUALCINA: Here I am, more than prepared to serve you.

10. A noteworthy or unusual situation; the florin was a gold coin in use then.

11. Indicates an extravagant wish. The original is "to make fig flowers": fig trees do not flower.

12. The word *cornelio* also meant "cornel," a wood known for its exceptional hardness; this reference is also found in Ruzante's *Prima oratione*.

MARIO: *Ma vedi, bisogna che tu me lo tenga secreto, perché l'è tanto importante quanto cosa che mai t' habbia conferito.*

GUALCINA: *Volete voi che non lo sappia persona, non lo dite voi ancora a me.*

MARIO: *Lasciamo il burlare, io dico che non è da manifestarlo a huomo nato et se io lo dico a te, lo fo che ho bisogno de' fatti tuoi.*

GUALCINA *Che bisogna tante parole, parrebbe che voi mi havessi a cognoscere ora, el ricordarmi quello che io fo per l'ordinario è un perdere tempo.*

MARIO: *Ora odi. Io so che t'è noto la grande amicitia che io ho contratta con Gismondo Castrucci lucchese, ancora che non sia più di tre mesi che qua per suo spasso venissi. La quale certamente è tale che quello che io non facessi per lui, ti poi rendere certo ch'io non farei per altro huomo. Et quantunque io habbia che fare da me per insino sopra i capegli niente di meno, tanto è l'amore che gli porto ch'io son forzato, postposto le mie faccende, pigliarmi le cure sue per mie proprie.*

GUALCINA: *É cosa lodevole, che già non è altro l'amico che un sé medesimo.*

MARIO: *Gismondo, addunque, essendo oltre modo innamorato d'una giovine che è in mano d' un certo Rinuccio còrso[22] et havendo fatto sì che gli pare havere guadagnato il suo amore, ha determinato per una via o per un'altra non restare mai fin che la gli venga nelle mani.*

GUALCINA: *Io vi romperò il parlare, o Gismondo non è egli parecchi giorni che partì per la volta di Lucca?*

MARIO: *Questo è quello che io voglio che tu mi tenga celato, Gismondo è in Roma, in casa Bergamino alla Scimmia.[23] Ma odi quello che gli ha fatto et in che termine si trova.*

GUALCINA: *Dite.*

---

22. Originario della Corsica.

23. La torre della Scimmia in palazzo Scapucci. Bergamino è il nome del protagonista di *Decameron*, I, 7.

MARIO: But look, you will have to keep it a secret for me, because it is the most important thing that I have ever asked of you.

GUALCINA: If you don't want anyone to know, then don't tell me.

MARIO: Stop kidding around. I'm saying that you are not to reveal it to any man on earth, and if I'm telling you, it is because I need your help.

GUALCINA: There's no need for so many words. It makes it seem like you just met me. Reminding me of my usual work is a waste of time.

MARIO: Listen up: I know that you are aware of the great friendship that I have formed with Gismondo Castrucci of Lucca even though it was only three months ago that he came here for his amusement. And the friendship is such that you can be certain that something that I would not do for him I would not do for anyone. And even though I am up to my ears with my own affairs, my love for him is so great that I must postpone dealing with my own and attend to his as if they were mine.

GUALCINA: That is praiseworthy, because a friend is another self.

MARIO: Gismondo, then, is head-over-heels in love with a young girl who is being held by Rinuccio the Corsican,[13] and having acted in such a way that he believes he has obtained her love, he has decided that he will not rest until in one way or another he has taken her into his own hands.

GUALCINA: I'm going to interrupt you. Isn't Gismondo the one who some days ago set out on the road to Lucca?

MARIO: This is what I want you to keep secret for me — Gismondo is in Rome, at the Bergamino house at the Monkey.[14] But listen to what he has done and what conditions he finds himself in.

GUALCINA: Tell me.

---

13. Italian *corso* means both "Corsican" and "corsair" (a private but state-authorized pirate).

14. This was the Monkey Tower in Palazzo Scapucci. Bergamino is the name of the lead character of *Decameron*, I, 7.

MARIO: *Havendo egli, per mezo di non so che donna, in questa sua partita quasi che condotta la corda in su la noce,[24] el suo huomo o che sia stato advertito o che se ne sia accorto, dove prima e' la teneva in casa, ora, a vedere et non vedere, l'ha cacciata nel monasterio delle Convertite[25] et da qualche inbasciata in fuori niente altro ne può havere.*

GUALCINA: *Et però si dice batti il ferro mentre è caldo.*

MARIO: *Ora Gismondo, cresciutogliene più la voglia quanto più vede la cosa essergli vietata, prese per expediente corrompere con denari questo Rinuccio.*

GUALCINA: *Buono, perché col mezzo de' denari s'ottiene ciò che l'huomo vole.*

MARIO: *Et fulli dato intentione che quando gli facesse una mancia di 150 o 200 scudi, gliene darebbe a ogni modo.*

GUALCINA: *Canchero, cotesta è un gran tasta,[26] ma torniamo un passo a dietro, donde è cotesta giovine?*

MARIO: *É figliuola d'un gentil' huomo pisano che si chiama Guicciardo Gualandi, el quale, faccendo vela da Palermo a Livorno, nel canale di Piombino dette ne' corsali et fatto prigione insieme con detta figliuola. Si pose 500 fiorini di taglia, infino non pagava dicta somma la lasciò loro in pegno. Costui che al presente la tiene appresso di sé la vorrebbe rendere al padre et con questo animo l'ha data in serbo alle suore.*

GUALCINA: *Come sa egli il nome del padre?*

24. Essendo sul punto di raggiungere il suo scopo.

25. Fondato da papa Leone X il monastero si trovava lungo l'attuale via del Corso.

26. Gran meraviglia.

MARIO: With the assistance of some woman or other on his quest, he had nearly gotten the string around the walnut[15] when his man, either because he was warned or because he noticed something, whereas he had earlier kept her in his home — now you see her now you don't — he stuck her in the Monastery of the Penitents[16] and except for a small number of guests from outside, she can see no one.

GUALCINA: And that is why they say, "strike while the iron is hot."

MARIO: And now Gismondo — since his desire increased as soon as the thing was forbidden — has decided on the tactic of buying off this Rinuccio.

GUALCINA: That's good, because money is the means by which a man can obtain anything he wishes.

MARIO: And he was given to understand that when he gave a tip of one hundred fifty or two hundred scudi, she would be given to him in one way or another.

GUALCINA: By the pox![17] This is a big deal! But let's go back a step: where is this young woman from?

MARIO: She is the daughter of a Pisan gentleman named Guicciardo Gualandi, who, while sailing from Palermo to Livorno, encountered corsairs in the Piombino Canal and was taken prisoner together with this daughter. A ransom of five hundred florins was put on his head, and he left her as his surety until he paid that sum. The guy, who has her at the moment, would like to turn her over to her father and with this in mind, he gave her to the sisters to keep.

GUALCINA: How does he know the father's name?

---

15. A proverbial expression that indicates being on the point of completing a difficult and tricky task.

16. The order was composed of reformed prostitutes. Founded by Pope Leo X, the monastery was located along the present via del Corso.

17. *Canchero* was an early term for syphilis, which had recently arrived in Italy and was spreading rapidly. An exclamation favored by Ruzante.

MARIO: *Perché quando la rimase a' corsali l'haveva 12 anni o più.*

GUALCINA: *Ben, ben, ell'era grande, ma come l'ha hora costui.*

MARIO: *Questo non ti so dire già, perché non mi è occorso il cercarne.*

GUALCINA: *Non importa, or seguitate di Gismondo.*

MARIO: *Gismondo, havuta questa intentione et non si trovando un denaio né havendo credito quantunque sia fratello di messer Lottieri, ricchissimo mercante, ha fatto una cosa ch'io per me non la pruovo, non di meno l'ha fatto constretto dalla necessità. Et questo si è che, havendo contraffatto le chiave del fondaco[27] del fratello et finto partirsi per Lucca, di lì a dua o tre sere entrò in detto fondaco et d'una cassa di drappi ne tolse tanto che vale 150 o 200 scudi, pensando che questi havessino a contentare quel Rinuccio, ma quando di poi e' tenta questa faccenda lo trova più discosto dal farlo che gennaio dalle more.[28] Onde trovandosi le mani piene di vento è in sul disperarsi et hiersera mandò per me et riferimi il tutto et pregommi che io vedessi se a te, che sei ingegnoso, ti dessi l'animo trarre questa giovine a quel còrso delle mani, quando egli habbia a mettere, oltre a' drappi, que' pochi denari che si trova.*

GUALCINA: *Che diavolo vuole egli se a sì fatta mancia non si piega?*

MARIO: *Ha incapato[29] volerla rendere al padre et a pena la darebbe ad altri per mille scudi.*

GUALCINA: *Pure la darebbe per danari, ma se gli ha tanta voglia di rendergliene, che non gliene mena egli fino a Pisa o egli gliene scriva acciò che e' si venga per essa?*

---

27. Magazzino, bottega.
28. Le more maturano nell'estate avanzata.
29. Si è messo in testa.

MARIO: Because when she was left with the corsairs, she was twelve years old or older.

GUALCINA: Well, then, she was a big girl, but how is it that he has her now?

MARIO: I can't tell you that, because I never needed to find out.

GUALCINA: Never mind. Now tell me more about Gismondo.

MARIO: Gismondo, after deciding on this strategy but having no money and no credit even though he is the brother of Signor Lottieri, a very rich merchant, did something that I myself do not approve of, but nonetheless he did it under pressure of necessity. Which is that he made a copy of the key to his brother's warehouse and pretended to leave for Lucca. Two or three evenings later, he entered the warehouse and from a chest of silk cloths he took enough to be worth one hundred fifty or two hundred scudi, thinking that this would be enough to satisfy Rinuccio. But when he later tried to complete the transaction, he found out that it was harder to accomplish than picking blackberries in January.[18] So, finding himself empty-handed,[19] he was on the point of despair, and yesterday evening he sent for me and told me everything and begged me to see if you, who are so ingenious, had the courage to rescue this girl from the hands of the Corsican, when he is able to add to the silk cloths what little money he can find.

GUALCINA: What the devil does he want if that kind of tip doesn't move him?

MARIO: He has gotten it into his head to turn her over to her father and can barely be convinced to give her to anyone else for a thousand scudi.

GUALCINA: Okay, so he will turn her over for money, but if he is so willing to turn her over, why doesn't he take her to Pisa or write there to get them to come for her?

18. Blackberries ripen in late summer.

19. The original is "with his hands full of wind."

MARIO: *Dice che gli e' n' ha mandato a dire più volte e qua non è mai capitato persona, che forse potrebbe essere morto, chi sa, et la non la mena perché si teme non haverla a rendere senza cavarne un baiocco,[30] che per adventura gli interverrebbe.*

GUALCINA: *Che direte voi se io gliene cavo di mano per manco che non ha voluto fare Gismondo?*

MARIO: *Come, Gualcina mio?*

GUALCINA: *State di buona voglia, che io son certo di servirvi a ogni modo et tosto tosto.*

MARIO: *Oh, ingegno felicissimo, oh, solo adiuto ne' mia bisogni, deh contami in che modo tu hai pensato.*

GUALCINA: *Bastivi, che io tengo buono in mano[31] et vi do la cosa per fatta.*

MARIO: *Dimmi ti priego il modo, acciò che io possa meglio pascermi di questa speranza con alcun verisimile, per amore dello amico mio.*

GUALCINA: *Udite, io mi voglio servire d'un mio conoscente spuletino[32] che ha nome il Zingaro, il più sufficente barro[33] che sia in Roma et tanto ben parlante et così accorto et sagace che darebbe a credere a ogni huomo ciò che gli paresse. Et dando ad intendere a cotesto Rinuccio d' esser egli il padre della fanciulla, gliene caverà di mano a ogni modo.*

MARIO: *Io dubito che la non ci verrà fatta.*

GUALCINA: *Di gratia, non vi date tanti pensieri, volete voi altro che Gismondo habbia lo attento suo?[34]*

MARIO: *Non altro quanto a Gismondo, ma vo' ben ora che si pensi al fatto mio, ch'io non vorrei però fare come colui che, rassegnando ogni sua cosa, lasciava indietro sé stesso. Tu vedi dove io mi trovo, la Cammilla è allo stretto di maritarsi a quel*

---

30. Moneta di rame, di scarso valore, in uso nella Roma pontificia.
31. Ho delle buone carte da giuocare.
32. Di Spoleto.
33. Baro, imbroglione.
34. Raggiunga il suo scopo.

MARIO: He says that he has sent word a number of times and no one has come. Perhaps her father is dead, who knows, and he will not take her there because he is afraid that he will have to turn her over without getting a penny out of it, which by chance could happen to him.

GUALCINA: What would you say if I got her out of his hands for less than what Gismondo was willing to give?

MARIO: How, my Gualcina?

GUALCINA: Keep your spirits up. I am certain I can assist you in one way or another and soon, very soon.

MARIO: Oh, most happy ingenuity, oh sole succor in my time of need, please tell me what you have thought up.

GUALCINA: Let it be enough for you to know that I have something good in hand[20] and can say that the thing is as good as done.

MARIO: Tell me, I beg you, how, so that I can better nourish myself with this hope by imagining it happening for the love of my friend.

GUALCINA: Listen, I want to use the services of an acquaintance of mine from Spoleto named the Gypsy, the most able con man in Rome, and such a good talker and so discerning and wise that he can get anyone to believe whatever he wants. And by convincing this Rinuccio that he, Gypsy, is the father of the girl, he will get her out of his hands in one way or another.

MARIO: I doubt that this will happen.

GUALCINA: Please, don't worry yourself about it. Do you want anything beside Gismondo's obtaining his goal?

MARIO: Nothing more for Gismondo, but now I really want us to think about my business, because I do not want to act like the guy who, while taking care of all his things, left himself out. You see where I am — Cammilla is being

20. A good hand of cards to play.

medico et hieri per la sua fante mi mandò a dire che temeva ch'
el parentado non si conchiudessi et mi pregava strettamente che
io la cavassi di casa, che più presto voleva fare ogni altra cosa che
essere sua moglie. Et in verità l' ha ragione, perché se non altro
gliè forzato ad esserne in tal modo geloso che non che altro alle
rondine sarà vietato l'entrata di casa. Et così non ci potren più
parlare et volendola menare via, come l'ho tenuta in speranza,
non mi trovo uno danaio et mal si può sanza danari pigliare
alcun partito.

GUALCINA: È vero, né di state, né di verno, dice il proverbio.

MARIO: Et non ho tempo a pensare di farne, perché, ogni poco
che io badi, in Roma mi potrò male liberare da mio padre, che
non mi lassa vivere di volermi dar per donna la vedova che
rimase di Valerio, figliuolo del medico, che pare che da quella
maladetta casa derivino tutti e' mia mali, se non fussi entrato in
questo farnetico di ripigliare moglie. Et se la nuora non havessi
tanta furia di volersi così tosto rimaritare, io harei tempo a ogni
mia difficultà, perché tu sai che chi ha tempo ha vita.

GUALCINA: Tagliatevi l'agno,[35] cavatevela di casa quanto più
presto meglio è. Et con Gismondo, che harà anche la sua,
andatevene a Lucca, di cosa nasce cosa.

MARIO: Sì, ma donde ho io a cavare i danari?

GUALCINA: Della borsa di vostro padre, donde pensate dal pesce
di San Piero?[36]

---

35. Prendete una coraggiosa risoluzione. L'*agno* era un bubbone
che si riproduceva nell'inguine.

36. Secondo la leggenda, dopo averlo pescato, san Pietro mise le
mani sul pesce, generando così le macchie che lo caratterizzano.

pressured to marry that doctor and yesterday had her maid bring me word that she feared that the family agreement was being concluded and begged me heartily that I get her out of her house, because she would do anything but become his wife. And in truth she is right, because if nothing else he will be forced to be so jealous of her that the only thing that won't be barred from the house will be swallows. And so we will not be able to speak to each other anymore and although I want to take her away, as I have kept her hoping I will, I find myself without a cent, and it is hard to work up a plan when you don't have any money.

GUALCINA: It's true, neither in summer nor in winter, as the proverb says.

MARIO: And I have no time to think about making any, because even when I pay a little attention to it, in Rome it will be hard to free myself from my father. He is always on my case about giving me as a wife the widow of Valerio, the doctor's son. It seems that that damned house is the source of all my troubles. If only he had not started this chatter about taking a second wife. And if the daughter-in-law were not in such a fury to remarry immediately, I would have time to resolve all of my difficulties, because you know that those who have time, have life.

GUALCINA: Burst the boil,[21] get her out of her house, the sooner the better. And with Gismondo, who will also get what he wants, go to Lucca because one thing leads to another.

MARIO: Yes, but where can I dig up the money?

GUALCINA: From your father's wallet, what do you think, from St. Peter's fish?[22]

---

21. To take courageous action to solve a problem. The Italian, *tagliatevi l'agno,* means literally "to burst [the plague] pustule [that formed] in the arm pit."

22. According to legend, St. Peter, after he caught the fish, took it in his hands, making its characteristic dark spots that resemble coins.

MARIO: *Per Dio, che tu ti fondi bene,[37] come se tu non cognoscessi che gliè sì misero che qual si voglia strettoio o mangano,[38] stringendolo, non ne caverebbono un picciòlo.[39]*

GUALCINA: *Una sola parola vi darà più danari che voi non volete et liberaretevi da tutti i fastidi, accadendo soprastare più uno dì che uno altro.*

MARIO: *Se non basta una parola io ne dirò mille, purché si sappia quello che ho a dire et a chi.*

GUALCINA: *Ben vi sbigottite per poco. Se voi dite a vostro padre d'esser contento a fare quanto egli vole et che per voi non sta di prender quella moglie che più li piace, pur che vi dia tanti danari alla mano che possiate sodisfare a qualche vostro debituzzo antico et voi stesso mettere in assetto, son certissimo che vostro padre non vi negarà quella somma di danari che voi gli adomanderete, tanto gran voglia ha di darvi questa moglie con questa buona dote, che lo avaro si piglia con l'avaritia come gli uccelli con gli uccelli.*

MARIO: *In fede mia che tu di' il vero, a ogni modo faccendogliene una gliene potrò ben anco fare dua, qualche santo in questo mezzo ci adiuterà. Va' tu dunque a mettere in ordine quello che hai pensato della cosa di Gismondo et io me n'andrò in casa a ritrovare il vecchio.*

GUALCINA: *Volete voi altro?*

MARIO: *Assai mi basta questo, Dio voglia che ci succeda bene.*

FINE DEL PRIMO ATTO

37. Ci fai assegnamento.
38. Argano.
39. Una moneta di scarso valore.

MARIO: By God, what a great idea, as if you didn't know that he is such a tightwad that whatever vise or winch you tightened around him, you would not get a penny from him.

GUALCINA: A single word will get you more money than you want and free you from all the troubles, because one day is more important than another.

MARIO: If one word is not enough, I will give a thousand, so long as I know what I have to say and to whom.

GUALCINA: You are losing your cool for so little. If you tell your father that you are happy to do what he wants and that as far as you are concerned, he should not hold off choosing whatever wife he likes best, as long as he puts enough cash in your hand to pay off some little old debts and put you in good shape. I am very certain that your father will not deny you whatever sum of money you ask, so great is his desire to give you this wife with her good dowry, because you catch a tightwad with his avarice just as you catch birds with birds.

MARIO: Upon my faith, you speak the truth, and anyway, if we pull one trick on him, we can pull two, some saint or other will help us in the meantime. So, go and organize the plan you have thought up for Gismondo's affair, and I will go home and find my old man.

GUALCINA: Do you want anything else?

MARIO: This is quite enough for me, God willing that it turns out well for us.

END OF THE FIRST ACT

Quanto sia dolce voglia
di lasciare dopo noi chi noi rasembri,
serbando in vita la paterna spoglia
Et come ad alte imprese Amore invoglia
pur ch'altri lo rimembri.
Giovinil core legato in salda rete
fino a qui udito havete.
Quel che di poi s'avoglia
in breve intenderete,
grati uditor, se voi ne presterete
l'orecchia intentte e quete.

Madrigal before the Second Act

What a sweet desire it is
to leave behind someone who resembles us,
keeping alive the father's mortal coil
and inspired by love to high achievements
so that others may remember him.
A youthful heart bound in a strong net
is what to this point you have heard.
What he will then desire,
you will soon learn,
welcome audience, if you will lend
your attentive and quiet ears.

Francesco Corteccia

Quanto sia dolce voglia

ga - t'in sal - da re - te fi - n'a qui u - di - t'ha - ve -
- da re - te fi - n'a qui u - di - t'ha - ve -
sal - da re - te fi - n'a qui u - di - t'ha - ve -
sal - da re - te fi - n'a qui u - di - t'ha - ve -
- te, Quel che di poi
- te, Quel che di poi
- te, Quel che di poi
- te, Quel che di poi
s'ac - co - glia in brie - v'in - ten - de - re - te, gra - t'u - di -
s'ac - co - glia in brie - v'in - ten - de - re - te, gra - t'u - di -
s'ac - co - glia in brie - v'in - ten - de - re - te, gra - t'u - di -
s'ac - co - glia in brie - v'in - ten - de - re - te, gra - t'u - di -

Quanto sia dolce voglia

Atto secondo

Scena prima

Gualcina, Zingaro et Mario

GUALCINA: *Io credetti che la professione tua fussi di barattieri,[1] cioè di buon compagno,[2] intendi, et tu mi riesci il maggior bravo[3] d'Italia.*

ZINGARO: *Pensa che chi vuole vivere come io, vive poco et male. A uno mio pari bisogna sapere tutte le professioni et tenere fermo questo punto: volere vivere sempre da ricco, non si curare del mondo, né del tempo, insomma da buon soldato che non pensa mai alla morte et venga quando vuole.*

GUALCINA: *A questo modo vogliono essere gli homini, a questi riesce ogni cosa. Ma tornando al fatto nostro, buon per te se tu servi el padrone mio, tu potresti forse cavarne tanto che tu non vorresti morire per qualche mese.*

ZINGARO: *L'opera loderà il maestro. Io so a punto quel che ho a fare et non mancherò del debito mio, non mancando voi, come tu prometti, del vostro.*

GUALCINA: *Tu sarai più che satisfatto, dico, ma vedilo là a punto.*

MARIO: *Se l'amore non fussi sempre accompagnato dalla gelosia, io sarei adesso più lieto che mai, non per cento ducati che mi ha dato mio padre, ma per la commodità che io ne spero.*

GUALCINA: *Et gliè lieto, debbe havere seco danari.*

ZINGARO: *Non può addunque la cosa succedere se non bene.*

---

1.   Truffatore.

2.   na «una buona compagna» era stata anche Sostrata, la madre di Lucrezia, nella *Mandragola* (I, 1) di Machiavelli.

3.   Prode, in senso implicitamente ironico.

Act Two

Scene One

Gualcina, Gypsy, and Mario

GUALCINA: I thought that your profession was glad hander, in other words a hail fellow well met, if you understand me, but I have figured out that you are the best strong man[1] in Italy.

GYPSY: You should know that a man who wants to live like I do lives a short time and badly. Someone who wants to be like me has to know all the professions and keep this point clear in his mind: you have to want to live like a rich man all the time, not care about the world or time, and, just like a good soldier, never think of death and let it come when it wants to.

GUALCINA: This is the way men want to be. These guys succeed at everything. But getting back to our situation, good for you if you serve my master, you might be able to make enough from it that you would not die for several months.

GYPSY: The work will praise the craftsman. I know exactly what I have to do, and I will not fail to do my duty as long as you, as you promise, do yours.

GUALCINA: You will be more than satisfied. I say, by the way, look, here he comes.

MARIO: If love were not always accompanied by jealousy, I would now be happier than ever, not for the one hundred ducats that my father gave me but for the way that I hope it will make things easier.

GUALCINA: And he is happy. He must have money with him.

GYPSY: Therefore the thing cannot go any other way than well.

1. A *bravo* was a kind of body guard or "goon" who carried out violent acts for the powerful, but here probably said with irony.

GUALCINA: *Non dubitare, a te non ha a mancare la debita provisione. Andiamo alla volta sua, patrone, oh, patrone.*

MARIO: *Oh, Gualcina.*

GUALCINA: *Ecco un conduttieri delli amori vostri.*

MARIO: *Questo è il Zingaro, quel valent'huomo che tu mi hai detto, eh?*

GUALCINA: *Messer sì.*

ZINGARO: *Al piacere di vostra signoria.*

GUALCINA: *Questo è il nostro invittissimo capitano Zingaro, che si dà vanto al primo assalto darci la terra[4] a man salva.*

MARIO: *Buono, a una spugnatione d'una città ha aguagliato quest'opera, gliè bene mantenerlo in su la data, ma gliè così, capitano?*

ZINGARO: *Signor sì, non si mancando dal canto della signoria vostra delle debite provisioni.*

MARIO: *È cosa giusta. Dite, capitano, per ordine tutto quello che occore et non si mancherà di nulla.*

ZINGARO: *Primieramente, perché il nervo della guerra è il danaio,[5] mi occorre ricordare che le provisioni de' danari sierno gagliarde et che e' soldati sierno ben pagati, acciò che per il patrone volentieri si sottomettino a tutti e' pericoli.*

GUALCINA: *Intendete voi, Mario?*

MARIO: *Benissimo, ma rispondigli tu che in questa impresa te ho fatto mio capitano et segretario.*

GUALCINA: *Danari ci sono, capitano, et pagherannosi i soldati avanti che eschino a combattere.*

---

4. Città.

5. Diversamente da Machiavelli, *Discorsi*, II, 10: «I danari non sono il nervo della guerra, secondo che è la comune opinione».

GUALCINA: Don't worry, you will be taken care of as promised. Let's go forward to meet him. Master, oh master!

MARIO: Oh, Gualcina.

GUALCINA: Meet someone who will command your love affairs.

MARIO: This is Gypsy, that gentleman that you spoke to me about, right?

GUALCINA: Yes, sir.

GYPSY: At your lordship's pleasure.

GUALCINA: This is our undefeated Captain Gypsy, who brags that on the first assault he will conquer the city for us with ease.

MARIO: Good. He has compared this undertaking to the conquest of a city. It is good to keep to the deal, is it not, captain?

GYPSY: Yes, sir, as long as on your lordship's part the promised provisions are not lacking.

MARIO: That is the right thing to do. Tell me in order, captain, everything that you need, and nothing will be lacking.

GYPSY: First of all, because the muscle of war is money,[2] I must remind you that the provision of money must be forthcoming and the soldiers must be paid well, so that they will willingly face all dangers for their master.

GUALCINA: Do you understand, Mario?

MARIO: I understand very well, but you must answer him that for this undertaking, I have made you my captain and secretary.

GUALCINA: The money is there, captain, and the soldiers will be paid before they go forth to combat.

---

2.   Because he was promoting local militias who would defend their homeland, Machiavelli, *Discorsi*, II, 10, discounted the importance of money in war, but by the time of this play, wars were fought by mercenaries.

ZINGARO: *Secondariamente fa mestiere d'arme, di scale, di briccole[6] et artiglierie, mediante le quali si possa, quando fia tempo, assaltare la muraglia et saltare dentro alla terra.*

GUALCINA: *Anche cotesto sarà in ordine, capitano.*

MARIO *Che intend'egli per tante artigliarie, bricchole et arme?*

GUALCINA: *Le vestimenta, vol dire, cappello, stivali et altre cose al proposito per dimostrare che gliè colui che vogliamo.*

MARIO: *Buono.*

ZINGARO: *Di poi fa bisogno di vettovaglia per rinfrescare i soldati prima et poi. Et questa è una delle più importante cose che accaggino nella guerra, perché si porteria troppo gran pericolo havendosi a combattere anche con la fame.*

GUALCINA: *Mi maravigliavo che lasciassi in dietro la gola. Non dubitate che la vettovaglia pioverà da tutte le bande. Seguitate pure, se gli occorre altro.*

ZINGARO: *Et perché mi pare intendere che nella terra vostra signoria ha qualche intelligentia, volendo che la cosa riesca bisogna tenere deste per vostre lettere quelle persone che ci hanno a servire, acciò che, quando daremo lo assalto, non manchi a quello che occorre.*

GUALCINA: *A tutto si provederà, state di buono animo.*

MARIO: *Che ha egli voluto dire in quest'ultimo?*

GUALCINA: *Che si faccia intendere alla fanciulla che, fingendo egli essere suo patre, dal canto suo facci bene gli atti suoi.*

MARIO: *Bene, per Dio, voi mi satisfate ogn'ora, capitano. Et per quello io veggio niente s'è lasciato indietro.*

ZINGARO: *Promettovi la vittoria.*

MARIO: *Horsù, Gualcina, che s'avanzi tempo. Mena il Zingaro a Gismondo e digli quel che accade. Egli è huomo a cui basterà*

6.   Macchine da guerra.

Gypsy: Secondly, there is need for arms, ladders, catapults, and artillery, by means of which, we can, when the time comes, assault the walls and drop down into the town.

Gualcina: This too will be ready, captain.

Mario: But what does he mean by so many pieces of artillery, catapults, and arms?

Gualcina: He means clothes, hat, boots, and other things needed to show that he is the kind of guy we want.

Mario: Okay.

Gypsy: Then we need food to refresh the soldiers before and after. And this is one of the most important things needed in war because it creates far too great a hazard when soldiers have to battle hunger too.

Gualcina: I was surprised that you had not mentioned the stomach before this. Do not fear. Food will rain down on you on every side. Keep going if anything more is necessary.

Gypsy: Because I seem to understand that your lordship has some means of gathering intelligence in the town, if you want the thing to succeed, you must use letters to alert the people who will be handling it for us, so that when we undertake the assault, we will not lack for anything that we need.

Gualcina: We will take care of everything. Keep your chin up.

Mario: What did he intend to say with this last thing?

Gualcina: That the girl should be made to understand that when he pretends he is her father, she for her part must act her role well.

Mario: Well done, by God! You are satisfying me on every point, captain. And that is why I will see that nothing is left out.

Gypsy: I promise you victory.

Mario: All right, Gualcina, time is passing. Take Gypsy to Gismondo, and tell him what is happening. He is the kind

un cenno et sopra tutto fa' che e' soldati si paghino, rinfreschinsi et arminsi et che il capitano si contenti in tutto et per tutto.

ZINGARO: *Oh, potere del cielo, questi sono homini da servire volentieri.*

MARIO: *Tornate di poi di qua con l'ordine, perché non passa mai un'ora che Rinuccio non sia qui intorno et io in tanto vedrò se potrò intendere nulla della cosa mia.*

GUALCINA: *Sta bene, venitene capitano Zingaro.*

ZINGARO: *Bacio la mano a vostra signoria.*

MARIO: *A Dio.*

SCENA SECONDA

Mario solo

MARIO: *Sempre pare che accaggia che più agevolmente si conchiudino le altrui faccende che le sue propie. Gismondo et io siamo aggravati d'una medesima infirmità. Et benché la sua molto più difficile apparisce, non di meno io gli ho saputo trovare la via alla salute et per me, ancora che io gli habbia tutti e' mezzi opportuni, non veggio spiraglio alchuno. Et tutto procede per non potere intendere il seguito del parentado della Cammilla et del medico. Gran cosa è certamente che in tutta questa mattina, che non mi sono mai partito di qui, non mi sia mai abbattuto rincontrare la fante, dalla quale io fussi tratto fuori di questo dubbio et mi potessi risolvere alla mia faccenda. Ma ecco a punto il medico, guarda chi mi fa,[7] horsù, ma io mi vo' levare di qui per non gli dare suspitione che m'havessi a nuocere.*

---

7.   Guarda per chi mi ha preso.

of man who needs only a small gesture, and above all make sure that the soldiers are paid, are fed, and are armed, and that the captain is happy about all things and in everything.

GYPSY: Oh, by the power of heaven, these are men that one is happy to serve.

MARIO: Come back here afterward with the order, because not an hour goes by that Rinuccio isn't hanging around here, and in the meanwhile, I will see if I can find out anything about this thing of mine.

GUALCINA: Be well. Come along, Captain Gypsy.

GYPSY: I kiss your lordship's hands.[3]

MARIO: Godspeed.

SCENE TWO

Mario alone

MARIO: It always seems to be the case that it is easier to bring other people's affairs to a conclusion than one's own. Gismondo and I are weighed down by the same illness. And although his seems much more difficult, I have managed to find the way to health for him. But for me, even though I have all of the right means, I don't see an opening at all. And all this is the consequence of not being able to learn what has happened in the family agreement regarding Cammilla and the doctor. It is very telling that in this entire morning, in which I have never left this spot, I have never happened to encounter her nurse, who could lift me out of this worry and give me a solution to my task. But here comes the doctor. Look at who he takes me for. Come on, I want to get out of here so as not to give rise to a suspicion in him that could hurt me.

3.   An expression of fealty, sometimes accompanied by the act.

Scena terza

Maestro Cornelio, Norchia suo servo

CORNELIO: *Che di' tu Norchia, né Scipione, né Cammillo non si trovano in casa, eh?*

NORCHIA: *Non vi dico io che stamattina l'uno et l'altro era cavalcato alla vigna.*

CORNELIO: *Per certo questo s'è fatto da loro in prova che, vedendomi hieri volto a questo parentado, per la invidia non ci sono potuti stare sotto. Infine, quando uno ha qualche cosa che sia sua, e' maggiori inimici sono e' più stretti parenti.*

NORCHIA: *Lasciate pure essere, gliè meglio essere invidiato che invidiare altri.*

CORNELIO: *Horsù, disporrenci a andar soli. Per questo non sarà che io non tolgha donna et che io non mi cavi questa voglia a dispetto di chi non vuole. Ma odi.*

NORCHIA: *Messere?*

CORNELIO: *Va' in casa et fa' ordinare di desinare,[8] ma sta, desinare no, fate un poco di colatione, che havendo stasera a uscire dell'ordinario col pasto, sarebbe errore caricarsi troppo col cibo.[9]*

NORCHIA: *Delle sua, stare sempre in su la regola.*

CORNELIO: *Che di' tu?*

NORCHIA: *Ch'el desinare che si è proveduto non è punto fuori della regola, né vi caricarete troppo, non dubitate.*

CORNELIO: *Or va,' fa' quel che io t'ho detto, in tanto darò una volta dallo spetiale.*

---

8.   Pranzo.

9.   Nota autografa a centro pagina in V, c. 26r: «Qui rimane maestro Cornelio in iscena et parla solo una scena e poi va in casa».

Act Two

SCENE THREE

Doctor Cornelio, Norchia his servant

DOCTOR CORNELIO: Norchia, what can you tell me — Scipione and Cammillo have both gone out, right?

NORCHIA: Let me tell you — this morning both of them went on horseback to the vineyard.

DOCTOR CORNELIO: They clearly did this because once they saw me intent on concluding this agreement with the family yesterday, they were so envious they couldn't stand it. In the end, when someone has something that is his, his greatest enemies are his closest relatives.

NORCHIA: Forget about them. It is better to be envied than to envy.

DOCTOR CORNELIO: All right. Let's prepare to go without them. This should not be a reason for me not to take a wife and not to satisfy this urge to spite those who don't want me to. But listen.

NORCHIA: Sir?

DOCTOR CORNELIO: Go home and order dinner to be prepared, but hang on, do not eat dinner, just get a snack, because this evening you will have to go beyond the usual with your meal, and it would be a mistake to weigh yourself down with too much food.

NORCHIA: (*aside*) *Just like him — always insisting on the rule.*

DOCTOR CORNELIO: What are you saying?

NORCHIA: That the dinner that has been provided is not at all outside the rule, nor will you weigh yourself down too much. Don't worry.[4]

DOCTOR CORNELIO: Get going. Do what I've told you, and in the meanwhile, I will head to the pharmacy.

---

4.   Florentines were legendary for their parsimonious eating habits.

NORCHIA: *Io vo.' Oh, meschino, gli ha paura in queste sue nozze non si aviluppare alla tavola,[10] pensa quel che farà nel lecto.*

Qui rimane maestro Cornelio in iscena et parla solo una scena et poi va in casa.

SCENA QUARTA[11]

Monna Appollonia fante, Cammilla

APPOLLONIA: *Deh, nella buon'ora non ti disperare tanto, sta' di buona voglia, che gliene darò in mano propia et anche gli dirò quattro parole che me intenderà.*

CAMMILLA: *Deh, sì fatelo, di gratia, madre mia cara.*

APPOLLONIA: *Lo farò, dico, vattene su, che sia benedetta, che madonna Ghostanza non habbia a pigliare sospetto di questo tuo stare qua giù tanto a l'uscio, che non ne segua maggiore scandalo.*

CAMMILLA: *Che maggiore scandalo volete voi che segua, mi po' ella fare peggio che darmi a un vecchio che potrebbe essere mio padre due volte. Vi pare che la me habbia fatto poco male a voi, eh?*

APPOLLONIA: *Mi pare male, pure troppo, ma che voi tu fare?*

CAMMILLA: *Rimediarci, se gliè è possibile.*

APPOLLONIA: *Beh, quale è il rimedio?*

CAMMILLA: *Uscirmi di questa casa prima che io possa.*

APPOLLONIA: *Che di' tu, isciagurata a te, dunque voi tu diventare femmina di mondo, eh?*

---

10. Riempirsi di cibo.

11. Nel manoscritto sia la quarta che la quinta scena sono intitolate 'quarta'.

Act Two

NORCHIA: I'm going. (*aside*) *Oh, poor guy, he is afraid that he will eat too much at the wedding feast. He's thinking about what he will do in bed.*

Here Doctor Cornelio remains on the stage and speaks alone for a scene and then enters his house.

SCENE FOUR[5]

Miss Appollonia (maid), Cammilla

APPOLLONIA: It is early days. Don't despair so much. Be of good cheer, I will put it right into his hand and will also say a few words so that he will understand me.

CAMMILLA: Oh, yes, please do so, my dear mother.

APPOLLONIA: I will do as I have said. Go on up, there's a good girl, so that Madam Gostanza will have no cause to suspect why you are standing so long at the door, so that it will not give rise to a greater scandal.[6]

CAMMILLA: What greater scandal would you like there to take place? Could she do worse than give me to an old man who could be my father twice over? Does it seem to you that she has done me little harm? Does it?

APPOLLONIA: It seems like a bad thing to me, unfortunately, but what do you want to do about it?

CAMMILLA: Find a remedy, if that is possible.

APPOLLONIA: What would that remedy be?

CAMMILLA: Get me out of this house as soon as possible.

APPOLLONIA: What are you saying, you disgraceful girl? Make you a woman of the streets?

---

5. In the manuscript, both this and the following scene are entitled *Scena quarta* (Scene Four).

6. Women of good character of the higher social classes were supposed to remain indoors and preferably upstairs to protect their virtue and reputations.

CAMMILLA: *Che dite voi, non mi ha egli promesso più volte et giurato di tormi per moglie et io similmente non ho promesso et giurato a lui?*

APPOLLONIA: *Sì, ma quante volte promettono et spromettono questi giovini.*

CAMMILLA: *Forse che gli altri sarebbono tali, il mio marito[12] non già, né credo in modo alchuno che egli sia per manchare di tanta fede, lo conosco, è tanto il bene che egli mi porta.*

APPOLLONIA: *Gli è vero, ma io non vorrei poi…*

CAMMILLA: *Che poi? Lasciatene la cura a me, ma per quanto bene vi voglio fate di trovarlo et dategli la lettera et pregatelo, se mi porta l'amor che mi ha sempre dimostro, mi cavi di questa casa, che io son disposta d'uscirne o d'uccidermi.*

APPOLLONIA: *Oh, che Dio ti perdoni, dice o d'uccidermi.*

CAMMILLA: *Uccidermi, sì, se non harò altro riparo.*

APPOLLONIA: *Ohimè, figliuola mia, tu mi dai nel core[13] a piangere a cotesto modo et a dire coteste cose. Vattene sù et levati la passione del cuore, che io te ne adiuterò quanto potrò.*

CAMMILLA: *Altri che Mario non me la può levare.*

APPOLLONIA: *Horsù, io farò tanto che tu gli parlerai innanti che sia sera, non piangere.*

12. S, fol. 8v: «il mio Mario».
13. Tu mi fai star male.

CAMMILLA: What are you saying? Hasn't he promised me many a time and sworn to take me as his wife and have I not promised and sworn myself to him in the same way?

APPOLLONIA: Yes, but how many times do these young men promise and overpromise.

CAMMILLA: The others might be this way but not my husband,[7] and there is no way that I will believe that he is about to fall short of his promises. I know him, and he loves me very much.

APPOLLONIA: That is true, but I would not want…

CAMMILLA: Want what? Let me take care of this. But if you want me to love you as much as I do, make sure that you find him and give him the letter and beg him, if he bears me the love that he has always shown me, to get me out of this house, because at this point either I leave or I kill myself.

APPOLLONIA: Oh, may God forgive you! She says "or kill myself."

CAMMILLA: Kill myself, yes, if I have no other way of protecting myself.

APPOLLONIA: Oh dear, my girl, you hurt my heart when you weep like this and say these things. Pull yourself together and remove this passion from your heart, and I will help you as much as I can.

CAMMILLA: No one other than Mario can remove it.

APPOLLONIA: Chin up. I will manage to have you speak with him before this evening. Don't cry.

---

7. The manuscript has *il mio marito* (my husband), while the print version, at fol. 8v, has *il mio Mario.* However, Cammilla's account of how she and Mario promised themselves to each other satisfied the Catholic requirements for the sacrament of matrimony prior to the Council of Trent (begun 1542). The Council added the required presence of a priest and two or three witnesses. The difference between the manuscript and the printed version may reflect that change.

CAMMILLA: *Oh, Dio ch'el volessi, monna Appollonia mia, ma come farete?*

APPOLLONIA: *Vè' come la s'è rischiarata, ti so dire che gliè del fine.*[14]

CAMMILLA: *Voi non mi rispondete.*

APPOLLONIA: *Darolli la lettera et dirolli che tu piangi et che ti disperi et che pensi a' casi tua presto, se non che tu la farai male.*

CAMMILLA: *Diteli pure che se mi vuole viva pensi di cavarmi di questa casa et che io andrò con lui in capo del mondo.*

APPOLLONIA: *Lascia fare a me che ti arrecherò qualche buona novella, oh, vatti sù!*

CAMMILLA: *Io andrò hora. Udite, monna Appollonia, raccomandatemeli un poco strettamente et diteli come io mi struggo per amore suo.*

APPOLLONIA: *Lo farò. Vattene sù in buon'hora, che io mi maraviglio che la non ti habbia già chiamata sei volte. Tu vuoi pure che se n'advegga tutto il mondo, gliè ben male fare il male, ma gliè ben peggio farlo alla scoperta.*

CAMMILLA: *Horsù, fate di recharmi buone novelle, che io non voglio altro marito che lui.*

APPOLLONIA: *Me ne ingegnerò.*

SCENA [QUINTA][15]

Monna Appollonia sola

APPOLLONIA: *Oh, poverina, ti so dire che la sta fresca.*[16] *Non gli bastava non trovare luogo per questo giovane, né che questa sua matrigna, che non vo' chiamare altrimenti, l'ha dato un vecchio*

---

14. Che la cosa avrà un buon esito.

15. Nel manoscritto sia questa che la scena precedente vengono intitolate 'quarta'.

16. Che ha un bel problema.

Cammilla: Oh, may God allow it, my Miss Appollonia. How will you manage it?

Appollonia: *(aside) See how she has brightened up.* I'm telling you that things will turn out all right.

Cammilla: You are not answering me.

Appollonia: I will give him the letter and tell him that you are crying and in despair and that he should do something about your situation soon, or you might do something bad.

Cammilla: Go ahead and tell him that if he wants me alive, he had better get me out of this house and then I will go to the ends of the earth with him.

Appollonia: Leave it to me, and I will bring you some good news. Go on upstairs!

Cammilla: I'm going now. Listen, Miss Appollonia, get close to him and recommend me to him, tell him that I am pining away for love of him.

Appollonia: I will do so. Go on up right away, because I am surprised that she has not already called you six times. You want the whole world to know, yet while it is quite bad to do something bad, it is worse to do it in the open.

Cammilla: Come on, now! Make sure you bring me good news, because I want no other husband but him.

Appollonia: I shall cudgel my brain.

Scene Five[8]

Miss Appollonia alone

Appollonia: Oh, the poor little thing. I can tell you that she is in trouble. It wasn't enough that she couldn't find a place for this young man, nor that her stepmother — whom I don't want to call anything else — gave her an old man of

---

8.   The manuscript erroneously labels this and the preceding scene as *Scena quarta* (Scene Four).

di 70 anni[17] per marito et dove l'altre si sogliono rallegrare questa da hiersera in qua che la lo seppe, non ha fatto altro che piangere, che è proprio una pietà el fatto suo. Et se Dio et suora Catherina non l'adiutano, io ho paura che la non capiti male, in modo gliè entrato il fistolo[18] adosso, naffe.[19] Iddio ne guardi le predelle[20] di questa maladictione. La padrona, che vede questa maninconia, m'ha mandato con queste cose al monasterio a fare oratione per lei che sia contenta, et ella mi manda al suo Mario, che solo vuole per marito, con una lettera, non so chi gioverà più. A iuditio suo, più la può fare contenta con uno solo cenno il suo Mario che quante monache ha il mondo. Oh, Dio, vedete poi dove si conduce una meschinella, che non ha persona che per lei sia et poco gli giova essere bella et di nobile sangue, che la sua sciagura cominciò dalle fasce. Dicono che l'è figlia d'un gentil'huomo di questa terra et al tempo del saccho[21] la capitò alle mani d'uno spagnolo che la non havea a pena 3 anni, il quale la lasciò a Napoli a questa mia patrona et ella, credendosi trovare il padre, circa a uno anno fa la menò qui, che era meglio che l'havesse menato presso ch'io non dissi, ch'el padre non s'è trovato altrimenti et la fanciulla ci capiterà male. Basta, che l'ha certi sua brevi[22] che li tiene con più sicumere che non si tengono le reliquie in contado et dice sono contrasegni[23] che l'havea quando la fu tolta. Voglio che la se li metta. Sono stata per dire a uno pelo una mala parola, che altro non farà ella mai, ma, uh sciagurata me, ecco non so che brigata qua, lasciami andare via.

17. In precedenza (I, 2), secondo Norchia, maestro Cornelio aveva 60 anni.

18. Il diavolo.

19. In fede mia.

20. Gli sgabelli.

21. Del sacco di Roma.

22. Scritture.

23. Segni di riconoscimento.

seventy[9] for a husband and where other girls are happy, this one, since yesterday evening when she found out, has done nothing but cry, so her life is just pitiable. And if God and Sister Catherine don't help her, I'm afraid she is going to end up badly. The devil has gotten into her, upon my faith. God protect the pews from this curse. My mistress, who sees this melancholy, has sent me with these things to the monastery to pray that she will find peace, and she sends me with a letter to her Mario, who is the only one she wants as a husband. I don't know who it will help more. In her opinion, her Mario can make her happier with a single gesture than all the nuns in the world. Oh God, see where a poor girl ends up who has no one on her side, and it is of little use to her that she is beautiful or of noble blood because her misfortune began when she was in diapers. They say that she is the daughter of a gentleman of this city and at the time of the Sack[10] she fell into the hands of a Spaniard, and she was barely three years old, and he left her in Naples with my mistress, and she, believing that she could find the father, about a year ago brought her here, and it would have been better if she had taken her to who knows whom, because the father has not been found and the girl is going to end up badly. I'll stop there, because she has certain documents that she keeps more securely than they keep relics in the countryside, and she says that it holds the proofs that she had when she was taken. I want her to put them forward. I was a hair's breadth from saying a bad word, because she will never do that with them, but oh, poor pitiful me, here comes some group that I don't know. Let me get out of here.

9.   In Act I, Scene 2, Norchia says that Cornelio is sixty years old.
10.   The 1527 Sack of Rome by the army of Holy Roman Emperor Charles V.

Atto secondo

SCENA *[SESTA]*

Zingaro, mutato d'habito, Mario, Gualcina, et Rinuccio[24]
còrso.

ZINGARO: *Messer Mario, non si affatichi vostra signoria in ricordarmi quel ch'io ho a fare, io vi riuscirò meglio a pane che a farina.*[25]

MARIO: *Ha inteso la fanciulla questo disegno?*

GUALCINA: *Tutto et ha risposto che non mancherà dal canto suo di quello che occorre et ne ha dati tutti e' contrasegni possibili.*

ZINGARO: *Non ci è dubbio alchuno, vi dico.*

MARIO: *Mi piace, ma vedi che non si starà troppo a disagio. Ecco qua Rinuccio, a punto non poteva giugnere a migliore tempo.*

ZINGARO: *Quanto più presto, meglio.*

MARIO: *Lascia prima muovere a me et tu andrai seguitando le mie parole.*

ZINGARO: *Sì, bene.*

MARIO: *Buon dì Rinuccio.*

RINUCCIO: *Buon dì et buon anno.*

MARIO: *Diteli hora e' casi vostri da voi, messere Guicciardo, questo è quel Rinuccio che voi havete tanto cerco.*

ZINGARO: *È quel Rinuccio còrso?*

RINUCCIO: *Al comando vostro.*

ZINGARO: *Oh, Rinuccio mio, le lacrime non mi lasciono parlare.*

RINUCCIO: *Che vogliono dire sì fatte accoglienze?*

ZINGARO: *Ringratiato sia Dio, che finalmente io vi ho trovato et che io harò pure questo contento innanzi che io muoia.*

---

24. Pochi anni dopo un altro Rinuccio, studente, sarà tra i protagonisti della commedia *L'Assiuolo* di Giovanni Maria Cecchi.
25. Riuscirò meglio con le opere che con le aspettative.

Act Two

Scene Six

Gypsy in different clothes, Mario, Gualcina, and Rinuccio the Corsican[11]

GYPSY: Signor Mario, your lordship should not tire yourself in reminding me what I need to do. My actions will speak louder than words.

MARIO: Has the girl been informed of this plan?

GUALCINA: Everything, and she has answered that she will not fail to do what is needed on her end, and she has given us all the proofs needed.

GYPSY: There is nothing to fear, I tell you.

MARIO: I like this, but make sure that things don't move too slowly. And here comes Rinuccio. He could not possibly have arrived at a better time.

GYPSY: The sooner, the better.

MARIO: Let me make the first move, and you follow my words.

GYPSY: Yes, okay.

MARIO: Good day, Rinuccio.

RINUCCIO: Good day and good year.

MARIO: Explain your situation to him yourself, Signor Guicciardo, this is that Rinuccio that you have sought for so long.

GYPSY: Is that Rinuccio the Corsican?

RINUCCIO: At your command.

GYPSY: Oh, my Rinuccio, my tears do not let me speak.

RINUCCIO: What does such a warm welcome mean?

GYPSY: May God be thanked, because I have finally found you, and I will have this happiness before I die.

11. A few years later, another Rinuccio, a student, will be among the main characters of *L'Assiuolo (The Owl)* by Giovanni Maria Cecchi.

RINUCCIO: *In fine che raccoglienze sono queste, che volete voi da me?*

GUALCINA: *Pel primo questo è stato un grande assalto.*

ZINGARO: *Son quel Guicciardo Gualandi a chi voi più volte havete fatto intendere che voi havete la sua figliuola.*

GUALCINA: *Oh, amore paterno, questo huomo non può exprimere quello vorrebbe per la letizia, oh, e' fa bene!*

ZINGARO: *Io sono venuto per lei, con animo di darvi quel guidardone[26] che voi stesso vorrete et di più starvi in eterno obligato.*

RINUCCIO: *Bisogna altro che parole a dare la fanciulla.*

MARIO: *Come pensi tu di torgli le cose sua?*

RINUCCIO: *Se sarà la sua, e' mi darà più d'un contrasegno. Huomo da bene, non pensate già che io voglia correre questa faccenda?*

ZINGARO: *E' parla benissimo. Quando voi facessi altrimenti non faresti l'ufitio vostro. Rinuccio, io son parato a darvi tutti e' contrasegni che voi ne adimanderete, che gliè bene ragione. Così volessi Dio che la mia figliuola fussi in quel grado che era quando la rimase a'corsali, come io vi saprò dire ciò che fa mestieri.*

RINUCCIO: *La fanciulla nelle mie mani è stata tenuta come una reliquia, non bisogna che voi ne dubitiate. Et perché voi sappiate bene lo intero, io l'ho tenuta et è al presente in un monasterio.*

ZINGARO: *Voi m'havete tutto riconsolato.*

RINUCCIO: *Ma ditemi un poco, huomo da bene, quale è la patria vostra?*

ZINGARO: *La ciptà di Pisa in Thoscana, quantunque io son nato et allevato in Palermo di Sicilia.*

RINUCCIO: *Il nome della fanciulla?*

ZINGARO: *Aurelia, sfortunata!*

26. Ricompensa.

RINUCCIO: Let's get to the point. What kind of welcome is this? What do you want from me?

GUALCINA: *(aside) As a first move, this is a big assault.*

GYPSY: I am that Guicciardo Gualandi to whom you have given to understand many times that you have his daughter.

GUALCINA: *(aside) Oh, a father's love! This man cannot express what he wants for the joy he is feeling. Oh, he is doing a good job!*

GYPSY: I came for her, with the intention of giving you the recompense that you yourself choose and then of being eternally obliged to you.

RINUCCIO: It will take more than words for me to give you the girl.

MARIO: How can you think of taking something that is his away from him?

RINUCCIO: If she is his, he will give me more than one item of proof. Good man, don't think that I want to hurry this matter.

GYPSY: *(aside) He speaks very well.* If you did anything else, you would not be doing your job. Rinuccio, I am prepared to give you all the proofs that you ask for because it is truly right. May it be God's will that my daughter is in the same condition she was in when I left her to the corsairs, and I will tell you that this needs to be determined.

RINUCCIO: The girl was preserved in my hands like a relic. Have no fear. And so that that you will know the entire truth, I placed her in a monastery, where she still is.

GYPSY: You have consoled me completely.

RINUCCIO: But tell me, good man, what is your home country?

GYPSY: The city of Pisa in Tuscany, even though I was born and raised in Palermo in Sicily.

RINUCCIO: The girl's name?

GYPSY: Aurelia, the unlucky girl!

MARIO: *Anzi, fortunata, poi che l'ha trovato suo padre, ma è così il nome, Rinuccio?*

RINUCCIO: *Aurelia è il nome, ma ci sono mille cose da intendere ancora.*

ZINGARO: *Domanda pure, ch'io sono parato a tutto rispondere, perciò che io delibero che tu resti satisfatto.*

RINUCCIO: *Quanto è che voi perdesti questa figliuola et dove et chi ve la tolse.*

ZINGARO: *Dirovi, io la persi son 4 anni finiti et va per cinque, quanto è da septembre in qua, et fummi rubata da Giusaffà, corsale da Tunisi, nel canale di Piombino, da cui mi fu tolta ella con ogni mia facultà. Et a cagione che voi non habbiate a durare fatica a dimandarmi di più cose, vi dirò sotto brevità come seguì il caso.*

MARIO: *Ditelo, messer Guicciardo, che oltre alla satisfatione sua tutti ne haremo piacere.*

ZINGARO: *L'anno '37, esercitando io la mercatura in Palermo, dove, come ho detto ero nato et allevato, hebbi adviso da Pisa che Rinieri Gualandi, mio consorte,[27] era morto. Et perciò che la heredità si atteneva a me più stretto parente, presi tutte le mia cose con questa mia figlioletta di anni circa a dodici, perciò che la madre si era morta, imbarchai per la volta di Livorno. Come volse la nostra mala fortuna demmo ne'corsali, i quali a'primi assalti guadagnorono il legno dove eravamo et così, con ogni mio havere, venimo loro nelle mani. All'hora io, veduto la mala parata, sperando pure della detta heredità trarne tanto che io acconciamente fare lo potessi, mi posi per dirvi la cosa come la sta: 500 scudi di taglia se me et la mia figliuola solamente*

<hr>

27. Familiare.

MARIO: On the contrary, lucky, since she found her father. But is that really her name, Rinuccio?

RINUCCIO: Her name is Aurelia, but there are a thousand things still to learn.

GYPSY: Ask away, for I am prepared to answer all questions because I have decided that you must be satisfied

RINUCCIO: How long ago was it that you lost this little daughter, and who took her and where?

GYPSY: I will tell you that I lost her over four years ago, going on five, as long as from September to now, and she was stolen from me by Giusaffà, a corsair out of Tunis, in the Piombino Canal, and she was taken from me together with all my goods. And so that you will not have to trouble yourself with asking me more questions, I will tell you briefly how the situation took place.

MARIO: Recount it, Signor Guicciardo, because in addition to your satisfaction, it will give all of us pleasure.

GYPSY: In the year 1537, as I was working as a merchant in Palermo, where, as I mentioned, I was born and raised, I received word from Pisa that Rinieri Gualandi, my business associate,[12] had died. And because the inheritance belonged to me as the nearest relative, I took all of my things, and, because her mother had died, my little daughter who was about twelve, and I set sail along the route to Livorno. As our bad luck would have it, we encountered corsairs, who in the first assaults took over the ship that we were on and so, with all my worldly goods, we fell into their hands. Then, seeing this bad turn of events and yet hoping that I could use enough of the inheritance to get out clean, I proposed — to tell you the situation as it stood — five hundred scudi of ransom if they would set me and my daughter free. The

12. The Italian, *consorte,* is the same as used above for a business associate.

volessero lassare in libertà. Il patrone acceptò l'offerta et così presonsi la mia figliuola,[28] *ohimè!*

MARIO: *Horsù, non piangete, voi l' havete riavuta horamai.*

ZINGARO: *Quel che di lei si seguisse non ti so dire.*

MARIO: *Che dici, Rinuccio?*

RINUCCIO: *Che volete voi che io dica. Se l'è sua io non gliene, né voglio, né posso, ritenere. La fanciulla lo vedrà ella, la quale se ne ricorderà et sempre l'ha in boccha.*

ZINGARO: *Voi fate come huomo da bene se aspetta, ma per maggior vostra satisfatione vi vo' dire ancora che l'ha uno neo nel fianco sinistro, a punto dove cominciono le costole, di questo non mi addomandavate voi?*

RINUCCIO: *Cotesto non ho io mai veduto già.*

ZINGARO: *Oh, s' io lo credessi, Rinuccio!*

RINUCCIO: *Ne potete essere certissimo et ella ancora ve ne farà buona testimonianza.*

ZINGARO: *Hora mi fate voi fede d'esserne strettamente huomo da bene.*

MARIO: *Non più. Tal quale ell' è, messere Guicciardo la vuole et tu gliene vuoi rendere. Et con tutto che ei potesse come cosa sua ripigliarsela senz'altro niente di meno come gentil'huomo, per le tua spese et per quello che tu mai addimandare li potessi, ti vuole donare cosa che tu sarà contento.*

RINUCCIO: *Io mi rimetto in voi. Penso che voi siate huomo da bene et discreto et potete pensare che ho speso per lei un thesoro, tenutola come mia figliuola, questo è noto a tutto il mondo. Et hora, come io vi ho già detto, l'ho in monasterio, che quanto si spenda lo sa ogni huomo. Donatemi quel che voi volete.*

---

28. I corsari hanno trattenuto la giovane in attesa del pagamento del riscatto.

head of the group accepted the offer, but yet they took my daughter.[13] Woe is me.

MARIO: Here, don't cry. You are getting her back again now.

GYPSY: What happened to her after that I don't know.

MARIO: What are you saying, Rinuccio?

RINUCCIO: What do you want me to tell you. If she is his, I will not, nor do I want, to keep her. The girl will see him and will remember him because she is always talking about him.

GYPSY: You are acting like a respectable man who waits, but to increase your satisfaction, I want to tell you in addition that she has a mole on her left side,[14] just where the ribs begin. Aren't you going to ask me about this?

RINUCCIO: I have never seen this.

GYPSY: Oh, if I could believe this, Rinuccio.

RINUCCIO: You can be certain of this, and she will give good witness of it to you.

GYPSY: Now you are swearing to me that you were a very strictly respectable man in this.

MARIO: Not any more. Whatever condition she is in, Signor Guicciardo wants her back, and you want to give her to him. And even though he could reclaim her as something of his without giving you anything, all the same, being a gentleman, he wants to make you happy by giving you something for your expenses and for whatever you could ask him.

RINUCCIO: I leave it up to you. I think that you are a good person and discreet and that you can understand that I spent a fortune on her, kept her as my daughter, this the whole world knows. And now, as I already mentioned, I have her in a monastery, and how much that costs everyone knows. Give me what you wish.

13. The corsairs kept the daughter so that the father would pay a ransom to get her back.

14. A crucial detail in *Decameron* II, 9.

ZINGARO: *Ben parla Rinuccio, io vi vo'donare 100 ducati alla mano et quel più che io vorrò quando io harò a presso di me la mia figliuola.*

MARIO: *Bella offerta è stata questa et degna d'un gentil'huomo come messere Guicciardo.*

GUALCINA: *Non ne fare parola.*

RINUCCIO: *Messere Guicciardo, non mi adiuti Dio!*

ZINGARO: *Non giurate, di gratia, che vi credo benissimo.*

RINUCCIO: *S'io non ho trovato chi m'ha voluto mettere in mano 150 scudi et che io gliene facessi copia et per salvare l'honore alla vostra figliuola et mantenere la fede al mio fratello, che, come per agio intenderete, la riscattò da'mori, non ho voluto fare nulla.*

ZINGARO: *Essendo vero cotesto, ingrato certamente sarei non ve ne dando ancora io 150, avenga che assai me disagino.*

MARIO: *Voi siate troppo credulo, messer Guicciardo.*

ZINGARO: *Chi non è uso a mentire pensa che ogn'uno dica il vero, ma notate, perché io non sono al presente in su'contanti, io vi darò in quel cambio una mercantia che dalla mattina alla sera ne farete denari.*

RINUCCIO: *Eh, io vorria denari contanti.*

MARIO: *Sta'a udire et poi parla.*

ZINGARO: *Et questi sono drappi che io ho portati da Lucca, bellissimi.*

MARIO: *Drappi! Oh, che vorrestù, forse che in Roma e' drappi non hanno spaccio*[29]*, che non è furfante che oggi non se vesta.*

29. Non hanno mercato.

GYPSY: *(aside) Rinuccio speaks well.* I want to give you one hundred ducats now and however much more I want to when my daughter is back with me.

MARIO: This is a good offer and worthy of a gentleman like Signor Guicciardo.

GUALCINA: Don't say a word.

RINUCCIO: Signor Guicciardo, may God not help me!

GYPSY: Don't swear, please, because I really believe you.

RINUCCIO: I wanted to do nothing more than find someone who would put one hundred fifty scudi in my hands with which I could generously save the honor of your daughter and maintain my promise to my brother who, as you will in time understand, ransomed her from the Moors.[15]

GYPSY: This being true, I would certainly be ungrateful if I did not give you one hundred fifty, even though this will cause me great difficulty.

MARIO: You are too gullible, Signor Guicciardo.

GYPSY: Those who are not in the habit of lying think that everyone tells the truth, but note that because I currently am out of cash, I will give you in exchange merchandise that you will convert into money between the morning and the evening.

RINUCCIO: Hey, I would like cash.

MARIO: Wait and listen, and then speak.

GYPSY: These are silk cloths that I brought from Lucca, very beautiful.

MARIO: Silk cloths! Oh, what do you think, that maybe here in Rome silk cloth isn't sold, that there isn't a scoundrel these days who doesn't wear silks?

15. The term *moro* was used to refer both to Turks and to north Africans. Historically the Moslems — both Turkish, north African, and those expelled from Spain — were the ones taking captives. In addition, a few lines above, the captor is identified as Giusaffà of Tunis, meaning that he is a Moslem.

ZINGARO: *Andian via, che io farò di sorte che ti chiamerai contento. Et di più, oltre ad ogni promessa et oltre a'drappi che montaranno 150 scudi, voglio donarti alla mano 25 scudi d'oro contanti.*

RINUCCIO: *Come piace a voi, ancora che…*

MARIO: *Non dite che voi siate trattato bene.*

ZINGARO: *Gualcina, piglia questo anello, vattene all'osteria del Pavone, dove io sono alloggiato, et di' all'hoste che ti dia que'drappi che io gli consegnai in serbo, togliete 3 pezze, queste credo che saranno d'avanzo.*

MARIO: *Quanto possono tirare l'una?*

ZINGARO: *45 o 50 braccia, alla misura nostra.*

MARIO: *Sì, sì, alla largha.*

ZINGARO: *Di' che pigli di quelle di sopra, che son più giuste.*

GUALCINA: *Io vo, ma fideramele egli?*

ZINGARO: *Come no, e' conosce l'anello benissimo, ma diteli voi, Rinuccio, dove ei l'ha a portare.*

RINUCCIO: *Al monasterio delle Convertite.*

MARIO: *Tu hai inteso?*

GUALCINA: *Sta bene.*

ZINGARO: *Hora andianne, che sia ringratiato Dio d'ogni cosa.*

GYPSY: Come on, I will handle this in such a way that you will call yourself content. And what's more, in addition to everything promised and to the silk cloths that are worth one hundred and fifty scudi, I want to give you twenty-five gold scudi in cash in hand.

RINUCCIO: As you wish, even though…

MARIO: Aren't you saying that you have been treated well?

GYPSY: Gualcina, take this ring, go off to the Peacock Tavern, where I have my lodgings, and tell the host to give you those silk cloths that I gave him to keep for me. Take three pieces. I believe that these will be more than enough.

MARIO: How long is each one?

GYPSY: Forty-five or fifty yards, in our measure.

MARIO: Yes, yes, approximately.

GYPSY: Tell him to take the ones on top, as they are closest to the measure.

GUALCINA: I'm going, but will he entrust them to me?

GYPSY: Why shouldn't he? He recognizes the ring very well, but tell him, Rinuccio, where he is to take them.

RINUCCIO: To the Monastery of the Penitents.

MARIO: Do you understand?

GUALCINA: That's fine.

GYPSY: Now let's get going, and God be thanked for everything.

SCENA [SETTIMA]

Gualcina solo

GUALCINA: *Vedi, vedi, che delle volpi si piglia costui. Per parer huomo da qualche cosa ha voluto mille contrasegni et mille novelle et poi se n'è lasciato menare pel naso come un bufalaccio. Pensati poi quello farà subito che la fanciulla vegga questo nuovo padre, di sorta ha ella havuta il vino.[30] Di sorte cred'io che la sappia ben fingere, che se nessuno altro contrasegno havessemo havuto per lo innanzi, le accoglienze sole di costei sarebbono state bastanti a dargli a credere ogni cosa. Ma lasciami ire, in cambio dell'hosteria, a trovare Gismondo per i drappi. In tanto gli darò nuova del primo successo, credo haverne ancora io una buona mancia, di poi per la più corta me n'andrò al monasterio.*

Fine del secondo atto

30. Ha avuto una bella fortuna.

Act Two

SCENE SEVEN

Gualcina alone

GUALCINA: Look, look how out of all the foxes this one gets picked. To seem like a man who knows what he is doing, he wanted a thousand proofs and a thousand facts, and then he lets himself be led around by the nose like a stupid buffalo. Think about what he will do as soon as the girl sees this new father, acting as if she had the good fortune to find some wine. She's the type, I believe, who knows well how to fake it, such that if we had had no other proof before, her welcome alone would have been enough to make him believe everything. But let me go, instead of to the tavern, to find Gismondo for the silk cloths. In the meanwhile, I will give him the news of the first success. I think that I will get a good tip out of it, then I'll get over to the monastery by the shortest route.

End of Act Two

Non le parole o l'herbe

non di Circe o Medea, sagace maga,

venenoso liquore,

ch'a tal uso si serbe,

ponno saldar quella amorosa piaga,

che s'inprime nel core,

ma solo animo pronto, aldace et forte

che non teme di morte.

Ardite amanti dove la voglia abonda,

che vostra amica sorte

sanerà la ferita aspra et profonda.

31. La parola *atto* manca nel manoscritto.

Madrigal before the Third Act

Neither the words nor the herbs
of either Circe or Medea, shrewd witch,
poisonous distillate,
kept for such use,
can heal this wound that love
has incised on the heart,
but only a soul that is quick, audacious and strong,
that fears not death.
Stay strong, lovers, where your desire abounds,
for a friendly fate
will heal the deep and harsh wound.

Francesco Corteccia

quo - re, ch'a tal u - so si ser - be, pon - no sal -
so li - quo - re, ch'a tal u - so si ser - be, pon - no sal -
so li - quo - re, ch'a tal u - so si ser - be, pon - no sal -
so li - quo - re, ch'a tal u - so si ser - be, pon - no sal -
dar quel - l'a - mo - ro - sa pia - ga, che s'im - pri - me nel
dar quel - l'a - mo - ro - sa pia - ga, che s'im - pri - me nel
dar quel - l'a - mo - ro - sa pia - ga, che s'im - pri - me nel co -
dar quel - l'a - mo - ro - sa pia - ga, che s'im - pri - me
co - re, ma so - l'a - ni - mo pron - t'al - da - c'et for -
co - re, ma so - l'a - ni - mo pron - t'al - da - c'et for -
re, ma so - l'a - ni - mo pron - t'al - da - c'et for -
nel co - re, ma so - l'a - ni - mo pron - t'al - da - c'et for -

te che non te - me di mor - te, che non te - me di mor - te.
te che non te - me di mor - te, che non te - me di mor - te.
te che non te - me di mor - te, che non te - me di mor - te.
te che non te - me di mor - te, che non te - me di mor - te.
Ar - di - t'a-man - t'o-ve la vo - gli'a-bon - da,
Ar - di - t'a-man - t'o-ve la vo - gli'a - bon - da,
Ar - di - t'a-man - t'o-ve la vo - gli'a - bon -
Ar - di - t'a-man - t'o-ve la vo - gli'a-bon - da,
che vo - str'a-mi - ca sor - te sa - ne-rà la fe - ri - t'as-pr'et pro-
che vo - str'a-mi - ca sor - te sa - ne-rà
da, che vo - str'a-mi - ca sor - te sa - ne-rà la fe - ri - t'as-pr'et pro-
che vo - str'a-mi - ca sor - te sa - ne-rà

fon - da, sa - ne - rà la fe - ri - t'a-spr'et pro - fon -
la fe - ri - t'as-pr'et pro - fon - da, sa - ne - rà la fe -
fon - da, sa - ne - rà la fe - ri - t'a-spr'et pro -
la fe - ri - t'as-pr'et pro - fon - da, sa - ne - rà la fe -
da.
ri - t'a - spr'et pro - fon - da.
- fon - da.
ri - t'a-spr'et pro - fon - da.

Atto terzo

Scena prima

Scena prima, Gualcina con Mario

GUALCINA: *Io per me credo che se al mondo fusse perduta ogni malitia, senza fallo si ritroverrebbe nelle donne. A posta loro hanno le lacrime su gl'occhi ogni volta che loro è commodo. Sanno di sorte hora piangere, hora ridere, che ad ogni persona darebbono agevolmente a credere di far da senno. Et se io di questo prima havessi punto dubitato, hora ne sarei certissimo, poi che ho veduto la maniera che tenne l'Aurelia riconoscendo o, per dire meglio, fingendo di riconoscere il finto padre suo alla presentia di quello balocco[1] di Rinuccio còrso. Ma infine di sorte seppe ella tenere a mente raccoglierlo hora con le risa, hora con le amorevoli lacrime che maggior barbassoro[2] che non è questo ci sarebbe stato allacciato, perché nel vero non è costui il più accorto huomo del mondo et per la gola di quelle 3 pezze et di quelli 25 ducati d'oro gli parse mill'anni[3] renderla al padre. Padre mi piacque, marito sì bene, anzi pure amante dolcissimo. Femmina et innamorata, eh, che cosa non ardisce uno amante, quale astutia finta non succede a una femmina? Ma che fo io, debbo trovare il mio padrone, che venendo qua amendua mi è sparito dinanzi. Maraviglierassi che io l'habbia smarrito, ma eccolo a punto. In fede mia, patrone, certamente ch'el vostro Gismondo haveva ragione di desiderare tanto Aurelia, che l'è una bella et gratiosa giovine.*

MARIO: *Fatto sta come accorta et di bellissime maniere. Notastù con che bel modo la fece accoglienza, con mille pietose lacrime et con altre tante dolcissime risa al Zingaro, io per me non aspettavo tanto da lei a gran pezzo.*

---

1. Balordo.
2. Persona che si ritiene dotta ed importante.
3. Non vedeva l'ora.

ACT THREE

SCENE ONE

Gualcina with Mario

GUALCINA: I for my part believe that if all the wiles of the world were lost, without a doubt they would be found again in women. On command, they get tears in their eyes every time it serves their purpose. They know when to weep and to laugh by turns such that they would easily convince anyone that they were doing it with sincerity. And if I had my doubts about this before, now I am very certain, since I have seen the way in which Aurelia recognized or, more accurately, pretended to recognize her fake father in the presence of that idiot Rinuccio the Corsican.[1] But in the end, she kept in mind how to welcome him in such a way, sometimes laughing, sometimes with loving tears, that a bigger know-it-all than this one would have been taken in by it, because to tell the truth, he is not the brightest man in the world and because of his hunger for those three pieces of silk cloth and those twenty-five gold ducats, he couldn't wait to turn her over to her father. Father I like, husband too, even a very sweet lover. A woman and in love, hey, what would a lover not dare? What fake trick would not occur to a woman? But what am I doing — I have to find my master, who, after we arrived together, disappeared from sight. People would be surprised that I lost him, but here he is right now. Upon my faith, master, your Gismondo certainly was right to desire Aurelia so much, because she is a beautiful and graceful young woman.

MARIO: It is a fact that she is discerning and has wonderful manners. Did you remark upon the lovely way she welcomed him, with a thousand tears of filial piety and as many sweet peals of laughter for Gypsy. I, for my part, was not expecting as much from her by a long shot.

1. Aurelia's response is being recounted by another character because unmarried girl characters did not generally appear on stage.

85

GUALCINA: *La badessa non poteva tenere le lacrime per la tenerezza.*

MARIO: *Vero et chiunque v'era.*

GUALCINA: *Il Zingaro similmente fece benissimo et prima et poi.*

MARIO: *Nel vero che noi ci servimo d'uno stromento tanto a proposito del mondo. Ma, venghiamo al fatto nostro, Gualcina, hora che Gismondo ha hauto il pien suo.*

GUALCINA: *Pieno harà il suo[4] l'Aurelia, oh, io lo credo, che dite?*

MARIO: *Quel che ti pare da fare hora ne'fatti mia?*

GUALCINA: *Che si cerchi di intendere il seguito del parentado della Camilla et secondo questo governarsi, benché, come vi dissi, fatto o non fatto, volendola voi ad ogni modo la leverei di quivi et me n'andrei un poco a spasso con Gismondo, hora che e' denari non mancono. Ma ecco a punto monna Appollonia, vedi che la non poteva giugnere più a tempo. Aspettiamola qui et parlato che noi le haremo, potrem pigliare quello expediente che parrà migliore.*

SCENA SECONDA

Monna Appollonia, Mario, Gualcina, messer Lucio

APPOLLONIA: *Uh, uh, uh, che triste le facci Dio quelle suore, le mi hanno con loro novelluzze[5] et loro favole intrattenuto tanto, che gliè passato l'hora di desinare et harò delle fatiche di trovare Mario.*

MARIO: *La mi cerca a punto, monna Appollonia?*

APPOLLONIA: *Chi mi chiama? Oh, Mario, di voi cercavo, Dio vi salvi.*

MARIO: *Et te similmente, che è della Cammilla, da cui sola mi può venire ogni salute?[6]*

---

4. Allusione oscena.

5. Chiacchere.

6. Possibile reminiscenza del dantesco «Vede perfettamente onne salute» (*Vita nuova*, XXVI).

Act Three

GUALCINA: The abbess could not hold back her tears of joy.

MARIO: That is true of everyone who was there.

GUALCINA: Gypsy similarly played his part well both before and after.

MARIO: It's true that we made use of the most appropriate instrument in the world. But let's get down to our business, Gualcina, now that Gismondo has been fully satisfied.

GUALCINA: His Aurelia will have full satisfaction,[2] I think. What do you say?

MARIO: What do you think we should now do about my business?

GUALCINA: We should try to find out what happened with the family agreement about Cammilla and make our decisions according to that, although, as I've already said, whether it has been concluded or not, if you are intent on getting her, I would take her away from here and would take a little trip with Gismondo, now that there is money. But à propos of that, here comes Miss Appollonia. See, she could not have arrived at a better time. Let's wait for her here, and once we have spoken with her, we can choose the expedient that seems best.

SCENE TWO

Miss Appollonia, Mario, Gualcina, Signor Lucio

APPOLLONIA: Oh, oh, oh! May God make those sisters sorry. They kept me so long with their tales and stories that it is past dinnertime, and I will have trouble finding Mario.

MARIO: Is it me you are looking for, Miss Appollonia?

APPOLLONIA: Who is calling me? Oh, Mario, it was you I was looking for. God save you.

MARIO: And the same to you. What word do you have of Cammilla, who is the sole source of all of my health.

2.   The reference is obscene.

APPOLLONIA: *Ne fia bene, se voi seguiterete d'amarla.*

MARIO: *Dunque, non istà ella hor bene, di' su, ti prego a un tratto.*

APPOLLONIA: *La lettera ve lo dirà ella, tenete et leggete.*

MARIO: *Che ha, di' tosto.*

APPOLLONIA: *Che voi l'havete concia male, ma leggete.*

GUALCINA: *Che le ha messo la rete torta.*[7]

APPOLLONIA: *Eh, che mettere ti possa! Sono stata per dirtelo, sempre vuole il dondolo*[8] *de' fatti nostri quest'altro.*

GUALCINA: *Il dondolo volete voi altre da noi.*

MARIO: *Ohimè, Gualcina, la va male.*

GUALCINA: *Che cosa è?*

MARIO: *La cosa è conchiusa, i' sono morto.*

APPOLLONIA: *Che chiusa la cosa, eh no, Mario, leggete bene.*

MARIO: *Dico che il parentado è conchiuso.*

APPOLLONIA: *Oh, cotesto si è così, gli venga la fistola*[9] *a quel vecchiaccio. Et però dissi io che hora bisognava che voi li volessi bene.*

GUALCINA: *Lasciatelo finire di leggere.*

MARIO: *Ne la caverò a ogni modo.*

APPOLLONIA: *Io ve la raccomando, Mario.*

MARIO: *Non mi raccomandate l'anima mia.*

GUALCINA: *Oh, oh, Mario, vedete là vostro patre. Monna Appollonia, andate via, presto.*

MARIO: *Ohimè, perché? Che furia è questa?*

GUALCINA: *Andate via dico, discostatevi da noi, andate via, voi, Mario, andate alla volta sua.*

---

7.   Che è di cattivo umore.
8.   Farsi beffe.
9.   Piaga incurabile.

Act Three

APPOLLONIA: She will be well if you continue to love her.

MARIO: So therefore is she not well now — come on, tell me right away.

APPOLLONIA: The letter will tell you. Here it is. Read it.

MARIO: What is her problem? Tell me immediately.

APPOLLONIA: That you have put her in a bad situation, but read on.

GUALCINA: Which has put her in a bad mood.

APPOLLONIA: *(to Gualcina)* I wish she could put you in one. *(to Mario)* I was about to tell you, this one here always wants to rock on about us.

GUALCINA: You women want another kind of rocking from us.

MARIO: Oh, my, Gualcina, this is going badly.

GUALCINA: What is it?

MARIO: The thing has been concluded. I am dead.

APPOLLONIA: What do you mean "concluded." No, Mario, read it carefully.

MARIO: I said that the family agreement has been concluded.

APPOLLONIA: Oh, if that is the way this has gone, may the old guy get an abcess. And this is why I said that now you have to be nice to him.

GUALCINA: Let him finish reading.

MARIO: I will get her out of there by hook or by crook.

APPOLLONIA: Make sure that you do, Mario.

MARIO: You don't need to tell me how to take care of my soul.

GUALCINA: Oh, oh, Mario, look! There's your father. Miss Appollonia, go away now.

MARIO: Oh, me, why? What's the rush?

GUALCINA: Go away, I say, get far away from us, go away. You, Mario, go to meet him.

APPOLLONIA: *Perché vuoi tu ch'io me ne vadia. Tu mi par pazzo a me et Mario anche se ne va via, bene d'cani si fa qui, hora vedi che amor è questo.*[10]

SCENA TERZA

Messer Lucio, Mario, Gualcina

LUCIO: *Che voleva quella fante?*

MARIO: *Non so, parlava con Gualcina.*

GUALCINA: *Voleva ch'io leggessi una soprascritta d'una lettera che la portava et non si ricordava a chi.*

LUCIO: *Servistila?*

GUALCINA: *Non vedesti voi che io la cacciai via.*

LUCIO: *Oh, perché? Si vuole essere cortese et maxime di quel che non costa.*

GUALCINA: *No, no, non volevo dare quel carico*[11] *a Mario che era presente.*

LUCIO: *Che carico?*

GUALCINA: *Come che? Volevate voi che si dicessi che la gli portassi e' polli,*[12] *che è in sul tor moglie, voi non sapete che lingue serpentine ci va a torno, eh!*

LUCIO: *In verità che tu hai hauto un buon discorso, Gualcina, tal'hora ha più accorgimento una persona idiota che uno savio, io non pensavo costì.*

MARIO: *Né io, in verità.*

---

10. In S, fol. 14r è aggiunta la seguente frase: «E' se ne sono iti tutti a dua senza farmi risposta alcuna. Oh, infelice Cammilla ti mancava questo, ma io le voglio dir così apunto ogni cosa, che la poveretta si morrebbe di dolore».

11. Incombenza.

12. Che le facesse da mezzana.

Act Three

Appollonia: Why do you want me to leave? You seem crazy to me, and Mario is leaving, too. Dogs really get treated well here. Do you see what kind of love this is?[3]

Scene Three

Signor Lucio, Mario, Gualcina

Lucio: What did that maidservant want?

Mario: I don't know. She was speaking with Gualcina.

Gualcina: She wanted me to read the address on a letter that she was taking to someone, and she didn't remember who.

Lucio: Did you help her?

Gualcina: Didn't you see that I sent her away?

Lucio: Oh, why? We should be courteous, especially when it doesn't cost anything.

Gualcina: No, no, I did not want to put that burden on Mario, who was present.

Lucio: What burden?

Gualcina: What do you mean, "what burden"? Did you want it said that she was the go-between in his taking a wife. You don't know what serpents' tongues there are out there.

Lucio: In truth, you have explained it well, Gualcina. Sometimes a simpleton has more insight than a wise man. I wasn't thinking about it that way.

Mario: Me neither, to tell the truth.

3.   In S, fol. 14r, the following sentence is added: "And they left together without responding to me at all. Oh, unhappy Cammilla, this was the last thing you needed, but for this reason I want to tell her everything, because the poor thing would die from the pain."

LUCIO: *Io vo' fare un po' di natta[13] a questo mio figliuolo. Hobbè[14] Mario, tu non mi addimandi quello che sia seguito della moglie?*

MARIO: *Aspettavo che voi me ne ragionassi voi*

LUCIO: *Diceva altro, perché, a dirti il vero, io non ti porto troppe buone novelle.*

MARIO: *Oh, Dio!*

LUCIO: *Che havesti?*

MARIO: *Niente, ma che vuol dire?*

LUCIO: *E' si è tutto cambiato, io gli ho toccho dove gli duole. Stimasi che Valerio,[15] suo primo marito, sia ancora vivo et per ciò la cosa è raffreddata un poco.*

GUALCINA: *Oh, vedi ventura che è questa, all'improvista!*

LUCIO: *Tu non rispondi?*

MARIO: *Che volete voi ch' io dica?*

LUCIO: *E' par così che tu ne sia mal contento.*

GUALCINA: *Pensate che la gli duole, che già se la stimava sua.*

LUCIO: *È vero, Mario?*

MARIO: *Duolmi per certo, ma che volete voi fare, qui bisogna accordarsi con la fortuna.*

LUCIO: *Horsù, io veggio che se affligge troppo, hor da' qua la mano.*

MARIO: *Sta' a vedere, che vuol dire questo?*

LUCIO: *Io ho voluto un poco di spasso del fatto tuo, buon prò ti faccia. Virginia de' Massimi è tua legiptima sposa et stasera ti troverai a cena con lei*

MARIO: *Ohimè!*

13. Prendere in giro.

14. Ebbene.

15. Qui messer Lucio si fa beffe di suo figlio Mario, il quale, innamorato di Cammilla, non intende sposare Virginia de' Massimi, presunta vedova di Valerio, che in realtà, come vedremo, era fratello proprio di Cammilla.

LUCIO: *(aside) I want to play a little joke on my son.* Eh, Mario, aren't you going to ask me what's happened about the wife?

MARIO: I was waiting for you to tell me.

LUCIO: I was talking about other things because, to tell you the truth, I'm not bringing very good news.

MARIO: Oh, God.

LUCIO: What's wrong?

MARIO: Nothing. What does this mean?

LUCIO: *(aside) He has completely changed. I have hit him where it hurts. He believes that Valerio,[4] her first husband, is still alive and for that reason things have cooled down a little.*

GUALCINA: *(aside) Oh, look what a stroke of luck this is, and unexpected!*

LUCIO: Aren't you going to answer?

MARIO: What do you want me to say?

LUCIO: It seems that you are unhappy about this.

GUALCINA: Think about how it hurts him, because he already thought of her as his.

LUCIO: Is that true, Mario?

MARIO: It hurts me, certainly, but what can you do. You must make your peace with fortune.

LUCIO: Come on. I see that you are beating yourself up about this. Give me your hand.

MARIO: Hang on. What does this mean?

LUCIO: I wanted a little fun out of your affairs. Take it as a learning experience. Virginia de' Massimi is your legitimate bride, and this evening you will be at supper with her.

MARIO: Oh, me!

4.   Here, Signor Lucio is playing a practical joke on his son Mario, who is in love with Cammilla and has no intention of marrying Virginia de' Massimi, the presumed widow of Valerio who, as will later be evident, is Cammilla's brother. Thus in S, fol. 14v the text reads "that another, her first husband."

Lucio: *Che hai tu havuto, gliè diventato come una cenere.*

Gualcina: *Padrone, avertite che la troppa allegrezza non gli habbia occupato il core, altri si sono trovati morti per questo.*

Lucio: *Certo costui non ha havuto altro. Mario, ripiglia gli spiriti. Come ti senti?*

Mario: *Non ho altro, no.*

Lucio: *Ringraziato sia Dio. Che te ne pare, non ho io condotto la cosa bene et presto?*

Mario: *Messer sì, ne son contento.*

Lucio: *Tu mi rispondi così a male in corpo. Infine io non veggio in te quella allegrezza che io harei voluto.*

Gualcina: *Parvi miracolo, e' gl'ha portato un gran pericolo per sì buona nuova. Di poi non sapete voi che come uno piglia moglie gl'entra nel pensatoio?[16]*

Lucio: *Gli pensieri et le brighe voglio che sieno tutte mie, Mario, et i piaceri sierno[17] tutti tua. Ma andianne a desinare et ragionaremo più all'agio.*

Mario: *Aviatevi voi, noi ne verremo.*

Lucio: *Horsù, io son contento. Tu ne vuoi ragionare un poco col Gualcina, io mi avio.*

Scena quarta

Mario et Gualcina servo

Mario: *Hor se' tu contento, Gualcina, vedi che per fare a tuo modo mi è intervenuto quello di che sempre ho temuto. Che partito ho io hora a pigliare, che io non ho più tempo che io mi possa mettere mani a bocca[18] et sono assediato da dua importantissimi casi, dal parentado della Cammilla et dal mio, che l'uno et l'altro harebbono bisogno d'un mese a pensarvi.*

16. Gli vengono i pensieri.
17. Siano.
18. Non ho tempo da perdere.

Act Three

Lucio: What hit you? You are as white as a sheet.

Gualcina: Master, what you are seeing is the excess of happiness that has taken over his heart. Others have been struck dead by this.

Lucio: Certainly he has not had any other news. Mario, pick your spirits up. How do you feel?

Mario: Nothing else is bothering me, not at all.

Lucio: Thank God. What do you think? Didn't I conclude everything well and quickly?

Mario: Yes, sir, it makes me happy.

Lucio: The answer that your body language gives me is bad. I just don't see in you the happiness that I wanted to see.

Gualcina: You marvel that such good news seems a great hazard to him. But then, don't you know that a man who is about to marry enters a worry chamber?

Lucio: I want the worries and the troubles to be all mine, Mario, and the pleasures to be all yours. But let's go to dinner and talk about this at our leisure.

Mario: You start off, and we'll follow you.

Lucio: Okay, that's fine. You want to talk about this a little with Gualcina. I'll get going.

Scene Four

Mario and Gualcina servant

Mario: Are you happy now, Gualcina? Do you see that by doing it your way, my worst fears have been realized? What option do I have, now that I have run out of time, and I am besieged by two important matters, Cammilla's family agreement and my own, with each one needing a month of thought.

GUALCINA: *Non dubitate, padrone, non vi disperate, che non è male alcuno che non habbia il suo rimedio.*

MARIO: *Sì, ma che mio prò se io non lo so trovare?*

GUALCINA: *Lasciate fare a me et non vi date maninconia.*

MARIO: *Delle nostre.*

GUALCINA: *Dice delle nostre anche, come che io non habbia pure hora condotto cosa che mai l' haresti creduta et pure è riuscita, n'è vero?*

MARIO: *Vero, ma qui non voglio rimedio più alchuno.*

GUALCINA: *Padrone, ben che questa cosa habbi dua capi, tuttavia uno solo rimedio li basta.*

MARIO: *Et qual'è questo? Cavami di questa molestia più tosto che tu puoi.*

GUALCINA: *Che dice ella, non è ella contenta di partirsi et venirsene con voi?*

MARIO: *Anzi, me ne prega, me ne scongiura.*

GAULCINA: *Il rimedio è dunque menarla via, prima che il medico vi vadia et così sarete libero d'ogni cosa, poi qual cosa fia.*

MARIO: *Troppo tardi ci siamo indugiati, hora mai debban essere 20 hore et non se gliè fatto intendere nulla di fermo.*

GUALCINA: *Poco importa questo, in una hora sola si leverebbe un exercito non che una fanciulla che altro non brama.*

MARIO: *Ma come faremo, che el medico per sorte non si ci abbattesse?[19]*

GUALCINA: *A questo ancora ho pensato.*

MARIO: *Dimmelo, di gratia.*

---

19. Non ci capitasse tra i piedi.

GUALCINA: Never fear, master. Don't despair, because there is no problem that is without a solution.

MARIO: Yes, but what good does that do me if I can't find it.

GUALCINA: Leave it to me and don't give in to melancholy.

MARIO: About our things.

GUALCINA: He even says "about our things," as if I had not just now brought to completion something that you would never have believed and yet it was concluded, wasn't it?

MARIO: That is true, but here I want no more remedies.

GUALCINA: Master, although this thing has two ends, it requires only one remedy.

MARIO: And what is that? Get me out of this troublesome predicament as soon as you can.

GUALCINA: What does she say? Is she not happy to leave and come away with you?

MARIO: Indeed, she begs me. She pleads with me.

GUALCINA: The remedy, therefore, is to take her away before the doctor goes to her house and that way you will be free of everything, whatever happens afterwards.

MARIO: We put it off too long. By now it must be twenty hours,[5] and no firm plan has been agreed upon.

GUALCINA: This matters very little. In an hour alone, one could raise an army, let alone a girl who wants this more than anything.

MARIO: But how will we manage to avoid the doctor running into us by chance?

GUALCINA: I have a plan for this too.

MARIO: Please, tell me.

5.   The time of day was calculated from sunset; assuming that the play was given during Carnival some time in February, sunset would have been around 5:00 p.m., and therefore twenty hours would be in the early afternoon.

GUALCINA: *Che el medico si trattenga dua o 3 hore, acciò che, senza sospetto del suo sopragiugnere, possiamo trarla di casa.*

MARIO: *Et chi sarà bastante a questo?*

GUALCINA: *Il Zingaro, se non altri.*

MARIO: *Poi, che modo?*

GUALCINA: *Oh, voi mi parete grosso,[20] perdonatemi, col richiederlo che vadia a qualche cura et aggirarlo[21] per tutta Roma o fuori, bisognando.*

MARIO: *El caso è che voglia andare, dovendo essere alle nozze.*

GUALCINA: *Dieci ducati lo farebbe trottare via fino a Napoli, non sapete che incantesimo è quello de'denari, eh, et maximamente in uno vecchio et medico.*

MARIO: *Horsù, piglisi questo partito per ultimo, ma come faremo a trovare il Zingaro?*

GUALCINA: *Io andrò a cercarlo in queste taverne et voi alla Scimia,[22] dove è Gismondo, che gliè forza che si sia ritirato a desinare.*

MARIO: *Hora va', che troppo ci importa et se'l vecchio vole aspettare, aspetti. Ma torna, odi, vogliamo noi però intrare in casa sua, che ogn'huomo ci vegga così sfacciatamente che altro si farebbe a una publica.[23]*

GUALCINA: *Questo niente rilieva, che agevole ne fia a travestirsi in qualche modo che l'intrare ne sia sicuro et sconosciuto.*

MARIO: *Ma come, Domine?*

GUALCINA: *Mancherà, che la casa di nozze pare sempre una sagra, tante persone entrano et n'escano sempre.*

20. Non volete capire.

21. Portarlo in giro.

22. La torre della Scimmia, in via dei Portoghesi, accanto a Palazzo Scapucci.

23. Una prostituta.

GUALCINA: The doctor should be held up for two or three hours so that we can get her out of the house without worrying that he will arrive in the middle of things.

MARIO: And who can pull that off?

GUALCINA: Gypsy, among others.

MARIO: And how will it be done?

GUALCINA: Oh, you seem thick-headed to me — excuse me for saying so — by asking him to go on some house call and sending him all around Rome and beyond if necessary.

MARIO: But what are the chances that he will want to do so just as he is about to get married.

GUALCINA: Ten ducats would get him to trot all the way to Naples. Don't you know what kind of a spell money casts, especially on an old man and a doctor.

MARIO: All right. We'll choose this last option. But how will we find Gypsy?

GUALCINA: I'll go look for him in these taverns, and you go to the Monkey,[6] where Gismondo is, because it is certain that he has retreated there to have his dinner.

MARIO: Now go! This is so important to us, and if the old man wants to wait, let him wait. But come back, listen. Do we want to enter her house? Because everyone will see us treating it as shamelessly as one does a common prostitute's.

GUALCINA: This raises no problem, because it is easy for us to disguise ourselves in such a way that entering will be secure and anonymous.

MARIO: But how, dear Lord?

GUALCINA: There will be no shortage of means because a house where there is a wedding always seems to be in festival time, so many people are going in and out all the time.

6.   The Torre della Scimmia (Monkey Tower), in via dei Portoghesi, near Palazzo Scapucci.

MARIO: *Và, dunque, spacciati.*

GUALCINA: *Non è da perder tempo et là aspettatemi.*[24]

   Qui dice certe parole necessarie il Gualcina.

SCENA QUINTA

Rinuccio solo

RINUCCIO: *Sciagurato a me, misera la vita mia, dove Domine potrò io mai trovare costui? Pensati pure che havendomi fatto una simile giunteria,[25] non si lascerà così tosto rivedere questo ladro assassino. Infine, quando la debbe andare male non ci è rimedio alchuno. Io me ne tornava con 3 pezze di raso che valevono poco manco di 200 ducati, che messer Guicciardo mi haveva donato per la rihauta della sua figliuola, quando a punto mi abbattei in uno che al viso et a'panni haveva cera di huomo più che da bene, ma poi a' fatti l'ho io provato peggio che un diavolo, un barro, un giuntatore, un assassino, il quale alla bella prova mi seppe cavare di boccha quello che io havevo fatto, quello che io facevo et quello che io havevo in atto di fare. Et detto che gliene hebbi d'havere que'drappi meco, mi dette ad intendere che fussi meglio che io me ne uscissi quanto prima potessi. Io, come un baloccho[26] che sono, poi che io comincio ad imparare a vivere hora alle spese mia, gli credetti et seco andai dove e' volle. Aggirommi un'hora intera, hora qua, hora là, hora con una persona, hora con un'altra, dal vedere al non vedere, io mi trovo manco gli drappi et lui non rivegho. Corro, grido, nulla non mi giova, ogn'uno mi dice: «Molto ben ti sta, tu eri col tuo huomo da bene». Misero me, dove son'io capitato, in un*

---

24. Nota marginale autografa in V, 25v: «Qui dice certe parole necessarie il Gualcina».

25. Inganno.

26. Sciocco, balordo.

Act Three

MARIO: Go, then, and hurry.

GUALCINA: Let's not waste time. Wait for me there.

Here Gualcina says certain necessary words.[7]

SCENE FIVE

Rinuccio alone

RINUCCIO: I am so unlucky. My life is a misery. Lord, where will I ever be able to find this guy? And think about the fact that since this thieving assassin has tricked me this way, he will not let himself be seen again soon. And then, when something must go wrong, there is no way of fixing it. I was returning with three satin cloths that were worth a little less than two hundred ducats that Signor Guicciardo gave me as a gift for getting his daughter back, and right at that moment I ran into a guy who from his face and his clothing had the appearance of a more than respectable man, but then when it came to deeds, I found that he was worse than a devil, a con man, a trickster, an assassin, who when it came down to it was able to extract from my mouth what I had done, what I was doing, and what I was planning to do. And once I had told him that I had those silk cloths with me, he gave me to understand that I should get rid of them as soon as I could. I, like the idiot I am since I began to learn to live at my own expense, believed him and went with him where he wanted. He led me around for an entire hour, here and there, now with one person, now with another, from seeing to not seeing, I found myself without the silk cloths, and I did not see him again. I run, I yell, nothing helps, everyone says, "It serves you right. You were with your trustworthy man."[8] Unlucky me! Where have I ended up? In

---

7.   This stage direction, at fol. 25v, may indicate the incorporation of a bit of the new art of improvisation or it may refer to language that would be considered too strong to write down; in other passages of the play, euphemisms are used rather than the stronger language one might hear in life.

8.   An ironic commentary on Rinuccio's failure to see that he was dealing with a con man.

punto ho perduto tutto quello che m'ero acquistato in parecchi anni con mille fatiche et con mille stenti. Pure beato, che messer Guicciardo mi donò, oltre a'drappi, una borsa con 25 scudi, che io mi troverrei del tutto brullo,[27] pur del male mi sono rimasti questi. Io so pure che son qui dentro per certo. Ohimè, ohimè, io non gli ritrovo, hoimè, ohimè, o ladri o assassini o ribaldi, anche questi e anche questi! Il cuore, se fussi d'oro, credo che io me lo troverrei manco! Povero a me, tristo et dolente a me, senza denari, senza li drappi et quello che è peggio et che più mi accora, senza la fanciulla ancora, che se io non l'havessi renduta così tosto, non mancherebbono né denari, né drappi. Hebbila, misero a me, da un mio fratello che ritornava da Tunisi, dove l'haveva rubbata al padrone propio di chi ell'era, et venendo a morte me la raccomandò come la vita sua propia, giurandomi che sempre in luogo di sorella era stata appresso di lui et così mi pregava che stessi appresso di me sino che ritrovassi il padre suo. Vero è che io l'ho resa al padre suo, ma dove sono le spese mie, dove le mia tante fatiche in allevarla et mantenerla, dove il merito che io ne dovevo cavare? Ohimè, rubbato, sono stato assassinato, andrò a cercarne et so non farò altro che affaticarme et martoriarme! Pure, se fortuna mi volesse aiutarmi quanto l'altrui malitia et la mia sciocchezza me ha fatto danno, forse, forse...

SCENA SESTA

Mario et Gismondo con la veste del Zingano[28]

MARIO: *E'gliè vero, Gismondo, che trovandomi io nel travaglio ch'io t'ho detto, né potendo havere il Zingaro, ho bisogno dell'aiuto tuo, non di meno per li inconvenienti che potrebbono nascere se tu fussi veduto dal tuo fratello o da altri di casa tua et maximamenete in questo habito tanto disforme da te quanto i costumi di chi n'è padrone da' tuoi.*

27. Spogliato.
28. L'intitolazione della scena manca nel manoscritto.

a moment I have lost everything that I had gained over many years with so much work and so many sacrifices. Yet I have one piece of luck, that Signor Guicciardo gave me, in addition to the silk cloths, a purse with twenty-five scudi, so that even if I find myself stripped bare, out of this bad situation I still have these. I know too that they certainly are inside here. Oh me, oh me! I can't find them! Oh thieves, oh assassins, oh criminals! These too, these too. My heart, if it were made of gold, I think that I would find it missing too! Poor me, sad and sorrowful me, no money, no cloths, and what is worse and what touches my heart more, no girl, because if I had not turned her over so soon, I would not be out of money and cloths. I had her, unlucky me, from a brother of mine who was returning from Tunisia, where he had stolen her from the master to whom she belonged, and as he was dying, he begged me to treat her as I would his life, swearing to me that she had always been treated like a sister by him, and he begged me to treat her the same while she was with me until I found her father. It is true that I turned her over to her father, but what about the expense to me, all the pains that I took raising her and keeping her. Where is the recompense that I should have gotten out of it? Oh me, robbed! I have been assassinated. I will go and keep looking, and I know that this will only be more work for me and more torture for me! However, if luck would like to help me out as much as the malice of others and my foolishness have harmed me, maybe, maybe…

Scene Six[9]

Mario and Gismondo wearing Gypsy's gown

MARIO: It is true, Gismondo, that finding myself in the difficulty that I told you about and not being able to call on Gypsy, I need your help, not least of all for the difficulties that could arise if you were to be seen by your brother or by others in your household, and especially in this get-up, which is as far from your usual as its owner's habits are from yours.

9.   The scene division is made in the published version but not in the manuscript.

Se Dio mi adiuti, voglio più presto che tu torni dalla tua Aurelia, acciò che tu almeno viva contento, poi che la mia fortuna vuole pure che io sempre stenti et mai non goda.

GISMONDO: *Mario, l'amore ch'io ti porto et di più li obligbi che io tengo teco sono tali che se io non ti veggio fruire di quanto brami et desideri, pensa che né io similmente posso viver contento. Maggiore cosa farei per amore tuo, perché in questa non veggio tanti pericoli quanti pare a te, anzi, essendo l'hora del desinare, niuno quasi si trova per le strade. Et se pure riscontrassi alchuno che mi conoscessi, havendo io questi panni addosso del Zingaro, potrò voltare un canto prima che da lui possa essere raffigurato, però dimmi solo quello che io debbo fare et non ti dare altro pensiero del fatto mio.*

MARIO: *Una volta io non ho altro rimedio se non che questo medico sia intertenuto due o tre hore, per potere in questo mezzo fare sicuramente quello che io t'ho detto.*

GISMONDO: *Stanne di buona voglia et quanto al trattenere il medico lasciane tutta la cura a me. Ma dimmi, faccendo io questo, potrai tu poi fare il restante per te medesimo?*

MARIO: *Al fermo, sì come io spero, con l'adiuto del Gualcina, che poco starà a comparire.*

GISMONDO: *Per Dio, ancora non m'è venuto alla mente, ma stanne sicuro che se io lo dovessi gittare in Tevere non ti verrà a dare noia. Lascia fare a me.*

MARIO: *A te lascio la cura in tutto di questo, io andrò incontro al Gualcina. Ritroverrenci alla stanza per cavalcare,[29] se fussi bene mezza notte.*

GISMONDO: *S'intende.*[30]

Resta qui Gismondo solo.

GISMONDO: *In verità che io vo più trasportato dalla voluntà di compiacere all'amico mio et renderli pare merito de' sua servigi,*

---

29. Ci ritroveremo presso la rimessa dei cavalli.

30. Nota autografa marginale in V, c. 27v: «Resta qui Gismondo solo».

God help me! I want you to return to your Aurelia as soon as possible, so that at least you may live happily, since, as my luck would have it, I always have to work and never have fun.

GISMONDO: Mario, the love that I bear you and even more the obligations that I have to you are such that if I don't see you enjoy all that you crave and desire, believe me when I say that I will be equally unable to live in peace. I would do even more for love of you, for in this I do not see as many dangers as you see. Indeed, since it is the dinner hour, there is almost no one on the street. And even if I ran into someone who knew me, with my wearing Gypsy's clothing, I could get around the corner faster than he could recognize me. So just tell me what I must do and do not give another thought to what happens to me.

MARIO: Now I have no other solution than having this doctor distracted for two or three hours so that in the meantime I am able to safely do what I told you about.

GISMONDO: Cheer up! And as far as distracting the doctor, I will take care of all that. But tell me, while I am doing this, will you be able to do the rest on your own?

MARIO: Certainly, if, as I hope, I have Gualcina's help. He should be here soon.

GISMONDO: By God, I had not yet thought of that, but rest assured that if I have to throw him in the Tiber, he will not cause you problems. Leave it to me.

MARIO: I will let you take care of all of this. I will go meet Gualcina. We will meet again at the horses' stables even if it is midnight.

GISMONDO: Understood.[10]

Gismondo remains here alone.

GISMONDO: In truth, I am carried along more by the desire to please my friend and to treat him as well as he treats me,

10. Here in the manuscript at fol. 27v there is a note in the margin in the author's hand that reads, *"Resta qui Gismondo solo"* (Gismondo remains here alone).

che dove io sappia in fatti di condurre questo medico, ma non di meno la prima cosa mi ingegnerò di cavarlo fuori di casa, di poi in qualche luogo lo menerò io meco, starà egli a ogni modo se io lo dovessi tenere a forza. Bussiamo la porta.

SCENA SETTIMA

Gismondo et Norchia

GISMONDO: *Tich, toch, vedi casa di noce,[31] qui mi pare addormentato ogn'uno, che sì che io gli desto, tich, toch.*

NORCHIA: *Che tempesta è questa, pensi tu d'haverci a tronare la porta un'altra volta, per certo che?*

GISMONDO: *Et tu come rispondi a chi reca guadagno al patrone.*

NORCHIA: *Che guadagno o non guadagno! Per la prima assai bel guadagno è questo, fracassare la porta. Che non di' tosto ciò che tu domandi, pensi che io habbia altro che fare che casi tua?*

GISMONDO: *Assai sono in casi tua quelli che tornano in utilità del tuo patrone. Possolo un po'vedere?*

NORCHIA: *Potrai, se prima non acciechi.*

GISMONDO: *Galante servitore è questo, gobbo di gentilezza et scrigniuto[32] di schiena et da fare honore a qualunque si vuole padrone.*

SCENA OTTAVA

Cornelio, Gismondo e Norchia

CORNELIO: *Chi mi domanda?*

GISMONDO: *Io, maestro Cornelio. Io son mandato da un gentil'huomo per caso assai importante.*

---

31. Riferimento all'antica usanza di gettare questi frutti in occasione delle feste nunziali.

32. Gobbo.

than by any real knowledge of where to take this doctor, but all the same, the first thing that I will figure out how to do is to get him out of the house, and then I will take him some place and get him to stay there one way or another, even if I have to use force. Let's knock at the door.

SCENE SEVEN

Gismondo and Norchia

GISMONDO: Knock, knock! Look, this is a wedding house,[11] and it seems to me that they are all sleeping, so I'll wake them up. Knock, knock.

NORCHIA: What tempest is this? Do you think that you have to bang on the door again? For what reason?

GISMONDO: And this is how you answer someone who is bringing profit to the owner.

NORCHIA: What do you mean profit or no profit? Just to start with, breaking down the door is quite a good profit. Why don't you say right away what you're after? Do you think that I have nothing else to do but deal with your business?

GISMONDO: There are many in your house who produce profit for your master. Can I see him for a minute?

NORCHIA: You can, if you don't go blind first.

GISMONDO: What a well-mannered servant, a hunchback of gentility, and curved of back, and one who honors whatever master he has.

SCENE EIGHT

Doctor Cornelio, Gismondo, and Norchia

DOCTOR CORNELIO: Who is asking for me?

GISMONDO: I, Doctor Cornelio. I am sent here by a gentleman on a rather important case.

11. The Italian *la casa di noce* (the walnut house) refers to the custom of eating walnuts at weddings.

CORNELIO: *Hor vengo a te. Va', Norchia, dove io t'ho detto et sopra tutto piglia uno cuoco pulito et oltre a quello che io t'ho detto, compera dua paia di starne et un paio di fagiani, potendosi havere.*

NORCHIA: *Bene dixisti.*

CORNELIO: *Bene, ben, tu parli ancora tu per lettera, eh!*

NORCHIA: *Chi usa col zoppo…*[33] *voi sapete, voi havete tanta conscienza che insino a'vostri letti si vagliono delle lettiere,*[34] *non che i vostri servidori.*

CORNELIO: *Scienza, bufolo, et non conscienza, per un'altra volta. Ma perché dicestù bene dixisti in fine?*

NORCHIA: *Che voi parlasti bene a dir potendosi havere, perché e' fagiani et le starne da noi altri a pena si possono vedere, mercè della gola dishabitata*[35] *di questi prelati, harpie famelice.*[36]

CORNELIO: *Anzi, habitata et bene, usando giornalmente cotesti cibi. Tant'è, farai il meglio che si può.*

NORCHIA: *Tanto farò.*

CORNELIO: *Hora, va' tosto. Che diciamo noi, huomo da bene?*

33. Chi va con uno zoppo impara a zoppicare.
34. Testiere dei letti.
35. Insaziabile.
36. In S, fol. 18v «barbassori» al posto di «prelati».

DOCTOR CORNELIO: I'm coming to see you. Go, Norchia, where I told you to, and above all get a clean cook, and in addition to what I told you, buy two pair of partridges and a pair of pheasants, if you can find them.

NORCHIA: Well said.[12]

DOCTOR CORNELIO: Well, well, you are still speaking in a learned fashion.

NORCHIA: If you hang out with a man who limps,[13]…you know, you have so much conscience[14] that even your beds use headboards,[15] as well as your servants.

DOCTOR CORNELIO: Science, you ox, not conscience, once again. But why did you say, "Well said"?

NORCHIA: Because you spoke aright when you said "if you can find them," because pheasants and partridges for us are hard to find, thanks to the insatiable appetite of these prelates, famished harpies.[16]

DOCTOR CORNELIO: On the contrary, usual and good appetite, eating these foods daily.[17] However, you will do the best you can.

NORCHIA: Yes, I will.

DOCTOR CORNELIO: Now get going. What do we say, good sir?

12. Norchia uses the Latinizing form *dixisti* to put himself on the level of Doctor Cornelio and his servants. Doctors were known for using Latin medical phrases, as Doctor Cornelio will do shortly.

13. According to the saying, if you hang out with a man who limps, you learn to limp.

14. Italian *coscienza* means "conscience," "awareness," and "knowledge"; in Doctor Cornelio's correction of *coscienza* to *scienza* (knowledge, science) there is a hint that he lacks conscience and awareness.

15. The exchange plays on *lettere* (letters or literature) and *lettiere* (headboards of a bed, *letto*).

16. S, fol. 18v has *barbassori* (clods, country bumpkins) in place of *prelati* (prelates).

17. Doctor Cornelio reverses Norchia's criticism of the prelates' practices.

GISMONDO: *Che gran bisogno è occorso a un gentil'huomo dell'opera vostra, correndo in uno medesimo tempo rischio la persona et l'honore d'una sua figliuola.*

CORNELIO: *I mali della persona si curano per l'arte nostra agevolmente, ma quelli dell'honore non può l'arte nostra sanare altrimente, né io vi metterei,[37] che tenera cosa è l'onore delle fanciulle maximamente, come sapete.*

GISMONDO: *Salvandosi la persona della fanciulla si viene insieme a salvare l'honore ancora. Udite il caso: costei, ancora che sia di buon parentado et ricco, o per sua cervellinaggine[38] o per poca advertenza della madre, si è trovata gravida.*

CORNELIO: *Per l'una cagione et per l'altra, spesse volte advengono simili dishordini, ma segui pure.*

GISMONDO: *Hora, essendo venuto el tempo del parturire et presole le doglie già 3 giorni sono, non può questa poverina in modo alchuno mandare fuori la creatura. Di che, trovandosi la madre e'l padre in quel grado che potete pensare, m'hanno mandato a pregarvi che con vostri instrumenti venghiate fin là, fidandosi et nella fede et nella virtù vostra.*

CORNELIO: *Mal volentieri posso venire, dovendo questo giorno andare a vedere la donna.[39]*

GISMONDO: *Ohimè, maestro mio, voi ruinate un casato intero e a quella meschina non socchorrete, che vi chiama et vi desidera. L'opera fia più breve che voi non pensate.*

CORNELIO: *La cosa può essere breve et longha, secondo la cagione onde procede el difetto, per ciò che puote advenire per dua cause, aut ex nimia angustia et strictitudine naturae aut extraversa fetus positura.[40]*

37. Me ne interesserei.

38. Leggerezza, irresponsabilità. Evidente ricordo di Machiavelli, *Mandragola,* III, 4: «È seguito che [...] per cervellinaggine della fanciulla, che si truova gravida di quattro mesi».

39. Cammilla, la sua promessa sposa.

40. Palese allusione a quanto dice Callimaco nella *Mandragola* (II, 2).

Gismondo: That a gentleman has a great need of your assistance, because at one and the same time, he is putting at risk his daughter's person and honor.

Doctor Cornelio: The ills of the body are treated easily with our craft, but it cannot cure those of honor in the same way, nor would I become involved, because the honor of girls is a most fragile thing, as you know.

Gismondo: Saving the body of the girl will also save her honor. Listen to what has happened: this girl, although she is of good family and wealthy, through her witlessness or by her mother's lack of attention finds herself pregnant.[18]

Doctor Cornelio: For both of those reasons, similar disorders arise often. But continue.

Gismondo: Now, the hour of the birth has arrived and although the contractions began three days ago, this poor girl cannot manage in any way to bring forth the child. As a result, the mother and the father, being in the state that you can imagine, have sent me to beg you to come with your instruments to their house, trusting in your loyalty and your skill.

Doctor Cornelio: I really don't want to go, since this is the day that I am going to see my intended.[19]

Gismondo: Oh me, Doctor, you will ruin an entire family, and you will fail to assist that poor girl, who is calling you and wants only you. The task will take less time than you think.

Doctor Cornelio: The thing might take a short while or a long while, according to the cause that gives rise to the problem, which could be one of two things, *aut ex nimia angustia et strictitudine naturae aut extraversa fetus positura.*[20]

---

18. The Italian, *cervellagine*, means "witlessness." This is a clear citation of Machiavelli, *Mandragola*, III, 4: "It happened that [...] through the witlessness of the girl, she found herself four months pregnant."

19. A reference to Cammilla, to whom at this point he is engaged.

20. A clear allusion to what Callimaco says in *Mandragola* (II, 2)

GISMONDO: *Questo è proprio uno parlare a' morti, che io per me non intendo di grammaticha.*[41]

CORNELIO: *Dico che questa difficultà del parturire può essere causata da due cosa.*

GISMONDO: *Sta bene.*

CORNELIO: *O dalla strettezza troppa di coteste parte da basso o dall'essersi attraversato il parto in orificio matricis. Hora gran differenza è quanto alla facilità de' rimedi, nascendo il difetto dalla prima o dalla seconda cagione.*

GISMONDO: *Io non vi so dire altro, se non che io credo che per strettezza a poche advenga questo caso, perché io l'ho tutte per assai ben capaci et larghe.*

CORNELIO: *Ah, ah, ah, tant'è, il caso é di grande importanza!*

GISMONDO: *Et però vi prego io tanto maggiormente che venghiate tosto et non manchiate, che anche a voi non si mancherà della mercede vostra.*

CORNELIO: *L'opera è lunga et fastidiosa.*

GISMONDO: *Tale premio vi sarà dato che voi ne sarete contento.*

CORNELIO: *Bisogna adoperare le mani in questa faccenda.*

GISMONDO: *Adoperate, se non basta, il capo e' piedi et venite.*

CORNELIO: *Non so, se tu m'intendi.*

GISMONDO: *Intendo d'avanzo. Dieci ducati d'oro vi saranno posti in mano avanti che voi entriate in camera da lei. Muoia o campi, quelli saranno vostri, di poi, salvandosi, harete cosa che vi sodisfarete di noi.*

CORNELIO: *No, no, io non guardo in denari, ma verrò a ogni modo, poi che tu me li profferi, dieci ducati, eh.*

GISMONDO: *Questi et meglio assai di poi.*

41. Non capisco il latino.

GISMONDO: This is really talking to the dead, because I don't understand Latin.

DOCTOR CORNELIO: I say that this difficulty in giving birth can be the result of two causes.

GISMONDO: Okay.

DOCTOR CORNELIO: Either from the excessive narrowness of those parts down below or from the birth going sidewise in *orificio matricis*. Now there is a great difference in how easy the remedy is, depending on whether the problem arises from the first or the second cause.

GISMONDO: I can't tell you any more except that I don't think that narrowness is the cause of this in many women, because I have found them all to be wide and roomy.

DOCTOR CORNELIO: Ah, ah, ah, this is why this case is of great importance!

GISMONDO: And this is why I beg you all the more to come quickly and not pass this up, as your mercy will not fail to be compensated.

DOCTOR CORNELIO: The task is long and difficult.

GISMONDO: The reward will be such that you will be satisfied.

DOCTOR CORNELIO: The hands must be used in this matter.

GISMONDO: If they are not enough, use your head and your feet, and come.

DOCTOR CORNELIO: I don't know if you understand me.

GISMONDO: I understand and more. Ten gold ducats will be put in your hands before you enter her room. Whether she lives or dies, those will be yours and then, if she lives, you will have something that will make you satisfied with us.

DOCTOR CORNELIO: No, no, I'm not considering the money, but I will come anyway, since you are making me an offer, ten ducats, eh.

GISMONDO: These and much better later.

CORNELIO: *Lasciami andare per i ferri che occorrono et fia buono che io prenda un mio palandrano[42] per non essere veduto entrare in cotesta casa in habito di medico.*

GISMONDO: *Anzi, ero un balordo io, che ve lo dovevo advertire.*

CORNELIO: *Io sono a bottega[43] a ogni cosa, che di questi casi ce ne intervengono ogni giorno. Io vo.*

SCENA NONA

Gismondo solo

GISMONDO: *Oh, come spesso d'una fantasia ne nasce un'altra, d'uno pensiero hauto ne viene uno megliore. Mentre che io ragiono con questo medico, m' è venuto nella mente dove io lo posso menare, che sarò almanco sicuro che tutta questa notte che segue non potrà impedire e' disegni di Mario. Et questo è il fondaco[44] di Lottieri, mio fratello, il quale come che habbia l'entrata principale in via molto frequentata, ha non di meno uno altro uscetto ancora, che riesce in un chiasso[45] tanto coperto del mondo, del quale ho io le chiavi appresso di me. Et, adiutami la fortuna, che doppo questa prima entrata si trova uno picciol cortile, nel quale è uno uscio che va nel fondaco, il quale ha una buona toppa saracinescha, si viene a serrar di sorte che né di dentro, né di fuori, si può senza le chiave aprire. Darò dunque ad intendere al medico che questa sia un'entrata secreta della casa dove è la fanciulla et poi che io l'harò nel cortiluzzo, aperto il secondo uscio et fingendo d'honorarlo, lo farò entrare dentro prima et di poi, tirato subito con forza a me l'uscio, chiami, gridi, arrovelli[46] a sua posta, nessuno potrà sentire. Mi rendo certo che prima che domattina, quando si aprirrà il banco e' potrebbe per adventura pagare i drappi al mio fratello, che io gli*

---

42. Veste ampia e pesante, con maniche lunghe.
43. A mio agio.
44. Magazzino, bottega.
45. Vicoletto tra due case.
46. Si arrabbi.

Act Three

DOCTOR CORNELIO: Let me go get the necessary instruments, and it would be a good idea for me to get my heavy cloak so that I am not seen entering this house dressed like a doctor.

GISMONDO: In fact, I was a fool for not having mentioned this to you.

DOCTOR CORNELIO: It's all in my wheelhouse, because cases like this arise every day. I'm on my way.

SCENE NINE

Gismondo alone

GISMONDO: Oh, how often does one fantasy give birth to another, from a thought that one has had a better one arises. While I was discussing with this doctor, an idea of where I can take him popped into my head, a place where I will at least be certain that for this entire night to come he will not be able to impede Mario's plan. And this is the warehouse of my brother Lottieri, who, because he has the main entrance on a street with a lot of traffic, has another small door that is located in an alley that is hidden from the world, and I have the keys to it with me. And, fortune help me, past this first entrance, there is a small courtyard in which there is a door that goes to the warehouse with a good Saracen-style key-hole that can be locked in such a way that it cannot be opened either from the inside or from the outside without the key. I will explain to the doctor that this is a secret entrance to the house where the girl lives, and once I get him in the little courtyard with the second door open, I will pretend to honor him by having him precede me and then, after I have pulled the door closed with a bang, he can call and yell and get upset as much as he wants. No one will be able to hear him. I am certain that no earlier than tomorrow morning when they open the store will he be able by chance to pay my brother for the silk cloths, the ones that

ho furati[47] per fare i fatti mia. Oh, che bello adviso, che pagherei io poterlo conferire a Mario, non ci mancherà tempo. Ma ecco il maestro impalandrato.

SCENA DECIMA

Maestro Cornelio et Gismondo

CORNELIO: *Quanto habbiano noi a ire lontano?*

GISMONDO: *Non ci è cento passi.*

CORNELIO: *Oh, se l'è così vicina, noi saremo veduti entrare, bene sai.*

GISMONDO: *La casa è bene in luogo frequentato, ma noi entrerremo per una certa entrata per fianco che non la troverrebbe.*

CORNELIO: *Hora oltre, al nome di Dio.*

Fine del terzo atto

47. Rubati.

I snuck out to take care of my business. Oh, what a great plan. I would pay money to be able to tell Mario about it. There will be time for that later. But here comes our doctor wrapped in his heavy cloak.

SCENE TEN

Doctor Cornelio and Gismondo

DOCTOR CORNELIO: How far do we have to go?

GISMONDO: Only about a hundred feet.

DOCTOR CORNELIO: Oh, if it is that close, people will see us go in, don't you know.

GISMONDO: The house is in a place with a lot of people, but we will enter by a certain side entrance that you wouldn't notice.

DOCTOR CORNELIO: Forward, in the name of God.

End of Act Three

A gran torto si lagnia,
giovine amante di sua fera sorte,
se colei che lo tien'legato a morte
presa ritien nella medesma ragnia.
O amanti felici,
o per sempre beati,
a cui volgonsi tanto i ciel'amici
che dolcemente amate e sete amati,
a voi ridono i prati
d'ogni intorno d'amor lieti et aprici.

Madrigal before the Fourth Act

The young lover is badly wrong
to complain of his savage fate,
if she who holds him in a deadly knot
becomes caught in the same kind of web.
O happy lovers,
O blessed for all time
to whom the heavens turn in such friendship,
who so sweetly love and are loved,
the meadows smile at you,
light-hearted and sunlit with love on all sides.

Francesco Corteccia

ga - t'a mor - te pre - sa ri - tien nel - la me - des - ma
ga - t'a mor - te pre - sa ri - tien, pre - sa ri - tien nel - la me -
tien le - ga - t'a mor - te pre - sa ri - tien nel -
ga - t'a mor - te pre - sa ri - tien nel - la me -
ra - gna, pre - sa ri - tien nel - la me - des - ma
des - ma ra - gna, pre - sa ri - tien nel - la me - des - ma
la me - des - ma ra - gna, pre - sa ri - tien nel - la me - des -
des - ma ra - gna, pre - sa ri - tien nel - la me - des - ma
ra - gna. O a - man - ti fe - li - ci,
ra - gna. O a - man - ti fe - li - ci,
ma - ra - gna. O a - man - ti fe - li - ci,
ra - gna. O a - man - ti fe - li - ci,

O, o per sem - pre be - a - ti, a cui vol -
O, o per sem - pre be - a - ti,________ a cui
O, o per sem - pre be - a - ti, a cui vol - gon -
O, o per sem - pre be - a - ti,________ a

- gon - si tan - t'i cie - l'a - mi - ci che dol - ce -
vol - gon - si tan - t'i cie - l'a - mi - ci che dol - ce -
si tan - t'i cie - l'a - mi - ci che dol - ce -
cui vol - gon - si tan - t'i cie - l'a - mi - ci che dol - ce -

men - t'a - ma - t'et se - t'a - ma - ti________ O
men - t'a - ma - t'et se - t'a - ma - ti________ O
men - t'a - ma - t'et se - t'a - ma - ti________ O
men - t'a - ma - t'et se - t'a - ma - ti________ O

a - man - ti fe - li - ci, o per sem - pre be - a -
a - man - ti fe - li - ci, o per sem - pre be - a -
a - man - ti fe - li - ci, o per sem - pre be - a -
a - man - ti fe - li - ci, o per sem - pre be - a -
ti a voi ri - don i pra - ti d'o - gn'in-tor -
ti a voi ri - don i pra - ti d'o-gn'in-tor-no d'a-mor, d'o-
ti a voi ri-don i pra - ti, a voi, a voi ri-don i pra - ti d'o - gn'in-tor -
ti a voi ri-don i pra - ti, a voi ri-don i pra - ti d'o-
no d'a - mor lie - t'et a - pri - ci,
gn'in - tor - no d'a - mor lie - t'et a - pri - ci, d'o - gn'in-tor -
no d'a - mor lie - t'et a - pri - ci, d'o - gn'in-tor -
gn'in-tor - no d'a - mor lie - t'et a - pri - ci,

d'o - gn'in-tor - no d'a - mor lie - t'et a - pri -
no d'a - mor, d'o - gn'in-tor - no d'a - mor lie - t'et a - pri -
no, d'o - gn'in-tor - no d'a - mor lie - t'et a - pri -
d'o - gn'in-tor - no d'a - mor lie - t'et a - pri -
ci, lie - t'et a - pri - ci.
ci, lie - t'et a - pri - ci.
ci.
ci, lie - t'et a - pri - ci.

ATTO QUARTO

SCENA PRIMA

Messer Lucio et Norchia servo

LUCIO: Non è senza gran cagione che Mario né 'l Gualcina non sono tornati a desinare, maximamente sappiendo quello che si doveva fare et di quante cose et di che importanza doveano ragionare insieme. Ne vo' andar cercando, che in fin che io non gli trovo non posso stare con l'animo in pace. Ma veggio, pare a me, il famiglio di maestro Cornacchia,[1] lo voglio dimandare per sorte gli havessi veduti. Tu non odi, oh là, tu non rispondi. A te dico, vieni un po' qua.

NORCHIA: Che vorrà da me questo vecchio, che addomandarmi?

LUCIO: Non se' tu il garzone di maestro Cornelio?

NORCHIA: Lo voglio un po' uccellare.[2] Messer no, maestro Cornelio non attende[3] al garzone.

LUCIO: Io vo' dire se tu stai con esso lui, io?

NORCHIA: Come posso stare seco stando con voi?

LUCIO: Meco non stai tu, né simili intronati vorrei per casa, che a ogni cosa rispondi a rovescio. Io ti domando se tu stai per servitore con maestro Cornelio, non so se tu intendi o pure non vuoi intendere.

NORCHIA: Ah, io hora intesi, messer sì, sono il suo servitore.

LUCIO: Vedi che mi ti pareva conoscere. Dimmi un poco, harestù veduto Mario, mio figliuolo o Gualcina, mio famiglio?

---

1. In S, fol. 20r «maestro Cornelio».
2. Prendere in giro.
3. Aspetta.

ACT FOUR

SCENE ONE

Signor Lucio and Norchia the servant

LUCIO: *(aside) There must be an important reason why neither Mario nor Gualcina returned for dinner, especially knowing what they were supposed to do and the number and importance of the things that they were to discuss together. I want to go and look for them, because until I find them, my heart will not rest. But I see, or so it seems to me, the servant of Doctor Crow.*[1] *I want to ask him if by chance he has seen them.* Don't you hear me, hello, you are not answering. I'm talking to you. Come over here.

NORCHIA: *(aside) What can this old man want from me? What is he asking me?*

LUCIO: Aren't you Doctor Cornelio's servant?

NORCHIA: *(aside) I want to have a little fun with him.*[2] No, sir, Doctor Cornelio does not wait on his servant.

LUCIO: I mean to say, are you with him?

NORCHIA: How can I be with him when I'm with you?

LUCIO: You are not with me, nor do I want people as confused as you around my house, people who give an upside down response to everything. I am asking you if you act as a servant for Doctor Cornelio. I don't know if you don't understand me or if you don't want to.

NORCHIA: Oh, now I understand. Yes, sir, I am his servant.

LUCIO: See — I thought I recognized you. Tell me, have you seen Mario my son and Gualcina my servant?

---

1.   In the manuscript version used here, Lucio sarcastically changes Cornelio's name to "Cornacchia" (crow). In S, fol. 20r "maestro Cornelio" (Doctor Cornelio).

2.   The Italian, *uccellare* (lit. to bird) means "to make fun of someone" or "to have fun at someone's expense," which correlates with "Doctor Crow."

NORCHIA: *Messer sì, gli viddi per insino per Pasqua di Ceppo,[4] quando el papa cantò la messa in san Piero.*

LUCIO: *Ah, costui ha cominciato a rispondere a rovescio. Fa' conto che io ho a fare con smemorati. Hagli tu veduti da dua hore in qua?*

NORCHIA: *Messer no, ma bene ho parlato a uno che gl' ha veduti hor hora.*

LUCIO: *Non importa, basta che tu mi sappia dire dove.*

NORCHIA: *Cotesto posso ben dirvi, sapete voi dove sta la Cassandra genoese?*

LUCIO: *Che Cassandra! Ti pensi forse che io tenga conto delle femmine, eh?*

NORCHIA: *Io dico, perché sono in casa sua.*

LUCIO: *Come in casa sua, non può essere, il mio Mario non va dietro a coteste cose. Cotestui è un frappatore,[5] non ne vo' vedere altro.*

NORCHIA: *Io ho parlato in cotesto come gli spiritati, fate hora voi.*

LUCIO: *Odi qua!*

NORCHIA: *Io lo vo' far rinnegare Dio, che dite?*

LUCIO: *Intendestù quel che si facessino in quella casa? Veghiamo un poco.*

NORCHIA: *Messer sì, giuchavono. Mi pare intendere che fra il servitore et lui havevon perso me[6] che 50 scudi.*

LUCIO: *Cinquanta scudi, ohimè! Oh, traditore, sarà vero, troppo quella ribalda gli harà fatto giochare que' danari. Oh, infelice a me, se gliè vero.*

---

4. Natale.

5. Imbroglione.

6. Più di.

NORCHIA: Yes, sir, I even saw them at Christmas[3] when the pope sang a High Mass at St. Peter's.

LUCIO: *(aside) Ah, this guy has started giving upside down answers. Take into account that I am dealing with idiots.* Have you seen them in the last two hours?

NORCHIA: No, sir, but I have spoken to someone who saw them just now.

LUCIO: That doesn't matter, just tell me if you know where they are.

NORCHIA: This I can tell you for sure — do you know where Cassandra from Genoa lives?

LUCIO: What Cassandra? Do you per chance think that I pay attention to women?

NORCHIA: I am saying that because I live in her house.

LUCIO: What do you mean in her house? That can't be. My Mario doesn't get mixed up in these things. *(aside) This guy is a trickster, I don't want to have anything more to do with him.*

NORCHIA: I have spoken in this matter like one possessed, now you do the same.

LUCIO: Listen here!

NORCHIA: *(aside) I want to get him to deny God, what do you say?*

LUCIO: Did you learn what they were doing in that house? Let's have it.

NORCHIA: Yes, sir, they were gambling. I seem to understand that between his servant and him, they have lost better than fifty scudi.

LUCIO: Fifty scudi, woe is me! Oh, the traitor! This is probably too true. That shameless woman must have gotten him to gamble too much money. Oh, my worse luck if it is true.

3.   The Italian, *Pasqua di Ceppo,* lit. "Easter of the Log," reflects the custom of using the term *Pasqua* to refer to numerous religious feast days and the association of Christmas with the burning of a log to keep the cold away.

NORCHIA: *Tu hai trovato Maria per Ravenna.[7]*

LUCIO: *Dimi di gratia dove sta questa ribalda.*

NORCHIA: *C'è un po' troppo.*

LUCIO: *Non importa, io voglio andare s'ella stessi in capo di mondo.*

NORCHIA: *Se tu mi credi, io ti trarrò la voglia d'andare.*

LUCIO: *Dove è?*

NORCHIA: *Dissi che vi parrà forse faticha l'andare.*

LUCIO: *Che faticha, no, no, quando mi monta il moscarino[8] io andrei fin al Sepolcro.[9] Mostrami pure la strada.*

NORCHIA: *Pigliate questa via di qua verso il Culiseo et, paxato il canto, voltate a man manca et lasciate la guglia spaccata a mezza la strada; sboccate poi a man destra et andate dua passi, date di petto nell'uscio che voi trovate, che quella è la casa. La via non si po' errare, ma è un po' lunga.*

LUCIO: *Sie, in buon'hora io vi voglio andare a ogni modo, che ne va il mio. Ohimè, 50 scudi, eh! Io non ho tanto d'entrata l'anno et si bado[10] troppo n'andranno anche tutti a 100.[11] Vedi quello fanno le male compagnie. Ohimè, ohimè!*

NORCHIA (solo): *Io so che tu sgranchierai[12] se tu vai dove t'ho mandato. Oh, come mi giova fare natte[13] a simili persone, che pare se le vadino cercando con lo steccarello.[14] Io gli ho tocca una corda ch'io lo farò andare 10 miglia per hora. Infine, e' non c'è il più efficace stimolo a fare andare un vecchio che toccharli la scarsella.[15] Io non cognosco questo Mario et manco il suo*

7.   Cercare cosa che non si può trovare.
8.   Mi arrabbio.
9.   Al santo Sepolcro di Gerusalemme.
10.   Indugio.
11.   Il prezzo arriverà a cento.
12.   Ti sveglierai.
13.   Burle.
14.   Fuscello, bastoncino.
15.   Borsa di cuoio.

NORCHIA: You found a needle in a haystack.

LUCIO: Tell me please where this shameless woman lives.

NORCHIA: That's a little far from here.

LUCIO: That doesn't matter. I want to go there even if she lives at the ends of the earth.

NORCHIA: If you believe me, I will make you stop wanting to go there.

LUCIO: Where is it?

NORCHIA: I said that it might seem to you like a lot of trouble to go there.

LUCIO: What trouble? No, no, when I get my dander up, I would go as far as the Holy Sepulchre.[4] Go ahead and show me the way.

NORCHIA: Take this road here toward the Coliseum, and when you have passed the corner, turn to your left and go until you pass the broken gargoyle in the middle of the street, turn off the road on the right side and go ahead a few steps, go straight toward the door that you find, because that is the house. You can't mistake the route, but it is a little long.

LUCIO: That's all right, I want to go soon anyway, because it involves something of mine. Woe is me, fifty scudi, wow! I bring in less than that in a year, and if I wait too long, they will all get it up to a hundred.[5] See what bad companionship does? Woe is me.

NORCHIA: *(alone)* I know that it will open your eyes if you go where I am sending you. Oh what good it does me to play jokes on people like this who seem to go around looking for them with a stick. I punched a button in him that will make him go ten miles an hour. In the end, there is no surer goad for making an old guy go fast than grabbing his wallet. I don't know this Mario or his

4. In Jerusalem.
5. The price will get up to one hundred.

servidore, ma quando io li conoscessi io m' harei fatto questo medesimo, perché io son tagliato a questa misura. Ma lasciami tornare al pollaiuolo, che per adventura mi harà provisto le starne et i fagiani che io gli chiesi. Ma io vegho venire in qua dua cuochi, o a nozze o a una signoria vanno questi.

SCENA SECONDA

Gualcina, Mario, due coqui,[16] Norchia

GUALCINA: *Per certo, Mario, ch' el vestirsi a questo modo è stato il migliore spediente che noi potessemo pigliare. Già siamo a casa et da nessuno siamo stati cognosciuti. Oh, oh, allentate il passo, fermatevi, fate le viste di rassettarvi a dosso coteste bagaglie.*

MARIO: *Per che cagione, Gualcina?*

GUALCINA: *Fate quel che io vi dico et state a vedere et non ridete se io parlassi da cuoco.*

NORCHIA: *Molto si fermano questi quochi qui intorno, sarebbono mandati dal padrone, che havessi fatto come il podestà di Sinigaglia.[17] Vo' domandare dove vanno et chi li manda. Olà, dalli stidioni.[18]*

GUALCINA: *Che addomandate?*

NORCHIA: *Dove si fanno le nozze, dove, dove?*

GUALCINA: *Non son nozze migha, ha da essere una cena.*

NORCHIA: *Dove si fa questa cena?*

GUALCINA: *Quinci, in casa la Cammilla napoletana.*

NORCHIA: *La Cammilla, eh! Chi vi manda, se gliè lecito?*

GUALCINA: *Lo capitano Musacchio, capitano de' cavaleggeri del papa.*

NORCHIA: *Che ha a fare ivi el capitano Musacchio?*

GUALCINA: *Oh, per certo tu non deggi essere da Roma già tu. Non è la Cammilla la sua femmina, che ne ha speso un mondo et*

---

16. Vestiti da cuochi.

17. Che voleva comandare e fare da sé.

18. Spiedi.

servant either, but if I did, I would do the same to them because that is the cloth I am cut from. But let me get back to the poultry seller, if by chance they have been able to provide the partridges and the pheasants that I asked them for. But coming toward me are two cooks, who are going either to a wedding or to a lord.

Scene Two

Gualcina, Mario, dressed as cooks, Norchia

GUALCINA: Certainly, Mario, dressing like this was the best means that we could have chosen. We are already home and have not been recognized by anyone. Oh, oh, slow down, stop, make it look like you are arranging this baggage to carry it.

MARIO: Why, Gualcina?

GUALCINA: Do what I tell you and wait and see. And don't laugh if I speak like a cook.

NORCHIA: These cooks are going to stay in this vicinity for a while. They were probably sent by their master, who acted like the mayor of Sinigaglia.[6] I want to ask them where they are going and who sent them. Hello there, you with the spits.

GUALCINA: What do you want to know?

NORCHIA: Where is the wedding being held, where, where?

GUALCINA: It is hardly a wedding. It must be a supper.

NORCHIA: Where is this supper being held?

GUALCINA: Here, in the home of Cammilla the Neapolitan.

NORCHIA: Our Cammilla, eh! Who sent you, if I may ask?

GUALCINA: Captain Musacchio, captain of the pope's cavalry.

NORCHIA: What is Captain Musacchio doing here?

GUALCINA: Oh, you certainly must not be from Rome. Isn't Cammilla his woman that he has spent a king's ransom

6. A proverbial expression for someone who wants to handle everything himself.

*stasera vi cena con quattro compagni de' sua homini. Vuo' tu
intendere chiù altro da me?*

NORCHIA: *No, no, và a tuo viaggio. Oh, questa è la bella cosa, ma
non vò dire nulla se non me ne chiarisco affatto.*

MARIO: *Che girandola è stata questa?*

GUALCINA: *State cheto, che noi ci siamo assicurati ch' el medico
non ci verrà a dare noia, il che importava, non sappiendo di
certo se Gismondo se l'ha trovato o no. Quello è il suo servidore.*

MARIO: *Io ho inteso, oh, questo è stato il buon colpo, l'uscio è
aperto, non accade bussare.*

GUALCINA: *Entrate, entrate, alla liberale.*

SCENA TERZA

Norchia solo

NORCHIA: *Questa non è stata favola, né canzone. Io posso dire
come messer Nicia, «di veduta»,[19] ma non queste mani, con
questi occhi. Vedi ch' io m'indovinava ch' el maestro vorrebbe
moglie per altri! Guarda come un huomo capita male, non
manchava altro a questo vecchio che in sua vecchiaia cacciarsi
di sua mano in testa un paio di corna. Se io non mi abbattevo
a riscontrare questi cuochi era facil cosa che vi fussi ammazzato.
Hora lasciamo stare i fagiani et cerchiamo di lui, acciò che pigli
quel partito che giudica migliore. Sarebb'egli un di questi che
vengono in qua? No, no, sono altre genti. Andiamo allo speziale
delle chiavi, che horamai è hora che tutti li spetiali[20] sieno
aperti.*

Qui Norchia va in casa.

---

19. Non è messer Nicia, bensì Ligurio che si esprime in questo
modo (*Mandragola*, I, 2).

20. Nota autografa a fondo pagina in V, c. 65r: «Qui Norchia va in
casa».

on? And this evening he is going to sup here with four companions from his division. Do you want to know anything more from me?

NORCHIA: No, no, continue on your way. Oh, this is a great thing, but I don't want to say anything until I get a clear idea of it.

MARIO: What kind of whirlygig was that?

GUALCINA: Keep quiet, because we have been assured that the doctor will not come to disturb us, which matters because we don't know for sure if Gismondo has found him or not. That is his servant.

MARIO: I understand — oh, well done. The door is open, we don't have to knock.

GUALCINA: Enter, enter, freely.

SCENE THREE

Norchia alone

NORCHIA: This was neither a fable nor a song. I, like Signor Nicia,[7] can tell you from having seen it, but not with these hands, with these eyes. See — I guessed that the doctor wanted a wife for someone else. Look at how a man can find himself in a bad situation. The last thing that this old man wanted in his old age was to stick a pair of horns on his forehead with his own hands.[8] If I had not happened to run into these two cooks, he could easily have been killed. Now, let's forget about the pheasants and go look for him, so that he makes the choice that he believes best. Would one of these guys coming toward me be him? No, no, these are other people. Let's go to the spice shop that has the keys, because by now it is time for all the spice shops to be open.

At this, Norchia enters the house.

7. A reference to a character in *Mandragola*, but it is not Signor Nicia but Ligurio who uses this expression (I, 2).
8. The sign of the cuckold.

Atto quarto

Scena quarta

Guicciardo vero et Lottieri Castrucci

Guicciardo: *In verità che questa città mi riesce molto magnifica et corrisponde al nome che l'ha per tutto il mondo.*

Lottieri: *Non ci siate stato forse mai più, eh, gentil'huomo?*

Guicciardo: *Messer no, io arrivai hiersera di notte.*

Lottieri: *Questa già si addomandava Roma caput mundi, ma l'è ben' oggi la coda o se altro membro si può dir più vile.*

Guicciardo: *Oh, perché?*

Lottieri: *Perché già soleva essere un ricepto de' virtuosi et buoni et oggi è una sentina de' vitiosi et di barri.*

Guicciardo: *In ogni luogo è più de' cattivi che de' buoni, che oggi il mondo è più che mai fusse incattivito.*

Lottieri: *Egli è il vero, ma per uno che altrove se ne trova, qui n'è un centinaio et tutto nasce per mali esempli di questi. Ma lasciamo ire, di che terra siete voi, se vi piace?*

Guicciardo: *Son pisano, al comando vostro.*

Lottieri: *Pisano, eh! Ben mi pareva che una certa affinità di sangue mi tirasse a parlare con voi.*

Guicciardo: *Siate forse pisano ancor voi, eh?*

Lottieri: *Messer no, io son lucchese, ma voi sapete che pisani et lucchesi per la vicinità son quasi una medesima cosa.*

Guicciardo: *É vero, ma come vi chiamate?*

Lottieri: *Lottiero Castrucci et son stato in questa terra tanto che a pena mi ricordo di Luccha.*

Act Four

Scene Four[9]

The real Guicciardo and Lottieri Castrucci

GUICCIARDO: In truth, this city comes across to me as truly magnificent and measures up to the reputation that it has in the entire world.

LOTTIERI: You have never been here before, perchance, sir?

GUICCIARDO: No, sir. I arrived yesterday, at night.

LOTTIERI: This city was once known as *Roma caput mundi* — Rome, the head of the world — but these days it's the tail, or you could say some other member that is more vulgar.

GUICCIARDO: Oh? Why?

LOTTIERI: Because it used to be a gathering place for the virtuous and good, and now it is a basin that collects the vice-ridden and con artists.

GUICCIARDO: Everywhere you go, there are more bad people than good, and the world today is worse off than ever before.

LOTTIERI: That is true, but whereas in other places there is one, here there are a hundred, and the bad example of these guys gives rise to it all. But let's drop it. What city are you from, if you please?

GUICCIARDO: I am from Pisa, at your service.

LOTTIERI: From Pisa, eh? It really seemed to me that an affinity of blood drew me to speak with you.

GUICCIARDO: Are you by chance Pisan as well, eh?

LOTTIERI: No, sir, I am from Lucca, but you know that because Pisa and Lucca are so close together, their people are almost one.

GUICCIARDO: That is true. But what is your name?

LOTTIERI: Lottiero Castrucci, and I have been in this city so long that I barely remember Lucca.

9.   In the manuscript, both this and the preceding scene are labeled "Scene Four."

GUICCIARDO: *Voi ve l'havete trovata forse buona stanza, eh?*

LOTTIERI: *Sì, bene, io ci ho avanzato qualche cosa. Voi come havete nome?*

GUICCIARDO: *Guicciardo Gualandi et come voi la maggior parte dell'età mia sono vissuto fuori della patria, cioè in Palermo. Pur in mia vecchiezza mi sono ripatriato.*

LOTTIERI: *Eh, buone faccende havete in Roma?*

GUICCIARDO: *Vi dirò il vero, io son venuto quasi come mosca sanza capo.[21] Son quattro anni o più che io lasciai una mia figliuola in mano de' corsali et hora m'è suto porto che l'è in questa terra, per il che son venuto per vedere se io la potessi trovare.*

LOTTIERI: *Sarà male agevole, non sapendo chi se l'ha. Pur si vuol cercare et se io vi posso giovare, sono pronto.*

GUICCIARDO: *Io fo capitale delle offerte vostre et già comincerò a servirmene.*

LOTTIERI: *In che cosa?*

GUICCIARDO: *Perché io penso starci qualche settimana, giudico che sarà buono che io mi rivesta un poco, che io non ho portato altri panni che voi vi vegghiate. Et essendo voi mercante et lucchese ho fatto pensiero di levare e' drappi che mi occorreranno da voi et non havendo vi affaticherò che mi indriziate dove fussi ben servito.*

LOTTIERI: *Voi non potevate abbattervi meglio. E' m'è stato mandato da Lucca pochi dì sono una cassa di drappi che non ci sono venuti un pezzo fa e' più belli et non c'è huomo che me' vi possa servire di me. Et a rivestirvi ve ne conforto, che in Roma chi non è ben vestito non è stimato un danaio.*

---

21. Sprovveduto di ogni cosa.

GUICCIARDO: So you have found a good place for yourself here, eh?

LOTTIERI: Yes, well, I have achieved a few things. What is your name?

GUICCIARDO: Guicciardo Gualandi, and like you I have lived most of my life away from my home town, in Palermo, that is. However, in my old age I returned home.

LOTTIERI: Do you do good business in Rome?

GUICCIARDO: To tell you the truth, I arrived here with nothing.[10] About four years ago or more, I left a daughter of mine in the hands of corsairs, and now I have been told that she is in this city, and that is why I came, to see if I could find her.

LOTTIERI: That will be hard to manage, not knowing who has her. And yet you want to look, and if I can be of assistance, I am happy to do so.

GUICCIARDO: I will take advantage of your offer and already make use of it.

LOTTIERI: In what way?

GUICCIARDO: Because I am thinking of staying here for a few weeks, I believe that it would be a good idea for me to get some new clothes, because I did not bring anything more than the clothes on my back. And because you are a merchant and from Lucca, I have thought about buying the cloth that I need from you, and if you don't have any, I will trouble you to direct me to where I will be well served.

LOTTIERI: You could not have landed better. I received from Lucca a few days ago a case of silk cloths more beautiful than any we have had for a while, and there is no man who can serve you better than me. And as for new clothes for yourself, I support you, because in Rome, the man who is not well dressed is not seen to be worth a dime.

10. The Italian, *come mosca senza capo,* (lit. like a fly without a head) is a proverbial expression meaning "lacking in everything."

GUICCIARDO: *Quando vi piaccia mostrarmeli, l'harò caro.*

LOTTIERI: *Ve li vo' mostrare ancora oggi et non importa che sia festa, che avanzare tempo in ogni faccenda è cosa lodevole. Domani non harete se non a tagliare le vesti.*

GUICCIARDO: *Voi dite bene, andianli a vedere a vostra posta.*

LOTTIERI: *Andiamo, questa qua è la [via] nostra, in tanto potrete succintamente narrarmi il caso della vostra figliuola.*

SCENA QUINTA

Lupo baro, solo

LUPO: *Gran piacere el mio per certo, ogni volta che venendomi rubato qualche cosa me abbatto a fare un bel tratto,[22] ma all'hora maximamente ghodo io meco medesimo quando rubbo i ladri et baro i barattieri. Io son baro et ladro et sempre sono per rubbare et imbolare[23] fin che io habbia un capestro alla gola. Sollo et quando mi advenga, non mi fia cosa nuova. Oggi mi abbattei a sorte in uno barbagianni, che, a pena mi posi a parlare seco, che mi disse tutti e' sua fatti, dove andava, dove stava, quello che faceva et quello che haveva. Io conoscendovi buon pastaccio,[24] occhiai 3 pezzi di raso rosso et una borsa piena di ducati et trovai inganni et bugie in chioccha,[25] delle quali bisognava essere grasso[26] chi fa questa arte. Insieme col Malitia mio compagno, il quale disse d'essere cassiere di messer Lottieri Castrucci, non restamo mai fino a tanto che l'una cosa et l'altra gli calleppolamo[27] suso. Ma questo è nulla, perché ingannare simili allocchi non è gran cosa, più bello è poi che essendo rimasi[28] col Malitia di dividere a mezzo ogni cosa, havendo*

22. Gli faccio un bel trattamento, nel senso di vendicarsi.

23. Derubare.

24. Una persona che può essere facilmente ingannata.

25. In abbondanza.

26. Ben fornito.

27. Rubammo segretamente (ringrazio Linda Carroll per il suggerimento).

28. Essendomi accordato.

Act Four

GUICCIARDO: I would be pleased for you to show them to me as soon as you would like.

LOTTIERI: I want to show them to you today, and it doesn't matter that it is a holiday, because getting a jump on time in every undertaking is to be praised. Tomorrow the only thing you will have to do is cut your garments out of the cloth.

GUICCIARDO: You are right. Let's go see the material as soon as it is convenient for you.

LOTTIERI: Let's go. This street right here is the one we need. In the meanwhile, you can give me a short summary of your daughter's situation.

SCENE FIVE

Wolf, a trickster, alone

WOLF: It certainly gives me great pleasure when, in the case that something is stolen from me, I find the way to get even, but I enjoy myself the most when I steal from thieves and trick the tricksters. I am a trickster and a thief, and I'll keep robbing and stealing until I have a noose around my neck. I know that, and when that happens, it won't be news to me. Today by chance I ran into an easy mark who as soon as I stopped to talk to him, told me his entire story, where he was going, where he was staying, what he was doing, and what he had. I recognized that he would be easy to fool. I spotted three pieces of red satin and a purse full of ducats, and I found tricks and lies in abundance, which you have to be fat with if you are in this profession. Together with my companion Malice, who said that he was the bookkeeper of Signor Lottieri Castrucci, we kept going until with one thing and another we snared him. But this is nothing, because tricking babes in the woods like this is not a big deal. The best is that after I was alone with Malice and we had agreed to divide everything in half

riposti i nostri trophei nel magazzino, del quale ha egli la vera chiave, io, mentre che egli badava a civettare[29] altrove, con altra chiave contraffatta ho alzato e' mazzi et voglio vendere questi drappi prima che io posso et andarmene con Dio, che maggior guadagno non posso fare. Guardo d'un certo messer Lottieri mercante, che mi parve pur hora vedermi innanzi, il quale, vedendo il guadagno pur d'un fiorino, lo compererà sanza fallo. Voglio vedere se fussi qui intorno, che poco lontano deve essere per certo.

SCENA SESTA

Lottieri, maestro Cornelio et Guicciardo vero

LOTTIERI: *A questo modo fanno gli huomini che tengano grado, a questo modo, eh?*

CORNELIO: *A questo modo fanno i mercanti, che vogliono mantenere il credito, a questo modo, eh?*

LOTTIERI: *Entrare per l'altrui botteghe et rubbare la roba del compagno, eh?*

CORNELIO: *Cavare gli huomini qualificati della casa sott'ombra di volere valersi di loro per mettergli poi in questi travagli, eh!*

LOTTIERI: *Che cavare di casa! Vi cavo di casa mia, pensate pure di restituirmi il mio, qui è un danno di dugento ducati.*

CORNELIO: *Pensa pure di restituirmi la fama et l' honore, che lo stimo più di 200 ducati.*

LOTTIERI: *E' sarà buono che io vi trovi a rubare il mio et ancho cerchi di salvarvi l'honore. Me ne vo' ire al governatore,[30] voglio s'intendano e' vostri buoni portamenti.*

---

29. Guardare in qua e là.
30. Massima autorità civile a Roma.

and placed our trophies in the warehouse, which he has a spare key for, and while he was spending his time looking around, I unlocked the door with an unauthorized copy, and I want to sell these silk cloths as soon as I can and get out of here with God's help, because I will never make more profit than this. I'm looking for a certain Signor Lottieri the merchant, whom I thought I saw here just now and who, when he sees that he could earn even a florin, will buy them without hesitation. I want to see if he's still here — he certainly can't be far away.

SCENE SIX

Lottieri, Doctor Cornelio, and the real Guicciardo

LOTTIERI: Is this the way that men of standing act? Is it really?

DOCTOR CORNELIO: Is this the way that merchants who want to maintain their credit act. Is it really?

LOTTIERI: Entering other people's shops and stealing their partner's goods, eh?

DOCTOR CORNELIO: Dragging professional men out of their homes under the pretence of wanting to make use of their skills but getting them in this kind of trouble, eh?

LOTTIERI: What do you mean, dragging them out of their homes! I got you out of my home, and you need to think about giving me back what is mine. This is a loss of two hundred ducats.

DOCTOR CORNELIO: You think about restoring my good reputation and honor, which to me has a value of more than two hundred ducats.

LOTTIERI: That's a good one. I find you stealing my stuff, and I have to try to save your honor. I want to get myself to the governor,[11] and I want people to hear all about your good behavior.

11. The highest civil authority in Rome.

CORNELIO: *Et io me n'andrò fino al papa et intenderannosi le vostre barerie.*

LOTTIERI: *Deh, guarda prosumptione d'huomo! L'ho trovato in sul manifesto furto, trovomi manco il mio et ardisce anche di parlare.*

CORNELIO: *Et che non trovò la scusa della fanciulla gravida!*

LOTTIERI: *Che fanciulla? Non facciamo il pazzo, e' vi sarà cavato la pazzia del capo. Che ve ne pare Guicciardo?*

GUICCIARDO: *Io non so che me ne dire.*

CORNELIO: *Non inporta tu[31] testimoni a me, la verità se ha a trovare.*

LOTTIERI: *Negheretemi voi che mai non vi habbia trovato nel fondaco mio in altro habito che di medico, con grimaldegli in mano et trovomi manco 3 pezze di drappo, se non altro. Ah, maestro Cornelio, maestro Cornelio, del suo bisogna vivere et non di quel d'altri.*

CORNELIO: *Se tu ti trovi manco il tuo, cerca di chi te l'ha rubato, non usare meco queste trappole, che le saranno conosciute, troffarello.*

LOTTIERI: *Mi dice anche troffarello, ladro, ladro, ladro scuro.[32]*

CORNELIO: *Tu ti menti per la gola, che io sono meglio huomo da bene che non sei tu.*

LOTTIERI: *Al corpo di…*

GUICCIARDO: *Non fate, non fate!*

31. Nel manoscritto "tuo."
32. Ignobile.

Act Four

DOCTOR CORNELIO: I'll go as high as the pope, and they will hear about your cheating.

LOTTIERI: Well, look at the man's presumption! I caught him stealing red handed, I find that I am missing goods, and yet he has the nerve to speak!

DOCTOR CORNELIO: And wasn't he the one who invented the excuse of the pregnant girl!

LOTTIERI: What girl? Let's not go crazy, the craziness will be driven right out of your head. What do you think, Guicciardo?

GUICCIARDO: I don't know what to say.

DOCTOR CORNELIO: It doesn't matter what you testify to me, it is important to find out the truth.

LOTTIERI: You will deny that I found you in my warehouse dressed in something other than what a doctor would wear, with picklocks in your hands, and with me missing three pieces of silk cloth, if nothing else. Ah, Doctor Cornelio, Doctor Cornelio, you have to live on what you have, not on what others have.

DOCTOR CORNELIO: If you find some of your stock missing, look for the person who robbed you, don't use these traps on me, because they will be recognized for what they are, you cheat.

LOTTIERI: You are calling me a cheat, thief, thief, lowdown thief.

DOCTOR CORNELIO: You are lying through your teeth, because I am a much more respectable man than you.

LOTTIERI: On the body of...[12]

GUICCIARDO: Don't do it! Don't do it!

---

12. The beginning of a number of blasphemous oaths.

CORNELIO: *Va' pure, la ti costerà questa cosa più che non vale cotesta bottega, catamuzzo[33] di merda. Ma io non vo' fare bella la piazza, me ne vo' ire in casa.*

LOTTIERI: *Io non me n'andrò già in casa, io al governatore me ne voglio andare. Guicciardo, di gratia, siatemi testimonio. Costui mi è entrato nel fondaco, toltomi la robba mia et hammi ingiuriato di parole. Si fanno queste cose a Roma, eh, siamo noi a Baccano.[34] Se non basterà al governatore andrò alla santità di pappa Diavolo[35] et voglio ire hor hora. Di gratia, Guicciardo, vi pregho, venite con esso meco.*

GUICCIARDO: *Lottieri, non voglio che voi corriate a furia, pensateci su un poco, né vi lasciate tanto vincere alla collora.*

LOTTIERI: *Che volete voi ch'io pensi più, che quanto più penso più mi trafigge.*

GUICCIARDO: *Forse che non gl'ha egli hauti, e' parlava molto audacemente.*

LOTTIERI: *Perché gliè huomo sanza faccia et sanza vergogna.*

GUICCIARDO: *Ah, non si vuole fare questi giudicij delle persone, che se le non sono buone, al manco ti hanno apparenza.*

LOTTIERI: *Mi maraviglio hora di voi, che giuditio è il mio a trovarlo in su 'l furto.*

GUICCIARDO: *Voi non lo lasciasti mai parlare, se voi stavate ascoltare haresti forse inteso in che modo e' v'era entrato, perché è, mi pare, un huomo da bene.*

LOTTIERI: *Ah, mi sono accorto che voi pigliate la parte sua.*

GUICCIARDO: *Io piglio la parte del dovere et non dico che voi non habbiate ragione, ma lasciate passare la collora et cercate che*

---

33. Il catamuzzo da catamita, cioè il partner passivo in un rapporto omosessuale (Linda Carroll).

34. Il bosco di Baccano, nei pressi di Roma, infestato dai briganti.

35. In S, fol. 24v: «Nostro Signore». Il papa era Paolo III Farnese.

DOCTOR CORNELIO: Go ahead! This will cost you more than the value of your shop, Mister shitty little catamite.[13] But I don't want to beautify the piazza, I want to go inside my house.

LOTTIERI: I'm not going to my house yet. It's the governor's that I want to go to. Guicciardo, please, be a witness for me. This guy entered my warehouse, took my stuff, and insulted me. Is this the way people act in Rome, eh, are we in Baccano?[14] If this isn't enough for the governor, I will go to His Holiness Pope Devil,[15] and I want to go right now. Please, Guicciardo, I beg you, come with me as I take him there.

GUICCIARDO: Lottieri, I don't want you to race off. Think this over a little. Don't let your anger get the best of you.

LOTTIERI: Why do you want me to think any more about it? The more I think about it, the deeper the wound goes.

GUICCIARDO: Maybe because he did not take them, and he was faking it with words.

LOTTIERI Because he is a man with no honor and no shame.

GUICCIARDO: Ah, we shouldn't judge people like this, because even if they aren't good, at least they present the appearance of being so.

LOTTIERI: I'm surprised at you, because my judgment is based on finding him while he was stealing.

GUICCIARDO: You never let him speak. If you had listened, perhaps you would have found out how he entered the warehouse, because he is, it seems to me, a respectable man.

LOTTIERI: Ah, now I understand. You have taken his side.

GUICCIARDO: I am taking the side of duty, and I'm not saying that you are not right, but let your anger cool down and try

13. A catamite was a passive homosexual. S, fol. 24v substitutes "shitty little merchant" *(mercantuzzo di merda)*.

14. Baccano was a wood near Rome that was full of robbers.

15. In S, fol. 24v: "Nostro Signore" (His Lordship). The pope was Paolo III, of the Farnese family.

non vi sia fatto torto et io ve ne adiuterò col far testimonianza di tutto quello che ho visto.

LOTTIERI: *Al nome di Dio, qualchosa sarà!*

GUICCIARDO: *Fate a mio modo.*

SCENA SETTIMA

Lupo, Lottieri, et Guicciardo

LUPO: *Torno a vedere se trovo messer Lottieri. Oh, ventura, per Dio, è esso. Lo voglio afrontare et sia seco chi essere vuole.[36] Messer Lottieri, potrebbevisi dire dua parole?*

LOTTIERI: *Puossi, di' ciò che tu vuoi.*

LUPO: *Io ho qui 3 pezze di raso nero spagniuolo, saretene voi comperatore?*

LOTTIERI: *Mostra un poco.*

GUICCIARDO: *Sta a vedere che cosa ha essere questa.*

LOTTIERI: *Questa è robba mia, donde hai tu hauti questi drappi?*

LUPO: *Come robba vostra! Voi pigliate herrore, sarà vostra se voi la mi pagherete.*

LOTTIERI: *Errore pigli tu se tu credi che io paghi quel che è mio. Di,' donde gl' ha tu hauti, dico?*

LUPO: *Voi non dovete volere comperargli. Rendetemi qua quelli drappi.*

LOTTIERI: *Adagio a rendergli, gl'è lecito dove si trova il suo ripigliarselo.*

36. Anche se c'è qualcuno con lui.

to make sure whether wrong was done to you, and I will help by giving testimony about everything that I saw.

LOTTIERI: In the name of God, there must be something there!

GUICCIARDO: Do it my way.

SCENE SEVEN

Wolf, Lottieri, and Guicciardo

WOLF: I'm going to try again to see if I can find Signor Lottieri. Oh, what are the chances! By God, it's him! I want to confront him, and it doesn't matter who is with him. Signor Lottieri, would it be possible to have a few words with you?

LOTTIERI: Yes, you may. Tell me what you want.

WOLF: I have here three pieces of black Spanish satin.[16] Will you be the one who buys them?

LOTTIERI: Show them to me.

GUICCIARDO: (*aside*) *Let's wait and see what is going on here.*

LOTTIERI: These are my goods. Where did you get these silk cloths?

WOLF: What do you mean your goods? You are mistaken. They will be yours if you pay me.

LOTTIERI: You are the one in error if you think that I am going to pay for my own goods. Tell me, where did you get them, I say.

WOLF: You must not want to buy them. Give those cloths back to me.

LOTTIERI: I will take my time in returning them. When one finds one's own, it is right to take it back.

16. In Scene 5, the satin was said to be red, although since red was the most expensive dye, it also came to mean "of highest quality." Satin is a weave of silk; at the time, with no synthetics, all satin was made from silk.

LUPO: *Io dubito che voi non mi vogliate fare Calandrino[37] et perché non m' ha essere lasciato il mio?*

LOTTIERI: *Il tuo, tanto harestù a fare del pane che tu mangi.[38]*

LUPO: *Messer Lottieri, se io son povero compagno io sono huomo da bene, nel grado mio.*

LOTTIERI: *Io non entro costì, io, ma io dico che questa è mia robba.*

LUPO: *Potta,[39] che mi faresti dire!*

GUICCIARDO: *Non bestemmiate, fate poco romore, questa cosa si può acconciare in dua parole. Di donde tu gl' ha hauti et sarà sgannato l'uno et l'altro.*

LUPO: *Io son contento.*

LOTTIERI: *Orbè, come ti son venuti in mano, chi te li ha dati?*

LUPO: *Un huomo da bene, pisano.*

GUICCIARDO: *Pisano?*

LUPO: *Messer sì, pisano, parvi ch' io vel sappi dire.*

GUICCIARDO: *Come ha nome costui?*

LUPO: *Guicciardo Gualandi.*

LOTTIERI: *Hora toccha a rispondere a voi.*

GUICCIARDO: *Hora dich' io bene che tu hai tutti e' torti et non puoi essere huomo da bene.*

LUPO: *Ah, voi vi siate accordati insieme, eh?*

GUICCIARDO: *Tu hai il torto, dich' io.*

37. Darmi a credere qualcosa per beffarmi, dal personaggio omonimo del *Decameron*.

38. Come se fosse il pane che tu mangi.

39. Interiezione per esprimere sdegno e rabbia.

Wolf: I'm afraid that you are trying to play me for a fool.[17] How come what is mine can't be given back to me?

Lottieri: Yours? As if this were bread for you to eat.[18]

Wolf: Signor Lottieri, I might be one of the poor folk, but I'm a respectable man within my rank.

Lottieri: I'm not going to get into that — I'm not — but I tell you that these are my goods.

Wolf: Fuck,[19] you're going to make me say stuff!

Guicciardo: Don't swear. Keep the noise down. This is something that can be resolved with a few words. Tell us where you got them and both of you will be undeceived.

Wolf: I'm happy to do so.

Lottieri: Okay, how did they end up in your hands? Who gave them to you?

Wolf: A respectable man, from Pisa.

Guicciardo: From Pisa?

Wolf: Yes, sir, a Pisan. Don't you think I know what I'm saying?

Guicciardo: What is this guy's name?

Wolf: Guicciardo Gualandi.

Lottieri: Now it's your turn to answer.

Guicciardo: Now I can tell you properly that you are completely wrong, and you cannot be a respectable man.

Wolf: Ah, the two of you had an arrangement, eh?

Guicciardo: You are wrong, I'm telling you.

17. Lit. "make me into a Calandrino," a simpleton character in the *Decameron* who was made to believe absurdities so that he could be the object of practical jokes.

18. The expensive silk cloths could not belong to Wolf because of his obvious poverty.

19. Lit. "cunt"; an interjection used to express contempt and anger, frequent in the works of Ruzante.

LUPO: *La cagione?*

GUICCIARDO: *Perché Guicciardo non te li ha dati.*

LOTTIERI: *Leviamoci da partito, parlategli apertamente Guicciardo.*

GUICCIARDO: *Guicciardo Gualandi sono io, né te li ho dati, né pensato, né sognato di darteli.*

LOTTIERI: *Che puo' tu dire hora?*

LUPO: *State forte, vi dirò la cosa come la sta.*

GUICCIARDO: *Oh, oh, costui confesserà senza duolo di fune.*[40]

LUPO: *E' drappi me ha dati infatti un Rinuccio còrso et egli dice haverli havuti da Guicciardo Gualandi pisano et così è la verità, come se io fussi innanzi al prete.*

GUICCIARDO: *Chi può essere questo Rinuccio?*

LOTTIERI: *Tanto lo conosco io quanto voi.*

GUICCIARDO: *Dimmi, valent'huomo, hattegli detto costui per che cagione gli riscevessi da Guicciardo?*

LUPO: *Messer sì.*

GUICCIARDO: *Hor dillo, che questo importa.*

LUPO: *In premio d'una sua figliuola.*

GUICCIARDO: *Oh, Lottieri, che dice costui?*

LUPO: *Vedi, vedi, che sarà pur vero che io non son ladro. Hora rendetemi qua e' mia drappi.*

LOTTIERI: *Tu l'hai pure con questo rendere. Bada un po' costì a Guicciardo.*

GUICCIARDO: *Che figliuola, sai tu particulare veruno?*

40. Senza essere sottoposto al tormento della fune.

WOLF: And your reason?

GUICCIARDO: Because Guicciardo did not give them to you.

LOTTIERI: Let's put aside our roles. Guicciardo, speak to him openly.

GUICCIARDO: I am Guicciardo Gualandi, and I never gave them to you, or thought or dreamed to do so.

LOTTIERI: What are you saying now?

WOLF: Hang on, I'll tell you how things are.

GUICCIARDO: Oh, oh, he will confess without yanks from the rope.[20]

WOLF: In fact, a certain Rinuccio the Corsican gave me the silk cloths, and he said that he had had them from Guicciardo Gualandi from Pisa and that's the truth, as if I were confessing to a priest.

GUICCIARDO: Who can this Rinuccio be?

LOTTIERI: I know as much about him as you do.

GUICCIARDO: Tell me, good man, did he tell you why he received them from Guicciardo.

WOLF: Yes, sir.

GUICCIARDO: Well tell us, because this is important.

WOLF: As a reward for his daughter.

GUICCIARDO: Oh, Lottieri, what is he saying?

WOLF: See, see, it must be true that I'm not a thief. Now give me back my cloths.

LOTTIERI: You will have them yet with this information. Pay a little attention to Guicciardo.

GUICCIARDO: What daughter? Do you know any details?

20. Refers to a common method of torture to obtain a confession. The suspects' hands were tied behind their backs with a long rope, by which they were pulled and then dropped, which caused intense pain and often dislocated the shoulder.

LUPO: *Una figliuola che voi, se voi siate desso, però lasciasti più anni sono in mano de' corsali.*

GUICCIARDO: *Fratel mio, io te ne vo' donare una, la più giusta, se tu mi fai parlare a questo Rinuccio.*

LOTTIERI: *Donate del vostro, che questo voglio per me.*

GUICCIARDO: *Tant'è, i' gli darò il prezzo et se non basterà d'una di due, fa' ch' io lo vegga un po,' di gratia.*

LUPO: *Farollo, ch' io mi vo' giustificare a tutto il mondo che io sono huomo da bene.*

GUICCIARDO: *Se lo farai, sì che tu sarai huomo da bene. Oltra che ti sarà paghato il tuo fino a un quattrino et io non ti mancherò della promessa, da vero gentil'huomo.*

LOTTIERI: *Va' via, fa quel che ti dice, che tu né io non ci habbiamo a perdere.*

LUPO: *Questa è una matassa scompigliata, ma poi che la pania non ha tenuto,[41] i' non vo' cercare cinque piè al montone.[42] Io ho fatte a mie' dì tante faldelle[43] che, havendosi a disputare questo caso alla corte, gl' è facil cosa ch' io dessi in un capestro. Per questa volta basti la buona volontà, andianci con Dio.*

SCENA OTTAVA

Guicciardo et Lottieri [et Vantaggio]

GUICCIARDO: *Che dite di questa cosa, Lottieri?*

LOTTIERI: *Dico che del male la m' è ita meglio ch' io non pensavo, poi che io ho ritrovato e' mia drappi.*

---

41. Modo per dire di non aver conseguito quello che si vuole. La pania era una sostanza adesiva, al tempo usata per catturare gli uccelli.

42. Mettere difficoltà quando non c'è.

43. Truffe.

WOLF: A daughter that you, if you really are who you say you are, left some years ago in the hands of the corsairs.

GUICCIARDO: My brother, I will give you something, and the most just, if you will arrange for me to speak with this Rinuccio.

LOTTIERI: Give your own money, because I want this for myself.

GUICCIARDO: Will do. I will give him the ransom, and if you can do two things as well as one, arrange for me to get a glimpse of him, please.

WOLF: I will do that, because I want to make the case to everyone that I am a respectable man.

GUICCIARDO: If you do it, you will indeed be a respectable man. In addition to paying you what is owed to you down to the penny, I will make sure to keep my promise like a true gentleman.

LOTTIERI: Go on your way. Do what he says, so that neither one of us loses.

WOLF: (*aside*) *This is a hot mess, but because the birdlime*[21] *didn't stick, I don't want to look for a fifth hoof on a ram.*[22] *I've pulled off so many cons in my day that if I were to dispute this case in court, it could easily turn out that I put my head in a noose. This time, a little good will should be enough. Let's go with God.*

SCENE EIGHT

Guicciardo, Lottieri and Vantaggio

GUICCIARDO: What do you think about this, Lottieri?

LOTTIERI: I think that the bad part of it went better than I anticipated because I found my cloths.

---

21. A sticky substance spread on branches to catch small birds.
22. Add a useless difficulty.

GUICCIARDO: *I' dico pure circa quel che ha detto costui della mia figliuola et di questo Rinuccio.*

LOTTIERI: *Io per me penso che questa sia una fintione, né giudico che ci sia da fare fondamento.*

GUICCIARDO: *Che haveva a muovere costui a fare mentione di me et della mia figliuola et di questo Rinuccio, che non ci sono a pena arrivato?*

LOTTIERI: *Io vi dirò come io l'intendo. I' penso che costui sia stato mandato da maestro Cornelio, il quale, temendo che io non mi vada a querelare di questo suo latrocinio, ha voluto rendermi il mio con questo arcighogholo[44] et a fine ch' io pensi che vengha da altri che da lui et tutto il carico del fatto redundi sopra di voi. Et credo che questo Rinuccio sia un nome finto et confermami in questo credere che questo ribaldo s'è quetato con due parole et che se la non stessi così, vedendosi fare la presaglia[45] del suo, hare' fatto più romore che in inferno.*

GUICCIARDO: *Che diavolo ho io fatto a questo maestro Cornelio che mi voglia dare questo carico?*

LOTTIERI: *L'ha fatto perché voi non possiate testimoniarli contra essendo in causa propia.*

GUICCIARDO: *Mi maraviglio che l' habbia possuto così presto sapere i casi mia.*

LOTTIERI: *Non è da maravigliarsene, come voi gl' havete detti a me, così gl' havete detti a gl'altri.*

GUICCIARDO: *Come ha egli fatto a mandare e' drappi, che poi che gl'entrò in casa non s'è mai visto tocchare l'uscio?*

LOTTIERI: *Non importa. Tutte queste case et bottheghe che voi vedete hanno l'uscita di dietro, anzi, se ben vi ricorda, costui che ce li arrechò venne per quello chiassolino che riesce dreto alla casa sua. Non di meno, per questo non vo' che perdiate la speranza et che vi togliate giù di cercare di questo Rinuccio.*

44. Arzigogolo.
45. L'appropriazione.

GUICCIARDO: I say the same about what he said about my daughter and this Rinuccio.

LOTTIERI: For my part, I think that this is a made-up tale, nor do I think that anyone should put their faith in it.

GUICCIARDO: What would have moved this guy to mention me and my daughter and this Rinuccio, when I have just arrived here.

LOTTIERI: I tell you how I understand it. I think that this guy was sent by Doctor Cornelio, who, fearing that I am going to sue him over this theft, wanted to give me back my belongings along with this tall tale so that I would think that it came from someone other than him and that therefore the charge for the action would fall back on you. And I think that this Rinuccio is a false name, and I find confirmation of my belief in this scoundrel's quieting down after a few words and if this was not how things stand, when he saw that his things were being appropriated, he would have made more noise than in hell.

GUICCIARDO: What the devil have I done to this Doctor Cornelio that he wants to burden me like this?

LOTTIERI: He did it so that you cannot bear witness against him because you are a party to the case.

GUICCIARDO: I'm surprised that he could have learned about my business so quickly.

LOTTIERI: It's nothing to be surprised at. Just as you told me about it, you told others about it.

GUICCIARDO: How did he manage to send the silk cloths when no one has seen him touch the door since he entered his home?

LOTTIERI: That's not a problem. All these houses and shops that you see have a back entrance. In fact, if you remember, the guy who brought them to us came out of that little alley that passes behind his house. All the same, I don't want you, for this reason, to lose hope and stop looking for this Rinuccio.

GUICCIARDO: *Lo vo' fare a ogni modo.*

LOTTIERI: *Dove siate voi alloggiato?*

GUICCIARDO: *All'hosteria del Paghone.*

LOTTIERI: *Oh, oh, al Pagone capita tutto il mondo et di costì questo ribaldo s'è informato di voi et delle faccende vostre. Et però vi conforto andare sin là adesso et domandate l'hoste se v'è stato persona a cercare de' casi vostri.*

GUICCIARDO: *Farollo.*[46]

Qui apparisce in scena il ragazzo di Lottieri.

LOTTIERI: *Oh, ecco a punto il mio ragazzo che mi sgraverà di questo peso. Togli qui, Vantaggio, porta questi drappi a casa et aspettami là. Voi, Guicciardo, andate via, che io me ne andrò pensando come mi debbo governare.*

SCENA NONA

Rinuccio còrso et Lottieri

RINUCCIO: *Bene mi sapea che cercare di questo malvagio era un zappare in rena,*[47] *perché è da credere che havendomi fatto una simile giunteria si dovessi in un subito dileguare. Non di meno, guidato dalla passione per havere perso la robba mia, indarno ho cercato tutta Roma. Restami solo, per non manchare d'alchuna diligentia circa questo caso, parlare a Lottieri Castrucci, di cui quello pessimo traforello disse esser cassiere, et ne vo' domandare a costui che vegho venire in qua. Ditemi, huomo da bene, e' m'è stato fatto una delle maggiori giunterie che voi udissi un'altra volta da uno ch'io non conosco se non per veduta.*

LOTTIERI: *Che volete voi che io ne faccia, se voi vi lassate giuntare.*

46. Nota autografa a centro pagina in V, c.79r: «Qui apparisce in scena il ragazzo di Lottieri».
47. Darsi da fare senza risultato.

Guicciardo: I want to get this done however I can.

Lottieri: Where are you staying?

Guicciardo: At the Peacock Inn

Lottieri: Oh, oh, everyone ends up at the Peacock and that is where this scoundrel got his information about you and your business. And so pluck up your courage to go down there now and ask the host if anyone has been asking after you and your business.

Guicciardo: Will do.

Here Lottieri's errand boy appears on stage.

Lottieri: Oh, here just now is my errand boy who will lift all of this weight off of me. Here you go, Vantaggio. Take these silk cloths home and wait for me there. You, Guicciardo, go on your way, and I will contemplate how I should handle this.

Scene Nine

Rinuccio the Corsican and Lottieri

Rinuccio: (*aside*) *It seemed clear to me that looking for this miscreant was like planting in the sand,*[23] *because you can believe that, having committed a fraud like this on me, he would immediately make himself scarce. However, led on by the passion I have about my stuff being taken, I looked for him all over Rome, but no luck. The only thing left to me, so as not to overlook any detail in this case, is to speak with Lottieri Castrucci, because this dirty little thief said that he was his bookkeeper, and I want to ask this guy that I see coming this way about it.* Tell me, my good man, one of the worst con jobs that you have ever heard about was played on me by one of the greatest con artists, whom I only know by sight.

Lottieri: What do you want me do do about it if you let yourself be cheated.

23. Lit. "hoeing in the sand": "to work hard but get no result."

RINUCCIO: *Non dich' altro, solo vorrei sapere da voi se per ventura conoscesti costui?*

LOTTIERI: *Dunque, mi fate voi baro e giuntatore, poi che io debbo conoscere i bari et giuntatori. Mi maraviglio assai di voi!*

RINUCCIO: *Non dico questo, io dico se voi havete veduto colui che me ha rubbato.*

LOTTIERI: *Che cosa vi è stata rubbata?*

RINUCCIO: *Tre pezze di raso et altro.*

LOTTIERI: *Che raso?*

RINUCCIO: *Raso nero.*

LOTTIERI: *Come è il nome vostro?*

RINUCCIO: *Rinuccio còrso.*

LOTTIERI: *Ditemi un poco, donde havesti voi questi rasi?*

RINUCCIO: *Da un certo Guicciardo Gualandi, pisano. Ma perché me ne ricerchate voi, di gratia?*

LOTTIERI: *Ve ne ricerco perché io ne credo havere qualche poco d'inditio. Rispondetemi pure a ciò che io vi domando, che tutto fo' in benefitio vostro.*

RINUCCIO: *Oh, huomo da bene, troppo grande obligo harei con esso voi se io gli ritrovassi. Domandate pure che a tutto risponderò.*

LOTTIERI: *Per che cagione ve li dette questo Guicciardo?*

RINUCCIO: *Dettemeli perché io li restituì una sua figliuola lasciata da lui in mano de' mori et riscattata poi da un mio fratello.*

LOTTIERI: *Dove è alloggiato costui?*

RINUCCIO: *Al Pagone et secondo ch' ei dice giunse hier sera al tardi.*

LOTTIERI: *La cosa sino a qui si riscontra. Ditemi un poco, che huomo è questo Guicciardo?*

RINUCCIO: I'm not going to say anything except I would like to know if you by chance would recognize him.

LOTTIERI: So then, you are making me out to be a cheat and a con artist since I must know cheats and con artists. I'm really surprised at you.

RINUCCIO: This is not what I'm saying. I'm asking if you have seen the guy who robbed me.

LOTTIERI: What were you robbed of?

RINUCCIO: Three pieces of satin and more.

LOTTIERI: What kind of satin?

RINUCCIO: Black satin

LOTTIERI: What is your name?

RINUCCIO: Rinuccio the Corsican.

LOTTIERI: Tell me something, where did you get this satin cloth?

RINUCCIO: From a certain Guicciardo Gualandi from Pisa. But why are you asking me about this, if I may?

LOTTIERI: I am looking for the cloths because I have some information about them. Come on and answer my question, which will be to your benefit.

RINUCCIO: Oh, good man, I would have too great an obligation to you if I found them. Go ahead and ask, I will answer all your questions.

LOTTIERI: Why did this Guicciardo give them to you?

RINUCCIO: He gave them to me so I would return to him a daughter left by him in the hands of some Moors and later ransomed by a brother of mine.

LOTTIERI: Where is he staying?

RINUCCIO: At the Peacock and according to what he said, he arrived there late yesterday evening.

LOTTIERI: Things up to this point match. Tell me something, what kind of man is this Guicciardo?

RINUCCIO: *Non vi ho io detto pisano?*

LOTTIERI: *Non ricerco cotesto io, vo' dire che taglia è la sua?*

RINUCCIO: *Io non so che gl' habbia taglia,[48] se già voi non volete dire quella che si puose egli stesso a' corsali, che furono 500 fiorini.*

LOTTIERI: *Buono, io ho inteso più che io non domandavo et così lui mi raccontò. No, no, i' vo dire che presentia era la sua?*

RINUCCIO: *Ah, la presenza sua.*

LOTTIERI: *Sì, come gliè fatto?*

RINUCCIO: *Quanto alla statura egli è simile a voi, la faccia pallida et non molta barba.*

LOTTIERI: *Costui l' ha dipinto più a punto che non l'harè fatto Giotto. L'abito?*

RINUCCIO: *Ha in dosso uno di questi gabbani[49] col bavero, come s' usa.*

LOTTIERI: *Io non ne vo' più, egli è desso.*

RINUCCIO: *Che ne dite voi, datemene voi speranza alchuna?*

LOTTIERI: *Huomo da bene, io non dico assolutamente che voi habbiate e' vostri drappi ritrovato, ma vi do buona speranza, se non accade altro, che voi gli ritroverete.*

RINUCCIO: *Oh, voi mi date la buona nuova, ma i mie' denari?*

LOTTIERI: *De' denari non so altro, andateli dreto voi. Ma ditemi, in vostro benefitio, quando e' ve gli dette, eravi testimonij?*

RINUCCIO: *Eravene ben dua.*

LOTTIERI: *Oh, fate a mio modo. Menatemi qui questo Guicciardo o al manco, il che verrebbe più a proposito, uno di que' testimoni che vi si trovorono, trovando qualche scusa, poi lasciate fare a me.*

---

48. Giuoco di parole tra *taglia* in quanto corporatura e *taglia* da pagare per un riscatto.

49. Pesanti mantelli, foderati di pelliccia, con maniche e cappuccio.

RINUCCIO: Didn't I say that he was Pisan?

LOTTIERI: This isn't what I was asking about. I mean was he bounteous?[24]

RINUCCIO: I don't know if he had a bounty on him, unless you mean the one that he proposed to the corsairs, which was five hundred florins.

LOTTIERI: *(aside) Good, I heard more than I asked and so he told me.* No, no, I was asking about his appearance.

RINUCCIO: Ah, his appearance.

LOTTIERI: Yes, what does he look like?

RINUCCIO: As far as height goes, he is about your height, with a pale face and not much beard.

LOTTIERI: This guy painted him more accurately than Giotto would have. His clothes?

RINUCCIO: He is wearing one of those long cloaks with a fur collar that are in style.

LOTTIERI: I don't need to know any more. That's him.

RINUCCIO: What are you saying? Are you giving me some hope?

LOTTIERI: My good man, I am not at all saying that you have found your silk cloths, but I offer you good hope that if nothing more happens, you will have them back again.

RINUCCIO: Oh, you are giving me good news. Now what about my money?

LOTTIERI: I don't know anything more about the money. Go after it yourself. But tell me — and it might benefit you — when you gave it to him, were there any witnesses?

RINUCCIO: There were two.

LOTTIERI: Oh, handle it this way. Bring me this Guicciardo or at least — and it would be more to the point — one of those witnesses that you found, using some kind of excuse, then leave it to me.

24. The Italian plays on the double meaning of *taglia,* both "size" and "bounty" or "ransom."

RINUCCIO: *Io lo farò se gli trovarrò, ma perché questo?*

LOTTIERI: *Ingegnatevene et non cercate altro, bastavi ch'io vi sono buon proccuratore.*

RINUCCIO: *Io vo,' ma dove vi troverrò io?*

LOTTIERI: *Qui intorno.*

SCENA DECIMA

Lottieri solo

LOTTIERI: *Hora veggho manifestamente che giudicio nessuno è più fallace di quello che si fa del huomo. Chi harebbe mai pensato questo Guicciardo, che pare la stessa bontà, havesse commesso questo furto et tenutoli mano. Et pure bisogna che sia così, perché questo Rinuccio si vede in fatti che è persona semplice et per la sua debolezza gli furono tolti e' drappi da quello ladroncello che mi dette nella ragna.[50] Bene si conoscono le sua parole non essere finte come quelle di Guicciardo. Non maraviglia che gli scusava il maestro et non voleva che io mi querelassi di lui. Fa' conto che questa debbe essere una medesima peverada,[51] ben che la trama è sì intrighata che io non la so intendere. Oh, eccolo, che per disegnare qualche nuovo tranello non mi si spiccha d'intorno. Io non mi vo' rompere seco fino a tanto che io non gli riprovo questa ribalderia. Vo' bene dimostrare che io sono informato chi è il ladro, acciò che e' non mi havessi però per uno simunito[52] affatto.*

---

50. Che mi ingannò facendomi cadere nella sua rete.
51. Una medesima cosa.
52. Scimunito.

Act Four

RINUCCIO: I will do that if I can find him But why do this?

LOTTIERI: Use your head and don't look for trouble. It is enough for you that I am a good provisioner.

RINUCCIO: I'm going, but where will I find you.

LOTTIERI: Around here.

SCENE TEN

Lottieri alone

LOTTIERI: Now I see clearly that no judgment is as faulty as the judgment that we make of our fellow man. Who would ever have thought that this Guicciardo, who seems to be goodness itself, would have commissioned this theft and given a hand. But that is the way it must be because it is obvious that this Rinuccio is a simple soul and because of his weakness, the silk cloths were taken from him by that little thief who tricked me to get me to fall into his net. His words are easily recognized as not being as fake as Guicciardo's. Do not be surprised that the doctor excused him and did not want me to make a case against him. Take into account that this must be all the same pepper sauce[25] even though the plot is so twisted that I can't follow it. Oh, here he is. Isn't he popping up near me to plot some new intrigue. I don't want to break with him until I can reprimand him for these bad deeds. I want to show him clearly that I am informed about who the thief is, so that he won't think I'm a total idiot.

25. The Italian, *la stessa peverada,* lit. "the same pepper sauce"; *peverada* was a sauce made with black pepper, used to flavor meat.

SCENA UNDICESIMA

Lottieri et Guicciardo

LOTTIERI: Siate qui, eh, Guicciardo, che havete fatto?

GUICCIARDO: La metà di non nulla, né hoste, né altri trovo havere notitia di costui, gl'è forza che sia un nome finto.

LOTTIERI: Non è finto migha, no.

GUICCIARDO: Perché, havetene poi inteso altro?

LOTTIERI: L'ho veduto et parlatogli.

GUICCIARDO: A questo Rinuccio?

LOTTIERI: A questo Rinuccio còrso propio.

GUICCIARDO: Oh, oh, oh!

LOTTIERI: Io l'ho [***],⁵³ che havesti?

GUICCIARDO: Duolmi che non me ci sono abbattuto, ma che dice, rallegratemi un poco.

LOTTIERI: Dice quello che non harei mai pensato.

GUICCIARDO: Che cosa?

LOTTIERI: Che e' drappi gli havete dati voi.

GUICCIARDO: Io?

LOTTIERI: Voi, sì! Guicciardo Gualandi, conoscetelo?

GUICCIARDO: Uno forse che pensa che sia Guicciardo Gualandi, ma non già Guicciardo.

LOTTIERI: Uno che vi somiglia et sa tutti e' vostri secreti.

GUICCIARDO: Oh, voi mi fate stupire.

53. S, fol. 28v: «trafitto».

Act Four

Scene Eleven

Lottieri and Guicciardo

LOTTIERI: Here you are, Guicciardo, and what have you accomplished?

GUICCIARDO: Half of nothing at all, I have found neither host nor anyone else who has information about this guy, so he must be using a false name.

LOTTIERI: No, it's not false, not at all.

GUICCIARDO: Why, have you heard more about him?

LOTTIERI: I have seen him, and I have spoken with him.

GUICCIARDO: With this Rinuccio?

LOTTIERI: With this Rinuccio the Corsican in the flesh.

GUICCIARDO: Oh, oh, oh!

LOTTIERI: I have speared[26] him. What's wrong with you?

GUICCIARDO: I'm sorry that I didn't run into him, but what did he say. Cheer me up a little.

LOTTIERI: He says something that I never would have thought.

GUICCIARDO: What?

LOTTIERI: That it was you who gave him the cloths.

GUICCIARDO: Me?

LOTTIERI: Yes, you! Guicciardo Gualandi. Do you know him?

GUICCIARDO: Someone whom he perhaps believes to be Guicciardo Gualandi, but not the real Guicciardo.

LOTTIERI: Someone who resembles you and who knows all your secrets.

GUICCIARDO: Oh, you amaze me.

---

26. Missing in manuscript, supplied from S, fol. 28v.

LOTTIERI: *Non mi havete ragionato di cosa che e' non mi habbia referito, dicendo haverla da voi. Oltre che mi ha dato tutti e' contrasegni di voi più a punto che non hareste fatto voi stesso.*

GUICCIARDO: *Questa è una gran cosa. Et della mia figliuola che dice?*

LOTTIERI: *Che ve l' ha renduta.*

GUICCIARDO: *M' ha renduto la mia figliuola?*

LOTTIERI: *L'Aurelia, vostra figliuola, sì.*

GUICCIARDO: *Oh, signor Dio, che mi dite voi!*

LOTTIERI: *Eh, Guicciardo, non accade fare tante maraviglie, noi conosciamo anche noi il bianco dal nero.*

GUICCIARDO: *Dunque, pensate voi che io vi habbia rubbato?*

LOTTIERI: *Come posso io non lo pensare.*

GUICCIARDO: *Oh, meschino a me! Lottieri, voi mi fate troppo grande ingiuria.*

LOTTIERI: *Ingiuria facesti voi a me a tormi la roba mia.*

GUICCIARDO: *Può essere che voi lo crediate.*

LOTTIERI: *Lo toccho con mano.*

GUICCIARDO: *Lottieri, mi voglio andare girando per tutta questa città come un pazzo tanto che io trovo questo giuntatore et vo' fare noto a ognuno questa ribalderia.*

LOTTIERI: *Non accaderà molto aggirarsi, che sarà qui hora et harà seco testimonij che furono presenti quando voi gli consegnasti e' mia drappi.*

GUICCIARDO: *Lo vo' aspettare a ogni modo et son parato non solo stargli a petto in presenza vostra, ma davanti a qual si vuole giudice di questa terra. Et starò al paragone seco et con qualunque mi testimonierà contra, sottomettendomi a ogni tormento pur che si trovi la verità, che qui mi cuoce più d'una cosa.*

LOTTIERI: *Voi non direte poi forse così.*

LOTTIERI: You did not discuss anything with me that he did not also convey to me, saying that he had it from you. In addition, he gave me all of your personal details more precisely than you would have done yourself.

GUICCIARDO: This is serious. And what does he say about my daughter?

LOTTIERI: That he has turned her over to you.

GUICCIARDO: That he has turned my daughter over to me?

LOTTIERI: Aurelia, your daughter, yes.

GUICCIARDO: Oh, Lord God, what are you saying?

LOTTIERI: Eh, Guicciardo, don't act so surprised. We too can tell black from white.

GUICCIARDO: So do you think that I stole from you?

LOTTIERI: How can I think anything else?

GUICCIARDO: Oh, poor me! Lottieri, this is too great an insult.

LOTTIERI: You insulted me by taking my goods.

GUICCIARDO: It is possible that you believe it.

LOTTIERI: I can touch it.

GUICCIARDO: Lottieri, I am going to search this city like a mad man until I find this con artist, and I want everyone to know of this evil deed.

LOTTIERI: You won't have to search much because he will be here soon, and he will have witnesses who were present when you turned over my silk cloths.

GUICCIARDO: I am going to wait for him as long as I have to, and I am prepared not only to confront him in your presence but in front of any judge of this city. And I will compare myself with him and with anyone who testifies against me, submitting to all torments so that the truth can be found, because it burns me up.

LOTTIERI: You might not say this later on.

GUICCIARDO: *Lo dirò et farollo, son d'un pezzo, Lottieri, così fossi io certo che ci tornassi.*

LOTTIERI: *Tornerà, non dubitate. Ma che vi dissi, eccolo et ha seco un testimone.*

GUICCIARDO: *Oh, traditori, oh ribaldi et che non venghono a testa ritta.*

LOTTIERI: *Fate una cosa, se voi volete che la verità si ritrovi. Non gridate innanzi tempo, aspettiamoli et ascontianli pianamente quel che vogliono dire.*

GUICCIARDO: *Son contento.*

SCENA DODICESIMA

Rinuccio, Zingaro, Lottieri et Guicciardo

RINUCCIO: *Come io vi ho detto, Guicciardo, voi havete solamente a dire messer Lottieri come e' drappi m' havete dato voi et basta.*

ZINGARO: *Che suspitione è questa?*

RINUCCIO: *Non è suspitione alchuna, ma una usanza, che quando e' comprano mercantie da chi e' non conoscono non le pagono senza la parola di chi l' ha date loro.*

ZINGARO: *Buona usanza questa, acciò che e' ladri non vendano e' loro furti, che, essendone per tutto, in questa terra ne è assaissimi, molto maggior piacere vi farei che questo.*

RINUCCIO: *Ne son certo, non staremo punto a disagio. Vedetelo là che spasseggia con quel gentil'huomo.*

ZINGARO: *Tanto meglio.*

GUICCIARDO: *Per Dio, uno di loro è 'l Zingaro, che hiersera era alloggiato al Pavone et ha mutato l' habito, oh, ribaldo.*

LOTTIERI: *Lasciateli venire, di gratia, che bene haverete tempo a gridare.*

RINUCCIO: *Che pensate voi?*

GUICCIARDO: I will say it, and I will do it because I am all of a piece, Lottieri, and I wish I were so sure that he will return.

LOTTIERI: He will return, never fear. But what did I say — here he is, and he brings a witness.

GUICCIARDO: Oh traitors and criminals, they are not coming with their heads held high.

LOTTIERI: Do one thing if you want the truth to be found. Don't call out too soon. Let's wait for them and listen quietly to what they have to say.

GUICCIARDO: I agree to that.

SCENE TWELVE

Rinuccio, Gypsy, Lottieri, and Guicciardo

RINUCCIO: As I told you, Guicciardo, all you have to do is tell Signor Lottieri how you gave me the silk cloths.

GYPSY: What suspicion is this?

RINUCCIO: There is no suspicion, but it is a custom that when someone buys merchandise from someone he doesn't know, the payment isn't made without the word of the person who gave it to them.

GYPSY: This is a good custom, so that thieves don't sell what they have stolen, and given that there are many everywhere in this city, I would give you an even greater pleasure.

RINUCCIO: I'm sure you would. We won't be in disagreement at all. Look at him over there, he is strolling with that gentleman.

GYPSY: So much the better.

GUICCIARDO: By God, one of them is Gypsy, who yesterday evening was lodged at the Peacock. But he has changed his clothes, the scoundrel.

LOTTIERI: Let them approach, please, because you will have plenty of time to call out.

RINUCCIO: What do you think?

ZINGARO: *Penso che io mi sono ricordato d'una mia faccenda importantissima. Rinuccio, faremo questa faccenda un'altra volta, che hora mi bisogna lasciarvi.*

RINUCCIO: *Come lasciarmi?*

ZINGARO: *Sarei rovinato se io badassi.*

RINUCCIO: *Una sola parola vi spedisce?*

ZINGARO: *L'importa troppo vi dico. Lasciatemi ire, a voi non dà noia tornare di qui a un' hora o dua?*

RINUCCIO: *Mi dà più noia che voi non pensate. Di gratia, non mi siate avaro di quattro passi et di due parole, di poi andate alle faccende vostre.*

ZINGARO: *Voi mi rovinate, Rinuccio, se Dio m' adiuti.*

RINUCCIO: *Voi rovinereste ben me voi se voi vi partissi, ma io non vi sono per lassare.*

GUICCIARDO: *Costui fa resistentia a venire, mi debbe havere conosciuto.*

LOTTIERI: *Havete forse ragione voi.*

ZINGARO: *Horsu, poi che voi mi sforzate, e' bisogna che io m' apra con esso voi, a dirne il vero io non voglio parlare a Lottiero se quel che è seco non si spiccha da lui.*

RINUCCIO: *Oh, perché, che vol' dire?*

ZINGARO: *Dirovelo et direte che io habbia ragione.*

GUICCIARDO: *Gran pratica è la loro, debbono pensare a qualche inganno.*

LOTTIERI: *Pensino a loro modo, la verità se ha a trovare non ci partendo di qui.*

ZINGARO: *Questo è uno della terra mia, al quale, son circa dua anni, fu imbolato[54] da un suo famiglio, detto il Zingaro, tra gioie, collane, danari, il valore forse di 1000 scudi. Di che e' ne prese tanto dispiacere et maninconia che ne impazzò. Et benché poi e' ne guarissi, non di meno spesso spesso gli torna questa pazzia et quando questa cosa gli dà noia ha per meno d'andare*

54. Rubato.

GYPSY: I think that I have remembered a very important task. Rinuccio, we will take care of this matter another time. Right now, I have to leave you.

RINUCCIO: What do you mean, leave me?

GYPSY: I would be ruined if I stayed.

RINUCCIO: A single word sends you on your way?

GYPSY: It matters too much, I tell you. Let me go. Would it be too much trouble for you to return in an hour or two?

RINUCCIO: It would be more trouble than you think. Please, don't deny me a short stroll and a few words, and then go about your business.

GYPSY: You are ruining me, Rinuccio. God help me.

RINUCCIO: You would quite ruin me if you left, but I am not about to let you.

GUICCIARDO: This guy is resisting coming. He must have recognized me.

LOTTIERI: You might be right.

GYPSY: All right, since you are forcing me, I must open myself to you about this, to tell the truth I do not wish to speak with Lottiero if the guy he is with does not leave him.

RINUCCIO: Oh, why? What does this mean?

GYPSY: I will tell you, and you will say that I am right.

GUICCIARDO: They are hunkering down together. They must be thinking up some trick.

LOTTIERI: Let them think up what they like. The truth will be found if we do not leave here.

GYPSY: This guy is someone from my home town, who, about two years ago, was robbed by a family servant, called Gypsy, of goods totaling perhaps one thousand scudi, including jewels, necklaces, and money. He was so upset and melancholy about this that he lost his mind. And even though he later got better, very often this madness returns to him and when this thing bothers him he must travel a

100 o 150 miglia che di sputare in terra, come gl' ha fatto hora, che vedete che gliè venuto [fino a Roma].[55] *Et mentre che gliè in viaggio (udite cosa fastidiosa), se non se abbatte a trovare chi conosca, non è huomo che non lo reputi savio, perché non fa altro herrore che domandare di questo Zingaro suo famiglio. Ma se trova uno che gli habbia un'altra volta veduto, come colui che ha quella albagia*[56] *nel capo, parendogli che sia quel che cerca, chiamandolo Zingaro gli fa le più belle moresche*[57] *intorno che voi vedessi mai. Et perché io so che mi conosce, per fuggire questa baia ho pensato noi lo lasciamo partire.*

RINUCCIO: *Mi pare gran fatto che messer Lottieri non si sia accorto che gliè pazzo.*

ZINGARO: *Non vi dich'io che non si abbattendo a chi conosca non fa una mattezza al mondo, ma se ne deve essere accorto, purtroppo, che gli stanno amendua in cagnesco senza parlarsi.*

RINUCCIO: *Io non vo' che per questo noi guastiamo e' fatti nostri. Lascerenlo dire et advertirenne messer Lottieri, se non se n'è advisto.*

---

55. Si inserisce tra parentesi quanto attestato da S, fol. 30r.

56. Superbia.

57. Balli.

hundred or a hundred and fifty miles, which is like spitting on the ground, as he did just now, as you can see he came as far as Rome.[27] And while he is traveling — listen to this bothersome aspect — if he doesn't happen to encounter someone he knows, he is held by all to be wise because he does nothing but ask about this Gypsy, his family servant. But if he sees someone whom he has seen before, like a person whose mind has been taken over by a fantasy,[28] he takes him for the man he is seeking, and calling him Gypsy, he dances the most beautiful *moresca* dances[29] around him that you have ever seen. And because I know that he knows me, I thought it would be best to let him go on his way, so as to avoid this problem.

RINUCCIO: It seems very important to me that Signor Lottieri has not realized that he is crazy.

GYPSY: I'm not saying that if he doesn't encounter someone he knows, he doesn't do anything strange, but he must have realized, unfortunately, that there are two men watching suspiciously and not speaking to each other.

RINUCCIO: I don't want us to mess up our business for this. Let's let him talk and then warn Signor Lottieri if he has not yet figured it out.

27. The manuscript does not have "as far as Rome"; supplied from S, fol. 30r.

28. The Italian, *albagia,* means "pride," here perhaps "proudful fantasy."

29. The *danza moresca* (Moorish dance), usually simply *moresca,* was a rhythmic dance originally representing a battle between Christian forces and encroaching Muslim ones. Popular from the fifteenth century on, it was included in numerous festivities, and the battle represented was extended to other religious challenges. For the history of the *moresca* with bibliography and a consideration of various views, see Anthony M. Cummings, "Dance and 'the Other': the *Moresca,*" in *Seventeenth Century Ballet: A Multi-Art Spectacle: An International Interdisciplinary Symposium,* ed. Barbara Grammeniati (Crossways, Dartford: Xlibris Corporation, 2011), 39–60; Anthony M. Cummings, "Leo X and Roman Carnival," *Studi musicali* 36 (2007): 289–341, esp. 309–37. Here it refers to this man's supposed tendency to physically attack anyone he believes to be Gypsy as described by Gypsy a few lines later.

ZINGARO: *Non basta, cotesto verrebbe forse a' fatti.*

RINUCCIO: *Che potrebbe ei fare?*

ZINGARO: *Potrebbe ei fare, dice? Venire in tanta collera che mi salterebbe a dosso con morsi et con graffi, voi non vedesti mai la più bestiale cosa.*

RINUCCIO: *Mi maraviglio che vi facci villania. Se gliè pazzo troverrà un pazzo e mezzo, andiam via pure.*

ZINGARO: *Horsu, io vegho che voi volete vedere questa festa. Andiamo, se io vi debbo fare piacere, forse non mi riconoscerà egli et se pure e' mi conosce non attendete a cosa che dica.*

GUICCIARDO: *Eccoli alla volta nostra, me' sarebbe che noi havessemo con noi un testimone, o dua, che potessi fare fede di questa giunteria, ch' i so che noi la scoprirremo.*

LOTTIERI: *Voi dite bene, io guardo se io ci vegho persona.*

RINUCCIO: *Ben trovato, messer Lottieri, questo è…*

LOTTIERI: *Aspettate, io vengo hora a voi. Io ho veduto qua uno a chi mi bisogna dire una parola sola.*

GUICCIARDO: *Tu se' qui, eh, Zingaro, molto presto sei diventato gentil'huomo.*

ZINGARO: *Che ti dissi, noi faremo pure delle nostre, oh, meschino!*

RINUCCIO: *Non è il Zingaro questo, no, voi pigliate errore. Egli è Guicciardo Gualandi, un della vostra terra.*

GUICCIARDO: *Come Guicciardo, oh, che è quel ch'io odo.*

ZINGARO: *Guicciardo son sì, così fussi voi in quello essere che voi vorresti.*

GUICCIARDO: *E' ti è bastato la vista attribuirti il nome d'altri, eh, pessimo giuntatore.*

ZINGARO: *Non vo' parlare con un matto, andianne, Rinuccio, qua a parlare a Lottieri et uscianne.*

GYPSY: That's not enough. This guy could start acting out.

RINUCCIO: What could he do?

GYPSY: What could he do, are you asking? He could become so enraged that he would jump me and bite and scratch me. You've never seen someone act like such an animal.

RINUCCIO: I'm surprised that he could treat you so savagely. If he is crazy, he will find someone who is crazy and a half. Let's just go.

GYPSY: All right. I see that you want to see this party. Let's go if I am to please you. Maybe he won't recognize me, and even if he does, pay no attention to what he says.

GUICCIARDO: Here he is, coming toward us. It would be better if we had a witness with us, or two, who could testify to this trickery, because I know that we are going to uncover it.

LOTTIERI: You are right. I'll look and see if I can find somebody.

RINUCCIO: Look who I've found, Signor Lottieri, this is…

LOTTIERI: Wait, let me come back to you. I have seen someone I have to say just a word to.

GUICCIARDO: You are here, too, eh, Gypsy? You have become a gentleman in a very short time.

GYPSY: What did I tell you? We will do what we have to, you poor guy.

RINUCCIO: This is not Gypsy. No, you are mistaken. This is Guicciardo Gualandi, someone from your hometown.

GUICCIARDO: What do you mean Guicciardo? What is it that I am hearing?

GYPSY: Yes, I am Guicciardo, and I wish that you were that person that you wish to be.

GUICCIARDO: All you had to do was look at someone to take their name, you wretched trickster.

GYPSY: I don't want to talk to a madman. Let's go, Rinuccio. Speak with Lottieri and then get out of here.

GUICCIARDO: *Vo' bene parlare io con un tristo, che importa assai.*

RINUCCIO: *Parlate modestamente con le persone da bene, che alla fine non sarete scusato per matto.*

GUICCIARDO: *Che scusato per matto, ti paio matto a cercare delle cose mia, eh, ma vegho bene che tu, non meno di me, se' stato trattato da matto et sciocco da cotesto baro.*

RINUCCIO: *Che vuole dire costui?*

ZINGARO: *Non attendete a lui, dico, andiamo a Lottieri.*

RINUCCIO: *Hora ne vengho.*

GUICCIARDO: *Ditemi un poco, che è venuto a fare qua questo Guicciardo?*

RINUCCIO: *Oh, oh, lo debbe forse riconoscere, e' sarà tornato in sé per la sua figliuola che gl'haveva perduta, la quale era appresso di me.*

GUICCIARDO: *Et tu gliela hai data?*

RINUCCIO: *Non era giusto, se l'era sua figliuola?*

GUICCIARDO: *Oh, traditore, oh, ribaldo, la mia figliuola ti se' usurpata per tua, eh, per vituperarla.*

ZINGARO: *Oh, oh, costui ha perso la robba et pargli havere perso la sua figliuola. Dio ne guardi ogn'uno da questo male!*

GUICCIARDO: *E' gli ha anche ardire di parlare, non so chi mi tiene, ch'io non gli cavi gl'occhi al ladroncello.*

RINUCCIO: *Io so che tu non gli farai villania.*

ZINGARO: *Per Dio, costui è il padre della fanciulla da dovero, lo stare qui non fa per me, io non voglio contendere con pazzi, a Dio, a Dio.*

GUICCIARDO: *Ohimè, a questo modo si fa a gl'huomini da bene. Lottieri soccorretemi, vogliono anche manomettermi.*

GUICCIARDO: And I really want to speak to a criminal, that matters a lot.

RINUCCIO: Speak quietly with respectable people, and in the end, you won't be dismissed as a madman.

GUICCIARDO: What do you mean, dismissed as a madman. Do I seem crazy to you to search for my goods, eh, but I see well that you, no less than I, have been treated as a madman and a fool by this fraudster.

RINUCCIO: What does he mean?

GYPSY: Pay no attention to him. Let's go see Lottieri.

RINUCCIO: I'm coming.

GUICCIARDO: Tell me something. What did this Guicciardo come here to do?

RINUCCIO: Oh, oh, he must recognize him. Perhaps, he must have gotten his sanity back because of the daughter that he lost who was staying with me.

GUICCIARDO: And you gave her to him?

RINUCCIO: Wasn't that the right thing to do if she was his daughter?

GUICCIARDO: Oh traitor, oh criminal, you usurped my daughter for your own, eh, to be able to ruin her.

GYPSY: Oh, oh, this guy has lost his goods, and he thinks that he has lost his daughter. God protect all of us from this illness.

GUICCIARDO: And he even has the temerity to speak. I don't know who will be able to hold me back to keep me from digging the eyes out of this little thief.

RINUCCIO: I know that you won't do anything bad to him.

GYPSY: (*aside*) *By God, this guy is the true father of the girl. Hanging around here isn't going to be good for me. I don't want to fight with madmen. Good-bye, good-bye.*

GUICCIARDO: Woe is me. Is this how respectable men are treated? Lottieri, help me. They want to put their hands on me.

Atto quarto

Lottieri, Rinuccio, Guicciardo, Fabio

Lottieri: Che cosa è, che questione è la vostra, e' non si fa così a' gentil'huomini.

Rinuccio: E' farà villania anche a voi se non si tiene, non vi siate voi accorto che gliè pazzo.

Guicciardo: Pazzo io, eh, lassami, oh, io non sono pazzo, ma bene sfortunato.

Fabio: Et lassalo, che t'ha ei fatto?

Rinuccio: Io farò a vostro modo et se vi fa male, vostro danno. Ma dove è Guicciardo, o Guicciardo, oh Dio, e' se n'è ito.

Lottieri: Io non so se tu ti sei ebro, non lo vedi tu costì. Dove vai, sì a punto vagli dreto.

Rinuccio: Se gli havessi pur detto una parola.

Lottieri: E' mi pare essere fra un monte di pazzi, chi va in qua, chi va in là, io non intendo questa girandola.

Fabio: Né io.

Guicciardo: Questa è la maggiore ribalderia che mai si facessi, ma non si doveva lasciare partire colui, che si è trovato il ladro che haveva rubbato me. Et voi chiamatelo et intenderete ogni cosa.

Lottieri: Ecco che torna.

Fabio: In fine, che travaglio è questo, non si po' egli intendere.

Rinuccio: Bontà delle pazzie di costui, non ho potuto giustificare de' mia drappi. Come faremo?

Guicciardo: Vedete dove io mi trovo et si da ad intendere che io sia matto. Parlategli un po' voialtri et diteli quel che s'è partito a voi ha rubbato la roba et a me la figliuola.

Act Four

SCENE THIRTEEN

Lottieri, Rinuccio, Guicciardo, Fabio

LOTTIERI: What is this? What are you quarreling about? Gentlemen are not treated this way.

RINUCCIO: He will treat you savagely as well if he is not held back. You have not realized that he is crazy.

GUICCIARDO: I am crazy, eh! Leave me alone. Oh, I am not crazy, just unlucky.

FABIO: Let him go. What has he done to you?

RINUCCIO: I will do as you ask, and if he harms you, that's your loss. But where is Guicciardo, oh, Guicciardo, oh God, he's left.

LOTTIERI: I don't know if you are drunk. Don't you see him here? Where are you going? Yes, go ahead and follow him.

RINUCCIO: If only I had said a word to him.

LOTTIERI: I feel like I'm in a pile of crazies, some going this way, some going that way. I don't understand this whirl.

FABIO: Neither do I.

GUICCIARDO: This is the worst fraud that was ever committed, but he should not have been allowed to leave, because he has been discovered to be the thief who stole from me. Call him and you will understand everything.

LOTTIERI: Look, he is coming back.

FABIO: In the end, it is impossible to understand what the problem is.

RINUCCIO: Thanks to his madness, I have not been able to get justice about my silk cloths. How will we handle this?

GUICCIARDO: Look at the situation I'm in. I am accused of being mad. You all speak to him a little and tell him that the guy who just left stole your goods from you and my daughter from me.

LOTTIERI: *Non dubitate de' drappi, Rinuccio, tiriamoci un po' qua che le vostre pazzie farebbono ragunate di popolo et faremo dir di noi.*

FABIO: *E'gliè bene, andiamocene dove pare a voi.*

RINUCCIO: *Sì, ma se costui ci viene dietro ce ne farà dell'altre.*

LOTTIERI: *Non dubitate, venitene Guicciardo.*

Fine del quarto atto. Comincia il quinto et ultimo

Act Four

LOTTIERI: Don't worry about the silk cloths, Rinuccio. Let's move over to the side because your craziness would attract a crowd, and we'll get ourselves talked about.

FABIO: That's a good idea. Let's go wherever you think is best.

RINUCCIO: Yes, but if this guy follows us, he will pull more stuff on us.

LOTTIERI: Don't worry. Come along, Guicciardo.

Act Four ends, the fifth and final act begins

Oh, come nulla vale
per adempire il nostro van disegnio
mortal forza et ingegnio.
Sola colei cui d'ogni cosa cale,
divina providenza,
tal volge il mondo ch'uno acerbo male
a dolcissimo ben subito sale.
Così crescendo sempre i nostri danni,
per i non giusti inganni,
fuor di nostra credenza,
huomo tornando dallo hispano Hibero,
tutti rallegrerà mostrando il vero.

Madrigal before the Fifth Act

O how mortal strength
and ingenuity do nothing
to fulfill our vain plan.
Only the one who cares for all things,
divine providence,
turns the world in such a way that
from a bitter ill it climbs swiftly
to a very sweet good.
Thus as the harm to us from unjust deceit
was growing by the hour,
what we could not have believed,
a man returning from Hispanic Iberia
will cheer us all by revealing the truth.

Francesco Corteccia

gno, So - la co - - - - - -
gno, So - la co - le -
gno, So - la co - le -
gno, So - la
le - i cui d'o - gni co - sa ca - le, di -
- - - - i cui d'o - gni co - sa ca - le, di -
- - - - i cui d'o - gni co - sa ca - le, di -
- co - le - i cui d'o - gni co - sa ca - le, di -
vi - na pro - vi - den - za, tal vo - lg'il mon - do
vi - na pro - vi - den - za, tal vo - lg'il mon - do
vi - na pro - vi - den - za, tal vo - lg'il mon - -
vi - na pro - vi - den - za, tal vo - lg'il mon - - -

ch'u - n'a - cer - bo ma - le a dol - cis - si - mo
ch'u - n'a - cer - bo ma - le a dol - cis - si - mo
do ch'u - n'a - cer - bo ma - le a dol - cis - si - mo
do ch'u - n'a - cer - bo ma - le a dol - cis - si - mo
ben su - bi - to sa - le. Co - sì cre - sce - nd'hor sem - pr'i no -
ben su - bi - to sa - le. Co - sì cre - sce - nd'hor sem - pr'i no -
ben su - bi - to sa - le. Co - sì cre - sce - nd'hor sem - pr'i no -
ben su - bi - to sa - le. Co - sì cre - sce - nd'hor sem - pr'i no -
- stri dan - ni, per i non giu - st'in - gan - ni, fuor
- stri dan - ni, per i non giu - st'in - gan - ni, fuor
- stri dan - ni, per i non giu - st'in - gan - ni, fuor
- stri dan - ni, per i non giu - st'in - gan - ni, fuor

di no - stra cre - den - za, huo - mo tor - nan - do dal -
di no - stra cre - den - za, huo - mo tor - nan -
di no - stra cre - den - za, huo - mo tor - nan - do
di no - stra cre - den - za, huo - mo tor - nan - do
- l'hi - spa - no Hi - be - ro, tut - ti ral -
do dal - l'hi - spa - no Hi - be - ro, tut - ti ral - le - grer - rà mo -
dal - l'hi - spa - no Hi - be - ro, tut -
dal - l'hi - spa - no Hi - be - ro, tut - ti ral - le - grer -
le - grer - rà mo - stran - do'l ve - ro, tut - ti ral - le - grer - rà mo -
stran - do'l ve - ro, tut - ti ral - le - grer - rà mo - stran - do'l ve -
- ti ral - le - grer - rà mo - stran - do'l ve - ro, tut - ti ral - le -
rà mo - stran - do'l ve - ro, mo - stran - do'l ve - ro, tut - ti ral - le - grer - rà mo - stran - do'l

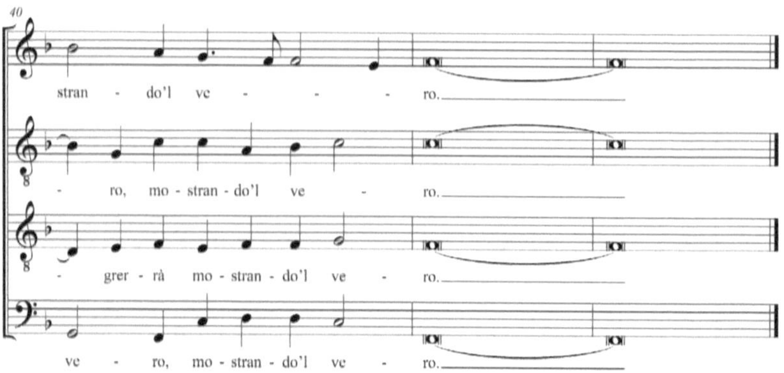

stran - do'l ve - - - ro.
- ro, mo - stran - do'l ve - ro.
- grer - rà mo - stran - do'l ve - ro.
ve - ro, mo - stran - do'l ve - ro.

Atto quinto

Scena prima

Messer Lucio solo

Lucio: Io sono stancho per essermi tanto aggirato cercando di questa Cassandra, che cassa[1] di vita possa esser ella et quello ladroncello del famiglio del medico che me insegnò la strada. Io andai et me aggirai un gran pezzo, poi, quando io penso essere giunto a luogo che egli mi dette ad intendere, non trovai né cane, né gatta che me ne sapesse dire parola, tanto ch'io tengo per certo che questa sia stata una natta[2] et forse fattami fare da maestro Cornelio per l'invidia che io ho dato per la moglie a Mario, mio figliuolo, quella che già era sua nuora. In fine, questa invidia è una gran maestra hoggi, ma guai a chi non è invidiato. Duolmi solo che io, in questo mentre, harei fatto mille faccende, trovato Mario et dato ordine a tutte le cose opportune. Ma ecco Fabio a tempo, fratello della mia nuora, parmi assai travagliato, Dio voglia che non si nata qualche disgratia.

Scena seconda

Fabio et messer Lucio

Fabio: Oh, come rest' io ingannato di questo Mario.

Lucio: E' gl'ha nomato Mario, trama c'è.

Fabio: Mi pareva una coppa d'oro.

---

1. Cancellata.
2. Burla.

Act Five

Scene One

Signor Lucio alone

LUCIO: I have tired myself out running around trying to find this Cassandra, and may she be cashiered[1] out of life, together with that little thief, the servant of the doctor, who told me what route to take. I went and looked around for a long time, and then when I thought that I had reached the place that he had given me to understand was the one, I found no one, not even a dog or a cat, who could tell me anything about it, so I am sure that this was a trick and maybe it was Doctor Cornelio who had it played on me because he was envious that I gave the girl who used to be his daughter-in-law to my son Mario as his wife. When you get down to it, this envy is the lady in charge these days, but it's worse for you if you are not envied.[2] I'm just sorry that in the time I spent running around, I could have gotten a thousand things done, found Mario, and put in order all the things that are needed. But here is Fabio just in time. He is my daughter-in-law's brother and he seems to me very agitated. May it be God's will that no misfortune has occurred.

Scene Two

Fabio and Signor Lucio

FABIO: Oh, how I was deceived by this Mario.

LUCIO: *(aside) He mentioned the name of Mario, there is intrigue afoot.*

FABIO: He seemed like a golden chalice to me.

---

1.   The term *cashiered* referred to the discharging of mercenary soldiers, either for defective performance or at the end of the war.
2.   When you have nothing for others to envy, you are worthless in their eyes.

LUCIO: *Che dice costui d'oro, che si sarà giuocati que' denari, Dio m'adiuti!*

FABIO: *Che dirà messer Lucio, quando lo saprà?*

LUCIO: *Non può essere altro, i' sono disfatto!*

FABIO: *Al manco lo trovassi io tosto.*

LUCIO: *E' mi cerca, voglio chiamarlo, o Fabio, o Fabio, che cosa è, che è del mio Mario?*

FABIO: *Oh, messer Lucio, a tempo ci sian ritrovati. La prima cosa che io vi ho da dire si è questa, che poi che fra noi non è seguito altro che parole quanto al parentado della mia sorella et del vostro figliuolo, io pretendo et voglio che sia a punto come se egli non se ne fusse mai ragionato.*

LUCIO: *Ohimè, che vole dire questo, che cosa ci è nata, che è di Mario mio?*

FABIO: *Et che il parentado sia annichilato et di fatto in tutto et per tutto.*

LUCIO: *Questa per certo deve essere una gran cosa. Ma ditemi presto che cosa ci è?*

FABIO: *Dove in altro io possa farvi piacere, non son per manchare, in questo fate conto che non ci fussimo mai conosciuti.*

LUCIO: *Domine, che voi mi diciate mai più che cosa sia nata io mi consumo.*

FABIO: *Oh, messer Lucio, vorrei piuttosto che ve lo dicessi un altro.*

LUCIO: *Dite, presto, non mi fate più stentare, vi pregho, che Domine po' egli havere fatto?*

FABIO: *Fatto, eh!*

LUCIO: *Che cosa harebbe costui mai rubbato?*

FABIO: *Rubbato et fatto ancora peggio.*

LUCIO: *Oh Signore, oh Signore.*

Lucio: *(aside) What is he saying about gold? If he has gambled that money away, God help me!*

Fabio: What will Signor Lucio say when he finds out?

Lucio: *(aside) It can't be anyone else. I am ruined!*

Fabio: At least if I could find him soon.

Lucio: (aside) *He is looking for me. I want to call out to him.* Oh, Fabio, oh Fabio. What is it? What has happened to my Mario?

Fabio: Oh, Signor Lucio. We have found each other in time. The first thing that I have to tell you is this, that because we did nothing but talk about the family agreement concerning my sister and your son, I insist and want the understanding to be exactly as it was, as if it had never been discussed.

Lucio: Oh, me! What does this mean? What has this caused? What has happened to my Mario?

Fabio: And the family agreement be nullified in word and deed in all things and everywhere.

Lucio: This certainly must be important. But tell me immediately what the problem is.

Fabio: In anything else where I can satisfy you, I will not fail, but in this matter, act as if we had never met.

Lucio: Lord, I am consumed with the desire to know what happened — what if you never get around to telling me?

Fabio: Oh, Signor Lucio, I would prefer it if someone else told you.

Lucio: Tell me immediately. Don't make me suffer any longer, I beg you. What in the Lord's name could he have done?

Fabio: Done, eh!

Lucio: What could he have stolen?

Fabio: Stolen and worse.

Lucio: Oh Lord, oh Lord!

FABIO: *Éssi trovato a rubbare più drappi a Lottieri Castrucci.*

LUCIO: *Ohimè, che mi dite voi!*

FABIO: *Et a uno povero gentil'huomo pisano una fanciulla.*

LUCIO: *Ahi, misero a me, una fanciulla anche!*

FABIO: *Et se tosto non si va con Dio, sarà preso.*

LUCIO: *Oh, Signore Dio, aiutatelo! Ma sapetelo voi di chiaro che la non fussi inventione di maestro Cornelio per dargli carico et guastare questo parentado?*

FABIO: *Come inventione di maestro Cornelio, che si è trovato ancora egli in sul fatto et porta non manco pericolo del vostro figliuolo?*

LUCIO: *Ohimè, figliuolo mio, che odo io de' fatti tua. Chi vi ha referito questa cosa, Fabio?*

FABIO: *Lottieri stesso et quel gentil'huomo pisano che ha perduto la figliuola.*

LUCIO: *Oh Dio, oh Dio, oh ruinato vecchio, va' allieva i figliuoli tu, va' hora, oh, oh!*

FABIO: *Non vi disperate, messer Lucio, che voi non siate il primo.*

LUCIO: *Et quando et in che modo è seguita la cosa?*

FABIO: *Sarebbe cosa lunga il narrarla, pensate più presto a' rimedij, prima che segua peggio.*

LUCIO: *Io mi vi raccomando, Fabio, non m'abbandonate, vi pregho adiutatemi et di favore et di consiglio, che questa cosa me ha fatto perdere la bussola.*

FABIO: *In questo non vi posso io mancare.*

LUCIO: *Che debbo io fare, che partito sarà il mio?*

FABIO: *Prima trovare Mario et fare ad ogni modo che questa fanciulla si renda a questo gentil'huomo et lui terrei ascoso qualche giorno, che poi ci sarà de' remedij, perché i drappi sono ritrovati nelle mani al padrone.*

FABIO: He was found to have stolen a number of cloths from Lottieri Castrucci.

LUCIO: Oh me! What are you telling me?

FABIO: And a girl from a poor gentleman from Pisa.

LUCIO: Oh, miserable me, a girl too!

FABIO: And if he is not soon on his way with God, he will be arrested.

LUCIO: Oh, Lord! God, help him! But do you know with certainty that this was not the invention of Doctor Cornelio to give him a boost in breaking this family agreement?

FABIO: How could it be an invention of Doctor Cornelio, who was there on the spot and to whom it poses no less danger than to your son?

LUCIO: Oh me, my son! What is it I am hearing about your affairs? Who told you about this, Fabio?

FABIO: Lottieri himself and that Pisan gentleman who lost his daughter.

LUCIO: Oh God, oh God! Oh ruined old man, go and raise your children now! Go now, oh, oh!

FABIO: Don't despair, Signor Lucio. You are not the first.

LUCIO: And when and in what way did this happen?

FABIO: It would take a long time to tell. It is better to think of remedies before something worse happens.

LUCIO: I beg of you, Fabio, don't abandon me. I beseech you. Help me with support and with counsel, because this thing has made me lose my compass.

FABIO: In this matter, I cannot fail you.

LUCIO: What should I do? Which option should I choose?

FABIO: First find Mario and do everything you can to get this girl turned over to this gentleman, and I would keep him hidden for a few days, and after that there must be a way to get the cloths back into the hands of their owner.

LUCIO: *Tanto farò, ma dove Domine lo potrò io trovare?*

FABIO: *A casa vostra, a casa gl' amici, ne' luoghi dove egli praticha. Non perdete tempo, andate, poi ci troverremo quando luce et io non mancherò d'adiutarvi.*

LUCIO: *Io ve ne prego quanto posso.*

FABIO: *Lo farò, dico, non perdete più tempo.*

LUCIO: *Ecco che io vo.*

FABIO: *Oh, infelice et sventurato vecchio! Non so io però di certo che Mario sia stato l'auttore di questo malefitio. Pure, essendo con quel ribaldo et in quel modo favorendolo, è da credere che ogni male siasi fatto per conto suo, ma, come la cosa si stia, non voglio tali homini per parenti già io.*

SCENA TERZA

Zingaro solo col suo habito[3]

ZINGARO: *Io vo' ben dire che oggi signoreggi qualche stella in cielo che mi favorisca da vero, poi che ogni cosa mi succede prosperamente. Io non fui levato a pena ch' el Gualcina mi messe quella pratica della fanciulla per le mani, la quale, rihuscendomi bene, tanto che meglio non si potea desiderare, ne spiccai una buona mancia. Et hora ch' el vero padre di lei ci è arrivato et io scampato dalle mani sua così destramente, un' altra maggiore ventura mi è capitata alle mani. Et questo è che havendo Gismondo inteso da me ogni cosa, mi ha fidato le chiavi del fondaco del suo fratello, acciò che io ne cavi stasera, fra dì et notte, un certo maestro Cornelio, che da lui fu oggi dentro rinchiuso. Et questo fa perciò che egli domattina delibera manifestarsi al padre della fanciulla et lei addomandare per sposa, né vorrebbe che questa cosa del medico, risapendosi, havesse a guastare il suo disegno. Zingaro, Zingaro, questa non è picciola ventura, perché, uscitone che n' è il medico, potrai fare un rastrello[4] di sorte che*

---

3. Non più travestito.
4. Portare via ogni cosa.

Act Five

LUCIO: I will do all of this, but where, Lord, may I find him?

FABIO: At your home, at friends' homes, in the places he frequents. Don't waste time. Go, then we will meet up when it is light, and I will not fail to help you.

LUCIO: I am begging you as much as I can.

FABIO: I will do it, I say. Don't waste any more time.

LUCIO: Look — I am on my way.

FABIO: Oh, unhappy and unfortunate old man! However, I don't know for certain that Mario was the author of this misdeed. Yet, because he is with that scoundrel and favoring him in that way, it is believable that every evil deed can be traced to him, but, that being the case, I do not want men like that as relatives. I don't.

SCENE THREE

Gypsy in his usual outfit[3]

GYPSY: I just want to say that today is under the rule of some star in the heavens that truly favors me, because everything I touch is turning out well. I had just gotten out of bed when Gualcina put that matter of the girl in my hands, which turned out so well for me that it could not have turned out better, and I popped a good tip out of it. And now that her true father has turned up and I have escaped his clutches with such agility, another and greater opportunity has fallen into my hands, which is that after Gismondo had heard everything from me, he entrusted to me the keys of his brother's warehouse, so that I could free from there, at nightfall, a certain Doctor Cornelio, whom he locked in there today. And he is doing this because he has decided that tomorrow morning, he will declare himself to the girl's father and ask for her as his wife, and he does not want this thing with the doctor to get out and ruin his plan. Gypsy, Gypsy, this is not a small venture, because once the doctor has gotten out, you will be able to rake in so much that

3.   He is no longer in disguise.

mai più non sarai povero. Gismondo a sua posta. Ad ogni modo, per questo fatto della fanciulla, non posso stare molto sicuro a Roma, il meglio fia che io rastrelli[5] et ambuli. Ma chi è questo che esce fuora? Parmi maestro Cornelio, che io cercho. Voglio stare a vedere se gl' è desso et intendere come sia fuori di quel fondaco, assai me ne maraviglio.

SCENA QUARTA

Maestro Cornelio, Norchia et Zingaro

CORNELIO: *Quanto rimescolamento me ne presi che, come tu hai veduto, mi s' è mosso il corpo, di sorte che mi è bisognato o per amore o per forza starmi più di dua hore in casa et continuamente, sì come tu hai veduto, in sul destro.[6]*

NORCHIA: *Mi maraviglio che vi sieno rimaste budella in corpo.*

ZINGARO: *Costui deve havere preso pillole, a quel che io intendo.*

CORNELIO: *Ma poi che tu mi hai conto questa altra faccenda che più mi preme, o che l'un male habbia cacciato l'altro o pure in qualunche altro modo si sia, la scorrenza[7] mi s' è stagnata, et io sono uscito fuori con animo di andare al governatore et narrarli il chaso, che è molto importante. Credo che Lottieri harà di già preso le mosse,[8] poi con l'animo alquanto più scarico penseremo a questa altra faccenda della moglie.*

ZINGARO: *Che dice costui della moglie, infine io non attingho.[9]*

NORCHIA: *Maestro Cornelio.*

ZINGARO: *Oh, oh, e' lo chiama maestro Cornelio, deve esser egli per certo.*

---

5.   Rubi e me ne vada.

6.   Sul water.

7.   Diarrea.

8.   La *mossa*, costituita da una corda di canapa tesa e poi lasciata cadere, era il luogo da dove partivano le corse dei cavalli. A tutt'oggi sopravvive nel Palio di Siena e in altre manifestazioni simili.

9.   Non capisco.

you will never be poor again. Gismondo wants it. Anyway, because of this affair of the girl, I'm not very safe in Rome. The best thing will be for me to rake in the profit and walk on. But who is this who has come out? It looks to me like Doctor Cornelio, the one I'm looking for. I want to see if it is really him and find out how he got out of the warehouse, which surprises me a lot.

Scene Four

Doctor Cornelio, Norchia, and Gypsy

Doctor Cornelio: What a mixing took me over when, as you saw, my body moved, in such a way that I needed by hook or by crook to stay at home for more than two hours spending all of that, as you saw, on the comode.

Norchia: I'm surprised that you have any guts left in your body.

Gypsy: (*aside*) *This guy must have taken some pills from what I am hearing.*

Doctor Cornelio: But since you told me about this other matter that is more important to me, either one bad thing has pushed the other out or in whatever way it happened, the runs have stopped, and I have left the house intent on going to the governor and giving him an account of the case, which is very important. I believe that Lottieri will have already made his move,[4] so with our souls much lighter, we will take care of this other matter of the wife.

Gypsy: (*aside*) *What is he saying about a wife? I'm not really getting it.*

Norchia: Doctor Cornelio.

Gypsy: (*aside*) *Oh, oh, he is calling him Doctor Cornelio, so it must be him for sure.*

---

4.   The Italian, *mossa*, refers to a rope that is drawn tight and then let fall at the point where the race begins, which is still done for the famous Palio of Siena and other similar kinds of races.

NORCHIA: *Pigliate quel partito che meglio vi pare, una volta la cosa sta come io vi ho detto.*

CORNELIO: *Tu, Norchia, sai ciò che tu hai a fare?*

NORCHIA: *Dite pure.*

CORNELIO: *Viemi dietro et da me non ti partir mai un' ugna.[10] Et come tu vedessi assassinamento nessuno, grida quanto tu puoi et chiama adiuto.*

Qui si levò.[11]

NORCHIA: *Questo posso io ben fare, ma di soccorrerlo non gli prometto io, gli imparerà a tor moglie di questa fatta.*

ZINGARO: *Io strabilio, trasecolo, spavento affatto. Questo è 'l medico che io dovevo andare a cavare, come diavolo è egli mai uscito? Questo voglio, che al mio disegno poco importi. Non ti credere già ch' io voglia che questo maestro Guazzaletto[12] sia cagione che io non faccia quanto io havevo in animo di fare. Andrommene nel fondaco con questa chiave et quivi fattone il miglior fardello delle migliori cose ch'io possa, a Lucca ti viddi.[13] Et se bene io rubbo lucchesi, Lucca è per tutto, pericolo non c'è nissuno, perché, essendo trovato, io son mandato da Gismondo, fratello del patrone del bancho. Zingaro, il guadagno è grande et il rischio sicurissimo, andian via.*

10. Un'unghia.
11. Nota marginale autografa in V, c. 49r: «Qui si levò».
12. Medicastro.
13. Sparirò, me ne andrò (modo di dire fiorentino).

NORCHIA: Take whatever course seems best to you once the thing is at the point that I told you.

DOCTOR CORNELIO: You, Norchia, do you know what you have to do?

NORCHIA: Tell me anyway.

DOCTOR CORNELIO: Follow me and do not put a hairsbreadth between us. And as soon as you see anything murderous, holler as loud as you can and call for help.

Here he gets up.[5]

NORCHIA: This I can easily do, but as for helping him, I don't promise him anything that will teach him to take a wife like this.

GYPSY: I am bowled over. I am shocked out of this world., I am greatly afeared. This is the doctor that I was supposed to go and free. How the devil is he already out? What I want is for it not to affect my plan very much. Don't you believe that I want this quack doctor[6] to be the reason that I don't manage to achieve everything that I have in my heart to do. I will get into the warehouse with this key, and after making the best bundle of the best stuff I can find, I saw you in Lucca.[7] And though I am robbing people from Lucca — Lucca is everywhere — there is no danger because if I am caught I have been sent by Gismondo, the brother of the head of the firm. Gypsy, the profit is great and very safe from risk. Let's get going.

Meanwhile the backdrop is being hung.

5.   This marginal note is on fol. 49r.
6.   The Italian, *maestro Guazzaletto,* is a byword for a "quack."
7.   A Florentine idiom meaning, "I'm out of here."

Atto quinto

SCENA QUINTA

Monna Appollonia sola

APPOLLONIA: Alla croce di Dio, che la medicina ha menato bene, non dica più alchuno che gli incanti non vaglino. Subito che io tornai a casa, li dissi d' havere data la lettera a Mario in mano propria. Di poi, inmantinente ella et io ci mettemmo a fare uno incanto che elli venisse presto, il quale mi fu già insegnato, essendo innamorata del mio prete, dalla buona memoria di monna Chrispophana. Togliemo incenso maschio[14] et fave dure, ricette assai al male delle fanciulle nubili, et con certe parole al proposito le gettamo in sul fuoco. Hor togli, se non vorrà venire per amore e' verrà per forza, ti so dire. Sammi ben male che io ci messi ben troppa maza,[15] bastava una letteruzza o che di notte ne venisse fino qua a consolarla un poco. Ma, ohimè, trist' a me, a pena fu fornita l'opera nostra che egli e' l suo Gualcina compariscono da cuochi, fingendo d'essere mandati dal maestro per ordinare il convito et, quello che è peggio, come si rabbuia la vuole menare via ad ogni modo et ella, pazzerella, vuole andare seco a tutte le vie del mondo, dicendo pure: «Non fia vero mai che io pigli altro marito che quello che io m' ho preso una volta». Io n' ho lasciato in fine il bel pensiero a lei.[16] Madonna Gostanza non gli conosce et, credendo che sieno mandati dal medico, ha tanta allegrezza che non cape nella pelle. Va' pure là, hammi mandato per certe novelluzze[17] che mancano alla cena, non mi poteva fare il maggior piacere, per non mi trovare a questi cimenti se nulla si scoprissi per mala disgratia. Di poi, ad ogni modo non ci vo' più stare un passo, andatasene lei, che dove io non ho simili intrattenimenti di fanciulle, non è la stanza mia, [che non mi mancano mai][18] le calze o pianelle[19]

14. Incenso in grani.

15. Dissi di più di quello che conveniva.

16. Ho lasciato che ci pensi lei.

17. Primizie.

18. Manca nel ms, recupero da S, fol. 35r.

19. Ciabatte.

Act Five

Scene Five

Miss Appollonia alone

APPOLLONIA: By God's crucifix, the medicine works very well. No one should ever again say that enchantments are worthless. As soon as I returned home, I told her I had put the letter right into Mario's hands. Then she and I immediately set about making a spell that would make him come right away, which was taught to me in the past by Miss Chrispophana of happy memory when I was in love with my priest. We took granulated incense and hard beans, recipes that are suited to the maladies of unmarried girls, and with certain words suited to our intent, cast them into the fire. Now get this — if he does not want to come for love, he will come by force, I can tell you. It seems to me that I did a bad thing, that I said too much. A little letter would have been enough, or during the night his coming to console her a little. But, oh me, unfortunately for me, as soon as our work was done, he and his Gualcina appeared dressed as cooks, pretending to have been sent by the doctor to organize the banquet, and, what is worse, when it gets dark, he wants to lead her away by hook or by crook, and she, the crazy little thing, wants to follow him wherever he goes in the world, saying, "Let it never be the case that I take a different husband from the one I already took." In the end, I left her with that lovely thought.[8] Madam Gostanza does not know them and, believing that they were sent by the doctor, is so happy that she is beside herself. Go on, she has sent me for certain fresh spring ingredients that are needed for the supper. She could not have done me a bigger favor, because I won't be around for any trouble if something were to turn up by some awful misfortune. And then, anyway, I don't want to stick around once she's left, because where I do not have these kinds of involvements with girls there is no place for me, and I'm never without[9] stockings or slippers or

8. The Italian phrase means "I left her to worry about it" or "to take care of it."

9. This phrase is missing from the manuscript, supplied from S, fol. 35r.

o altro che mi facci di bisogno, tant'è, bisogna vivere o per un modo o per un altro.

SCENA SESTA

Gismondo solo[20]

GISMONDO: *Ahi, infelice, ahi misero me, quanto poco è durata la mia beatitudine, quanto è stata breve la mia felicità, come in un punto mi sono lasciato perdere ogni mio bene. Io, lasso, me ne ritornava alla stanza dove have' lasciata la mia Aurelia et per la via riscontro Lottieri, mio fratello, et Guicciardo, vero padre di lei, come io penso, et seco havevono, ahi lasso me, colei che più bramo che gl' occhi miei, né so in che modo possa mai essere questo. Ahi, fortuna, non bastava fare giungnere il padre vero, contro ogni nostro disegno, che tu gli hai saputo discoprire il luogho dove io la tenevo. Vedendo io costoro, per la conscienza de' falli comessi, non hebbi ardire di parlare pure solo una parola, ma seguitandoli appresso come uno mentecapto, udii, ahi misero me, il mio fratello che irato verso di me disse: «Indarno ti affatichi dreto a costei che troppo hai offeso et Guicciardo qui, patre suo». Io, humile quanto potevo, me li raccomandavo chiedendoli per donna. Egli alla fine mi disse d'accordo con Guicciardo: «Ogni tua preghiera, ogni tua fatica è vana se prima non operi di sorte che maestro Cornelio ti perdoni allora et noi forse ancora ti perdoneremo». Ahi, ahi, cruda mia ventura, qual più dura et più iniqua conditione mi poteva imporre il mio fratello che questa! Troppo ho io, misero me, offeso il medico et talmente che niuna speranza spero di potere impetrare perdono da lui. Ma ecco Rinuccio còrso, so che egli non mi conosce, voglio vedere se io potessi intendere da lui cosa alcuna di questo fatto.*

20. Questa scena manca in S.

anything else that I need. And that's the way it is. You have to make your living one way or another.

Scene Six

Gismondo alone[10]

GISMONDO: Ah, unhappy man, miserable me! How short was the time of my blessedness. How brief was my happiness, for I allowed my every good to slip away in a moment. I, alas, was returning to the room where I had left my Aurelia and on the street I ran into Lottieri, my brother, and Guicciardo, her true father — I think — and they had with them, alas for me, the woman whom I desire more than my own eyes, nor do I know how this came to be. Oh, woe, fortune. It wasn't enough for her true father to appear — contrary to all of our plans — for you helped him discover where I was keeping her. When I saw them, my conscience was pricking me for the mistakes that I had made, to the point that I lacked the spirit to say even a single word, but I followed behind them like an idiot, and, oh miserable me, I heard my brother, who was angry with me, say, "You are laboring in vain after this girl, whom you have offended too much, just as you have offended Guicciardo here, her father." I, as humbly as I could, beseeched them and asked for her as my wife. In the end, he said that he had made an agreement with Guicciardo. "Every prayer of yours, every labor, is in vain if beforehand you have not managed to get Doctor Cornelio to forgive you and then we maybe will forgive you." Oh, woe, oh woe, my cruel fate! What harsher and more unfair condition could my brother have imposed on me than this! I, miserable me, have offended Doctor Cornelio too much and in too many ways that no hope do I have to petition him for pardon. But here comes Rinuccio the Corsican, and I know that he does not recognize me. I want to see if I can learn something about this situation from him.

10. This scene is missing from S.

SCENA SETTIMA

Rinuccio et Gismondo

RINUCCIO: *Oh, come gli sta bene, vedi, vedi che la giustitia ha hora il luogo suo.*

GISMONDO: *Che Domin fia?*

RINUCCIO: *Si troverrà pure il ladro che ha rubbato messer Lottieri.*

GISMONDO: *Che nomina costui il mio fratello, non voglio più tardare a domandarlo quell' huomo da bene che cosa è stata.*

RINUCCIO: *El bargello,[21] che n'ha menato hor hora el maggiore baro del mondo et hallo trovato in sul furto nel fondaco di messer Lottieri Castrucci.*

GISMONDO: *Chi è egli, conoscilo tu?*

RINUCCIO: *Il Zingaro si chiama et hollo conosciuto a mio gran danno, ben che di tutto[22] sarà ghastigato, in luogo è.*

GISMONDO: *Che danno ti ha fatto mai costui?*

RINUCCIO: *Danno et assassinamento, che m' ha giuntato togliendomi una fanciulla da bene fingendosi essere il padre di lei et a messer Lottieri ha rubato pezze di raso et di nuovo è stato trovato nel suo fondaco.*

GISMONDO: *Come, Domine?*

RINUCCIO: *Fatto che m' hebbe la giunteria della fanciulla et conosciutasi la cosa per la sopragiunta del padre vero di lei, messer Lottieri a caso entrato nel fondaco, vi trovò dentro un medico che sta qui oltre, in questa casa.*

GISMONDO: *Di' pure, ch'io lo conosco.*

RINUCCIO: *Andossene messer Lottieri al governatore a querelarsi del medico, il quale esso ancora si querelava d'un ministro[23]*

---

21. Capo della polizia cittadina.
22. Scritto due volte nel manoscritto (ben che di tutto ben che di tutto).
23. Una persona al servizio di messer Lottieri.

Act Five

Scene Seven

Rinuccio and Gismondo

RINUCCIO: Oh, he deserves it. Look, look, justice is now taking place.

GISMONDO: What in heaven is it?

RINUCCIO: The thief who stole from Signor Lottieri will be found now.

GISMONDO: *(aside) Since he is referring to my brother, I will not put off any longer asking that respectable man.* What happened?

RINUCCIO: The chief of police just now led away the biggest fraudster in the world, and he caught him red-handed in Signor Lottieri Castrucci's warehouse.

GISMONDO: Who is he? Do you know him?

RINUCCIO: He is called Gypsy, and it was my great misfortune to meet him, but now he will be punished for everything. He is in that place.

GISMONDO: What damage did he do to you?

RINUCCIO: Damage and murder because he tricked me into taking from me a respectable girl by pretending to be her father, and he stole pieces of silk cloth from Signor Lottieri, and he was found again in his warehouse.

GISMONDO: How, dear Lord?

RINUCCIO: Once he had tricked me about the girl — and this had been revealed by the arrival of her true father — Signor Lottieri by chance entered the warehouse and found there a doctor who lives over here, in this house.

GISMONDO: Go on, I know him.

RINUCCIO: Signor Lottieri went to the governor to lodge a complaint about the doctor, who himself was making a

di messer Lottieri che ve lo haveva condotto per inganno. Il governatore, per intendere la cosa a punto et vedere chi di loro havesse ragione, ha mandato il bargello, il quale giunse nel fondaco, vi trovò quel ladro che faceva a punto un fardello. Et è quello che vi condusse maestro Cornelio, secondo che il medico divisò al bargello le vestimenta sua et quello che a me ha rubbato et tranellato[24] la mia fanciulla, che solo veniva per renderla al padre. Spero che per la tortura si troverrà il vero a punto et io non ne farò male affatto,[25] anzi riharò tutto quello che io ho perduto et meglio.

GISMONDO: *Piacemi ch' e' tristi sieno castigati et che tu non ne faccia male. Io ti ringrazio.*

RINUCCIO: *Non accade, al comando vostro.*

GISMONDO (solo): *Oh, misero et dolente a me, che partito fia il mio, chi mi consiglia, chi mi adiuta! Al meno trovassi io Mario, per cui solo sono in tanti travagli. Voglio andare a cercare di messer Lucio, suo patre, il quale, essendo amico del medico, potrà forse rimediare a questi mali. Ma chi veggo io là oltre, che spade son quelle? Forz'è ch' io tema, così fa chi è consapevole di qualche errore.*

SCENA OTTAVA

Valerio, figliuolo del medico, don Diego spagnuolo,
et uno servidore[26]

VALERIO: *Per mia fé signor Diego, che più lungo et più fastidioso viaggio mi è parso questo poco da Napoli a qui che tutto quello che noi facemo da Cartaginea[27] a Napoli.*

---

24. Fatta oggetto di un tranello.

25. Non ne avrò alcun danno

26. In S, fol. 36r: «uno servitore che dietro ha una valigia».

27. Cartagena, nel sud della Spagna, dove erano approdati i superstiti della spedizione di Algeri.

complaint against an employee[11] of Signor Lottieri's who had tricked him into going there. The governor, so as to get to the bottom of things and figure out which of them was in the right, sent the chief of police who, when he arrived at the warehouse, found that thief, who was bundling up the goods. And he is the one who took Doctor Cornelio there — according to how the doctor identified his clothing to the chief of police — and the one who robbed me of my girl and made her the object of a plot, when he was only coming to turn her over to her father. I hope that torture will reveal the truth and that I won't suffer any harm and in fact that I will get back everything that I lost and more.

GISMONDO: I am pleased that the evildoers will be punished, and you won't suffer any harm. I thank you.

RINUCCIO: There is no need. I am at your service.

GISMONDO: *(alone)* Oh miserable and sorrowful me, what option do I have? Who will advise me? Who will help me? If only I could find Mario, who alone is the reason for all my travails. I want to go seek out Signor Lucio, his father, who, being a friend of the doctor, perhaps will be able to find a remedy for these ills. But whom do I see over there? What swords are those? I must fear them, because they are acting the way people do when they know something is wrong.

SCENE EIGHT

Valerio, the doctor's son, Don Diego the Spaniard, and his servant, who is carrying a suitcase[12]

VALERIO: Upon my faith, Signor Diego, how much longer and more tedious a journey this little bit from Naples to here has seemed to me than the entire one that we made from Cartagena[13] to Naples.

11. The Italian, *ministro*, refers to someone who is in service to Lottieri, probably in an administrative capacity.

12. Missing from the manuscript, supplied from S, fol. 6r.

13. Cartagena, in southern Spain, is where the survivors of the failed Algerian expedition returned to Europe.

DIEGO: *Non è maraviglia, perché tenendo noi alto mare havemo il vento più gagliardo sempre.*

VALERIO: *Non il vento, ma il gran desiderio ch' io tengho di vedere la mia sorella, la quale, havendo inteso essere venuta a Roma, non credevo vivere mai tanto ch' io ci arrivassi.*

DIEGO Credolo, perché io so benissimo quanta possanza habbia l'amore fraterno.[28] Quanto dobbiamo noi ire ancora per ritrovare la casa che ne fu disegnata?*

VALERIO: *Questa piazza è Campo di fiore, bisogna che la stia qui appresso, secondo che mi fu detto.*

DIEGO: *Giur' a Dio, signor Valerio, che io riconosco questo luogo. Questa è quella piazza dove era a punto l'alloggiamento de' lanzi, de' quali io riscattai quella puttina che voi dite essere vostra sorella.*

VALERIO: *Questa certo è la piazza, eh, signor Diegho.*

DIEGO: *Signor sì.*

VALERIO: *Ma riconosceresti voi la casa così a punto?*

DIEGO: *A punto consideravo io hora questo, signor sì, vedete voi quella che è là in sul cantone, quella è dessa.*

VALERIO: *Oh, signor Diegho mio!*

DIEGO: *Che vogliono dire queste lacrime, signor Valerio, non piangete.*

VALERIO: *Non piango, anzi mi rallegro, perché mi son certificato che veramente questa è la mia sorella, perciò che quella che voi ne havete divisato è la casa di maestro Cornelio, mio patre, hora piaccia a Dio che noi la troviano viva et in buono stato.*

DIEGO: *Non dubitate, signore, perché ella è appresso di donna che l'amava come propia sua figliuola.*

---

28. In ms, c. 52r: «l'amore paterno», evidente svista dell'autore, corretta in S, fol. 36.

Diego: This is no surprise, because when we were on the high sea, we always had a strong wind.

Valerio: Not the wind but the great desire that I have to see my sister, who, as I have heard, has come to Rome, and I never believed she would still be alive when I got here.

Diego: I believe it, because I know the power of brotherly[14] love. How much farther do we have to go before we get to the house that we were told was hers?

Valerio: This piazza is Campo de' fiori. She must be staying around here, according to what I was told.

Diego: I swear to God, Signor Valerio, that I recognize this place. This is the piazza where the German soldiers had their lodging, where I ransomed that little girl that you said was your sister.

Valerio: This certainly is that piazza, eh, Signor Diego.

Diego: Yes, sir.

Valerio: But would you recognize the specific house[15]?

Diego: I was just considering that, yes, sir. Do you see that one in the corner? That's the one.

Valerio: Oh, Signor Diego!

Diego: What do these tears mean, Signor Valerio? Don't cry.

Valerio: I'm not crying, I am joyful, because I have verified to myself that this truly is my sister, because the house that you pointed out is the house of Doctor Cornelio, my father. Now may it please God that we have found her well and in good condition.

Diego: Have no fear, sir, because she is staying with a woman who loved her like her own daughter.

---

14. The manuscript on fol. 52r has "fatherly love," a copyist's slip, corrected in S, fol. 36.

15. Soldiers lodged in the homes of civilians, either billetted there or taking them by force.

Atto quinto

Scena nona[29]

Gualcina da cuoco, Valerio et Diego

GUALCINA: *Ringratiato sia Dio, che hora mai è appresso sera, che presto potremo cavare costei di questa casa. Io vo per i panni et alla mia tornata sarà l'hora a punto conveniente. Ma che gente è questa, deono venire di fuori, poi che hanno valligie con esso loro.*

VALERIO: *Io vo' domandare questo cuoco[30] che me lo saprà insegnare benissimo.*

DIEGO: *Domandalo, di gratia, che mi pare mill' anni di veder madonna Ghostanza.*

VALERIO: *Oh, cuoco, oh là, oh cuoco!*

GUALCINA: *E' mi chiamano, voglio usare il parlare da cuoco. Che ci è, che mi vuostù dicere?*

VALERIO: *Sapestù insegnarmi la casa d'una certa madonna Ghostanza napolitana, che ha una figliuola chiamata Cammilla?*

GUALCINA: *Me, deh, no, sono praticissimo in su questa piazza et non ci saccio[31] nessuna persona di cotesto nome qui intorno.*

VALERIO: *E' m' è pure stato detto che la stava in su questa piazza.*

GUALCINA: *Qualche d'uno harà voluto il giambo dello fatto tuo,[32] sì certo.*

DIEGO: *Che dice costui?*

VALERIO: *Dice non la conoscere. Ma sta, che romore è quello?*

29. Nel manoscritto 'decima'.

30. In S, fol. 36v: «zanaiuolo», chi servendo di una cesta (*zana*) portava cibi a domicilio.

31. Non conosco, in napoletano.

32. Avrà voluto prendersi giuoco di te.

Act Five

SCENE NINE[16]

Gualcina as a cook, Valerio, and Diego

GUALCINA: Thanks be to God that now it is almost evening and we will soon be able to get her out of this house. I am going for the cloths and when I return the time will be right. But who are these people? They must have come from out of town because they have baggage with them.

VALERIO: I want to ask this cook.[17] He will be able to give me good information.

DIEGO: Ask him, please, because it seems to me that a thousand years will pass before I see Madam Gostanza.

VALERIO: Oh cook, you there, cook!

GUALCINA: (*aside*) *They are calling me. I need to speak like a cook.* What is it? What do y'all want to say to me[18]?

VALERIO: Could ya show me the house of a certain Madam Gostanza from Naples, who has a daughter named Cammilla?

GUALCINA: Me, well, no. I am familiar with this piazza and I don't know anyone with a name like that around here.

VALERIO: And yet I was told that she lives on this piazza.

GUALCINA: Someone was certainly having a joke at your expense. Yes indeed.

DIEGO: What is he saying?

VALERIO: He says he doesn't know her. But wait, what is that noise?

16. The manuscript mistakenly labels it as Scene Ten.

17. In S, fol. 36v: "zanaiuolo," a person who used a basket (*zana*) to deliver food to people's homes.

18. He incorporates details of different dialects, including Venetian, in his speech; Valerio responds in kind.

SCENA DECIMA

Madonna Gostanza, Valerio, Diego, et Gualcina

GOSTANZA: *Ahi ribaldo, ahi tristo, a questo modo si fa alle fanciulle da bene?*

DIEGO: *Sta, sta, questa è una donna che grida molto forte.*

VALERIO: *Sento ancora io gridare, stiamo a vedere che cosa è questa.*

GOSTANZA: *Via, brutto ribaldo, escimi di casa, a chi dich' io, vanne fuori manigoldone.*

GUALCINA: *Ohimè, io sento gridare in casa, che Domine sarà?*

GOSTANZA: *Aiutatemi, oh, huomini da bene, soccorretemi!*

VALERIO: *Che havete, madonna?*

DIEGO: *Madonna, che havete voi?*

GOSTANZA: *Un poltrone d'un cuoco, che gliè bastata la vista, manomettere la mia figliuola. Di gratia, soccorretemi gentil'huomini.*

DIEGO: *Giuro a Dio che questa è madonna Gostanza che io cerco.*

GOSTANZA: *Oh, signor Diego, Dio mi vi ha mandato a tempo, aiutatemi, che io sono sforzata.*

DIEGO: *Venite dentro, signor Valerio, vedremo et soccorreremo.*

VALERIO: *Eccomi.*

GUALCINA: *Ohimè, ohimè, che son spacciato. Costoro ammazzeranno il mio patrone. Oh, patrone mio, se vi potessi aiutare! Ohimè, parmi di sentire un gran fracasso di spade. Oh, oh, sfortunato Gualcina, di questo male se' tu la cagione. Maladetto sia quel pensiero che ti indusse a consigliarlo di questo fatto. Oh, infelice, oh, misero sfortunato vecchio, quando harà questa nuova. Oh, povero Mario mio, potessi io al meno trovare tosto tuo patre che ti potesse soccorrere. Oh, Signore, aiutami. Ma eccolo, in fede mia a punto, insieme con Fabio.*

Act Five

Scene Ten

Madam Gostanza, Valerio, Diego, and Gualcina

GOSTANZA: Woe to you, you criminal! You evil man! Is this the way that respectable girls are treated?

DIEGO: Hang on, hang on, it's a woman who is yelling loudly!

VALERIO: I still hear yelling. Let's see what it is.

GOSTANZA: Go away, you ugly criminal, get out of my house! I'm talking to you! Get out, you big louse.

GUALCINA: Woe is me! I hear yelling in the house. What in heaven is it?

GOSTANZA: Help me, you good men, assist me!

VALERIO: What is the problem, madam?

DIEGO: Madam, what is the problem?

GOSTANZA: A ne'er-do-well of a cook, the minute he saw her, put his hands on my daughter. Please, gentlemen, help me.

DIEGO: I swear to God that this is the Madam Gostanza that I am looking for.

GOSTANZA: Oh, Signor Diego, God sent you to me in the nick of time. Help me, because force is being used against me.

DIEGO: Come inside, Signor Valerio. Let's see, and let's help.

VALERIO: Here I am.

GUALCINA: Oh me, oh me, I am done for. These guys will kill my boss. Oh boss, if only I could help you! Oh me, I seem to hear a great clashing of swords. Oh, oh, unlucky Gualcina, you are the cause of these problems. Cursed be the thought that led you to advise him to do this. Oh how unhappy, oh how miserable will this unlucky old man be when he hears of this. Oh my poor Mario! If only I could find your father now so he could help you. Oh, Lord, help me. But here he is, upon my faith, together with Fabio.

Scena undicesima

Messer Lucio, Gualcina, Fabio

Lucio: Dico che Gismondo Castrucci è stato a me.

Gualcina: Non mi basta l'animo andarli innanzi con questo habito.

Lucio: Et hammi detto che la fanciulla fu tolta a quel còrso per conto suo.

Gualcina: Che fo io, non è da indugiare.

Lucio: Et che il patre l' ha rihauta.

Gualcina: Io vo' ire, infine io non m'arrischio.

Lucio: Et che Mario non ci ha che fare.

Fabio: Mi piace se la sta così.

Gualcina: Vo io o non vo?

Lucio: Ben' è vero che egli vagheggiava questa fanciulla, che sta qui maritata a maestro Cornelio, pare a me.

Gualcina: Io voglio andare, vadane che vuole. Padrone?

Lucio: Che vuole questo cuoco?

Fabio: Non so, non vogliamo niente, no, va via, va.

Gualcina: Oh, Dio, non mi riconoscono, che debb' io fare!

Lucio: Et dice che fu egli che rinchiuse il medico nel fondaco per fare questo piacere a Mario. Et mi ha pregato che io gli faccia perdonare, perché altramente non può havere quella fanciulla per donna che egli desidera et in quello scambio promette di fare che Mario lascerà questa sua dama.

Fabio: Tutto mi piace se la sta in cotesto modo et non ci è pericolo alcuno.

Gualcina: Voglio tornare un'altra volta, oh padrone!

Act Five

Scene Eleven

Signor Lucio, Gualcina, Fabio

LUCIO: I say that Gismondo Castrucci has been to see me.

GUALCINA: (*aside*) *I don't have the courage to go meet him in this get-up.*

LUCIO: And he said that the girl was taken away from that corsair on his behalf.

GUALCINA: (*aside*) *What should I do? I shouldn't hang around.*

LUCIO: And that her father got her back.

GUALCINA: (*aside*) *I want to go — in the end I'm not going to take any risks.*

LUCIO: And that Mario is not involved.

FABIO: I am happy that things are this way.

GUALCINA: (*aside*) *Do I go or do I stay?*

LUCIO: It is in fact true that he had feelings for this girl, who lives here married to Doctor Cornelio, it seems to me.

GUALCINA: (*aside*) *I want to go, let's get going.* Boss?

LUCIO: What does this cook want?

FABIO: I don't know. We don't want anything. No, go away, go.

GUALCINA: (*aside*) *Oh, God, they don't recognize me. What should I do?*

LUCIO: And he says that he was the one who locked the doctor in the warehouse to do a favor for Mario. And he begged me to get him pardoned, because otherwise he will never have that girl that he desires for his wife, and in exchange for that, he promises to make it so that Mario will leave this lady of his.

FABIO: All of this pleases me if this is the way it really is and there is no danger.

GUALCINA: (*aside*) *I want to come back later.* Hey, master!

LUCIO: *Che importunità è questa, noi non vogliamo cosa alcuna.*

GUALCINA: *Padrone, io sono il Gualcina.*

LUCIO: *Oh, Gualcina, che abito è questo?*

GUALCINA: *Habbian fatto mascare, ma ascoltate.*

LUCIO: *Mario dov'è?*

GUALCINA: *Ascoltate, ve lo dirò, ma non voglio che voi ne diate la colpa a me, perché non ne son cagione io.*

LUCIO: *Che vuole dire questo scusarsi, dov'è Mario, dico?*

FABIO: *Excusarsi senza bisogno è un manifesto accusarsi.*

GUALCINA: *È là, in quella casa, è il pericolo grande et poi grande, e' bisogna che voi l'aiutate.*

LUCIO: *Dio mi aiuti, con tante battisoffiole[33] che vi fa egli, che pericolo è questo, di' su a un tratto.*

FABIO: *Questo sarà altro che vagheggiare.*

GUALCINA: *Bene sapete che noi eravamo in maschera, perché vi si fa nozze, ma come vi ho detto io per me non ne son cagione.*

LUCIO: *In fine, che è seguito, di' su.*

GUALCINA: *Et mentre che stavano così a sollazzo…*

LUCIO: *Diavolo, che fu, lo dici?*

GUALCINA: *Eccoti venire tre armati.*

LUCIO: *Armati et che feciono?*

GUALCINA: *Io me ne saltai fuora per paura, dubito non habbino fatto villania a Mario.*

LUCIO: *Et tu lo lassasti solo?*

---

33. Timori, paure.

Lucio: Why does he keep bothering us? We don't want anything.

Gualcina: Boss, I am Gualcina.

Lucio: Oh, Gualcina! What's this get-up?

Gualcina: We disguised ourselves. Listen.

Lucio: Where is Mario?

Gualcina: Listen. I will tell you but don't blame me because I am not the cause of it.

Lucio: Why are you making excuses? Where is Mario, I say?

Fabio: People who make excuses when there is no need are plainly accusing themselves.

Gualcina: He is there, in that house, and there is great danger, really great danger, and you have to help him.

Lucio: God help me! With all the frights that he is giving you, what danger is this? Come on, spit it out.

Fabio: This will be something more than make-believe.

Gualcina: You know that we were in costume because of the wedding, but as I told you, I am not the reason for it, according to me.

Lucio: Keep going! What happened— tell us!

Gualcina: And while they were having a good time…

Lucio: By the devil, what happened? Will you tell us?

Gualcina: Along come three armed men.[19]

Lucio: Armed men, and what did they do?

Gualcina: I jumped out,[20] from fear. I was afraid that they were going to do some harm to Mario.

Lucio: And you left him alone?

19. Valerio, Don Diego, and Don Diego's servant.

20. Gualcina and Mario had been inside Madam Gostanza's house to rescue Cammilla. Gualcina apparently jumped out a window to avoid the fray.

GUALCINA: *Che havevo io a fare non havendo altr' arme che queste dita, tempo non era da riparare con la mia pelle.*

LUCIO: *Dunque cacciorno mano per le spade.*

GUALCINA: *Io, per me, credo di sì.*

LUCIO: *Che di' tu asino, non vedestù se cacciorno o non cacciorno?*

GUALCINA: *Non veddi questo, che ero fuora.*

LUCIO: *Che di' tu, fuori, traditore pessimo, non dicestù che eri seco in casa?*

GUALCINA: *Sì, ma quando vidi entrare costoro bravando et minacciando, me ne saltai fuori alla prima.*

LUCIO: *Oh, assassino, quanto è che fu questo?*

GUALCINA: *Hor hora, a pena eravate voi qui giunto ch' io saltai fuora.*

LUCIO: *Che gente può essere questa, Fabio, che io so ch' el mio Mario non ha questione con persona.*

FABIO: *Potrebbe forse essere gli sbirri, che debbono havere hauto commissione di pigliarlo.*

LUCIO: *Certo, voi dite bene. Andiamo, non badian più, ma, di gratia, fatemi compagnia.*

FABIO: *Sì, bene, entriamo, poi che l'uscio è aperto.*

GUALCINA: *Non ho fatto poco a spignerci questi dua. Io per me non voglio entrarvi altrimenti, perché, bene o male che la si sia ita, tutta la roba si rovescerebbe a dosso a me, né mi potrebbe lavare tutta l'acqua del Tevere. Il meglio fia ch' io mi pigli puleggio,[34] ma ecco il medico a punto, altro non mancherà, ti so dire.*

---

34. Che me ne vada.

GUALCINA: And what was I supposed to do? Since I have no other weapons but these fingers, it was not the time to deal with it by risking my own skin.

LUCIO: So they grabbed their swords.

GUALCINA: I think so.

LUCIO: Tell me, you donkey! Did you see them grab them or not?

GUALCINA: I did not see it because I was outside.

LUCIO: What are you saying, outside? You nasty traitor! Didn't you say that you were with her in the house?

GUALCINA: Yes, but when I saw those guys come in swaggering and threatening, I jumped out as soon as I could.

LUCIO: Oh, murderer! How long ago did this happen?

GUALCINA: Just now! As soon as you arrived, that was when I jumped out.

LUCIO: What people can these be, Fabio, because I know that my Mario does not have disputes with anyone?

FABIO: It might be the cops, who must have been ordered to take him.

LUCIO: Yes, you are right! Let's go! Let's not wait any longer, but please come with me.

FABIO: Yes, okay. Let's enter the house, since the door is open.

GUALCINA: It took me more than a little to push these two this far. I, for my part, don't want to enter without them because, whether it goes well or ill, all the blame will be placed on me and all the water of the Tiber could not wash me clean. The best thing for me to do is to get out of here. But here comes the doctor. There is more to come, I can tell you.

SCENA DODICESIMA

Norchia et maestro Cornelio

NORCHIA: *Non vi diss' io, maestro, che venendose di giorno non ci era un pericolo al mondo?*

CORNELIO: *Ringratio Dio, che de' travagli ch' io ho havuti questo giorno fino a qui, ne sono riuscito meglio ch'io non pensava.*

NORCHIA: *Et andrete ancora di bene in meglio se voi vi liberarete da questo morbo di questa vostra moglie.*

CORNELIO: *No, no, io me ne sono lavato le mani a questa hora.*

NORCHIA: *Et voi savio.*

CORNELIO: *Et benché io habbia sottoscritto la scritta et hobligatomi a 500 fiorini di dota, intendendosi i sua buoni portamenti, ogni cosa tornerà a' sua termini.*

NORCHIA: *Siate sicuro di cotesto.*

CORNELIO: *Ma quando io ci havessi a mettere dua contanti non mi dorrebbono, pur che la non habbi a fare meco. Ma chi è quello che esce di casa sua, messer Lucio, per mia fé.*

NORCHIA: *Non vi diss'io che l'era la pilla della acqua benedetta?*[35]

CORNELIO: *Che ha a fare un suo pari ivi?*

NORCHIA: *Sollacciarsi, ogn'uno va dietro a' sua piaceri.*

CORNELIO: *Oh, se vi è il capitano Musacchio, come vi è entrato costui?*

NORCHIA: *Debbe tenere sua amicitia, chi sa.*

---

35. La pila dell'acqua benedetta in chiesa, dove tutti mettono le mani (allusione volgare all'ipotetica disponibilità delle donne di quella casa).

Act Five

Scene Twelve

Norchia and Doctor Cornelio

Norchia: Didn't I tell you, doctor, that if we came here during the day there would not be a danger in the world?

Doctor Cornelio: I thank God that the troubles that I have had today up until now have turned out better than I thought.

Norchia: And they will continue to go even better if you free yourself from this disease of your wife.

Doctor Cornelio: No, no! I have washed my hands of her by now.

Norchia: And you are wise.

Doctor Cornelio: And even though I have signed the paper and committed myself to five hundred florins of dowry, conditioned upon her good behavior, everything will reach its conclusion.

Norchia: Make sure that this is how it goes.

Doctor Cornelio: Even if I have to put a few coins into it, this does not bother me, as long as she leaves me alone. But who is that who is leaving her house? Signor Lucio, upon my faith.

Norchia: Didn't I tell you that she was a very holy water font?[21]

Doctor Cornelio: What is someone of his ilk doing here?

Norchia: Having a good time! Everyone pursues their own pleasures.

Doctor Cornelio: Oh, if Captain Musacchio is there, how did he get admitted?

Norchia: He must be a friend of hers. Who knows?

---

21. Referring to the holy water font that churchgoers dip their fingers in to bless themselves, here meant ironically as a woman available to everyone.

Cornelio *Io lo voglio aspettare qui et parlargli un poco, perché è grande mio amico.*

Norchia: *Io vegho rappiccare la pratica.*[36]

Cornelio: *Non farò.*

Norchia: *Tiratevi più presto in casa, che già si comincia a far buio.*

Cornelio: *Ancora non è hora pericolosa, benché io non mi sono per discostare troppo da bonba.*[37]

Norchia: *Gliè meglio ch' io vadia ad aprire l'uscio et porvi a canto un pezzo d'arme, se bisognasse.*

Cornelio: *Fa' ciò che tu vuoi.*

Norchia: *Questo è quel messer Lucio che io mandai oggi a spasso et per questa cagione mi sono levato di qui volentieri.*

Scena tredicesima

Messer Lucio et maestro Cornelio.

Lucio: *Vedi, che doppo una gran pioggia si è rasserenato ogni cosa d'intorno. Oh, che allegrezza harà di questo maestro Cornelio. Ma eccolo a punto, oh, felice vecchio! Voglio in prima darli questa buona nuova, di poi andrò a casa a contarlo a mogliama, che io la lasciai mezza morta per quel che di Mario haveva inteso. Maestro Cornelio, Iddio vi dia la buona sera, date qua la mano.*

Cornelio: *Per che cagione?*

Lucio: *Perché vi vo' dire buon prò vi faccia et darvi buone nuove, che non havesti un pezzo fa le migliori.*

Cornelio: *So quello che voi volete dire et vi rispondo che non la voglio per conto nessuno.*

Lucio: *Chi non volete voi, maestro?*

36. Ricominciare la discussione.

37. Da casa, come messer Nicia nella *Mandragola* (I, 2). Per richiami ad altri autori (Ariosto, Aretino), Fido, *La scena del principe a Firenze*, 268.

DOCTOR CORNELIO: I want to wait here a moment and speak with him a little, because he is a great friend of mine.

NORCHIA: I see the discussion being reopened.

DOCTOR CORNELIO: I won't do it.

NORCHIA: Get back home immediately, because it is already beginning to get dark.

DOCTOR CORNELIO: It is not yet a dangerous hour, although I am not about to get too far away from home.[22]

NORCHIA: It's better if I go and open the door and put a weapon next to it in case it's needed.

DOCTOR CORNELIO: Do as you wish.

NORCHIA: (*aside*) *Here comes that Signor Lucio that I took for a spin today, and that is why I was so happy to get out of here.*

SCENE THIRTEEN

Signor Lucio and Doctor Cornelio

LUCIO: You see, after a heavy rain, the sun has come out all over. Oh, how happy Doctor Cornelio will be. But here he comes, the lucky old man! I want to be the first to give him this good news, and then I will go home to tell my wife, whom I left half dead because of what she had heard about Mario. Doctor Cornelio, may God grant you a pleasant evening. Give me your hand.

DOCTOR CORNELIO: For what reason?

LUCIO: Because I want to tell you "good for you" and give you good news, and better than this you haven't had for a while.

DOCTOR CORNELIO: I know what you want to tell me, and my answer is that I don't want her for any reason.

LUCIO: Whom don't you want, doctor?

---

22. He uses the expression *da bonba* used by messer Nicia in *Mandragola* I, 2. For references to other authors (Ariosto, Aretino), see Fido, *La scena del principe a Firenze*, 268.

CORNELIO: *Cotesta Cammilla et non ha che fare meco.*

LUCIO: *Oh, perché, se l'è vostra?*

CORNELIO: *Mia non è ella, lasciatevi dire et sturisi gl'orecchi ogn' uno.*

LUCIO: *Che dite voi, che ci siamo certificati che l'è veramente vostra, né ve ne potete discostare.*

CORNELIO: *Vi parrà, che io me ne discosti.*

LUCIO: *E' ci sono le scritture, i testimonij, e' vostri più attinenti li prestano fede.*

CORNELIO: *A sua posta chi fa il carro lo sa disfare. Questa festa non si ha a fare senza me et se io ci dovessi mettere lo stato mio, io non la torrò mai et se voi non volevate altro da me, addio.*

LUCIO: *Io non so se costui ha notitia del seguito o se pure egli non intende. Io gli vo' parlare altramente. Maestro Cornelio, ascoltate un po' me, non ve ne andate così subito, io dirò forse cosa che più vi piacerà. Sapete voi ch' el vostro figliuolo Valerio è vivo et sano?*

CORNELIO: *È vivo il mio Valerio?*

LUCIO: *Et è tornato in Roma.*

CORNELIO: *Il mio figliuolo Valerio è tornato!*

LUCIO: *È tornato et gli ho tocco la mano.*

CORNELIO: *A Valerio, mio figliuolo, havete parlato voi?*

LUCIO: *Sì, dico, non so come io me ho a dire.*

CORNELIO: *Oh, messer Lucio, hora voglio bene che mi tocchiate la mano et vi vo' basciare et stringere. Ma dove è egli, il mio figliuolo, in che lato l'havete voi veduto?*

LUCIO: *Qui, in casa questa napoletana.*

CORNELIO: *Et evvi al presente?*

DOCTOR CORNELIO: This Cammilla, and she has nothing to do with me.

LUCIO: Oh, why, if she is yours?

DOCTOR CORNELIO: Mine she is not! People may talk, but let everyone plug their ears.

LUCIO: What are you saying — we have made certain that she is truly yours, and you cannot distance yourself from her.

DOCTOR CORNELIO: Just watch and see if I don't distance myself.

LUCIO: There are documents and witnesses. Those who are closest to you swear to it.

DOCTOR CORNELIO: If he wants to, the man who made the cart can unmake it. This feast cannot be held without me and if I had to consider my state of mind, I will never take her as my wife, and if this is all you wanted from me, good-bye.

LUCIO: (*aside*) *I don't know whether he has been informed of what happened or if he doesn't understand. I want to approach it from a different angle.* Doctor Cornelio, listen to me for a bit. Don't leave right away. I have something to tell you that you might like. Do you know that your son Valerio is alive and well?

DOCTOR CORNELIO: My Valerio is alive?

LUCIO: And he has returned to Rome.

DOCTOR CORNELIO: My son Valerio has returned?

LUCIO: He has returned, and I have shaken hands with him.

DOCTOR CORNELIO: You have spoken with my son Valerio?

LUCIO: Yes, I say! I don't know what I have to say to convince you.

DOCTOR CORNELIO: Oh, Signor Lucio, now I really want you to shake my hand, and I want to kiss and hug you. But where is my son, and where did you see him?

LUCIO: Here in this Neapolitan house.

DOCTOR CORNELIO: And is he here right now?

LUCIO: *Messer sì!*

CORNELIO: *Et che vi fa egli?*

LUCIO: *Ve l'havevo cominciato a dire, ma, o che voi non mi intendesti o che voi non mi volessi dare udienza.*

CORNELIO: *Dite, dite, che io vi ascolterò bene hora, perché voi dite cose che mi piacciono.*

LUCIO: *Ha trovato quella fanciulla, che è quivi, essere vostra figliuola et sua sorella.*

CORNELIO: *La Cammilla del capitano Musacchio?*

LUCIO: *Come del capitano Musacchio? Dico vostra figliuola io.*

CORNELIO: *Come, io non hebbi figliuola mai di cotesto nome. Ne hebbi bene una che si chiamò Lucretia, la quale, come più volte vi ho detto, di 3 anni insieme con la madre sua fu da' lanzi uccisa.*

LUCIO: *Questa è quella Lucretia che voi pensavate essere morta.*

CORNELIO: *Voi mi fate stupire! Et in che modo è ella qui hora?*

LUCIO: *Dirovelo. Quando e' lanzi, per lo sdegno della vostra fuggita, hebbeno uccisa la vostra donna, volendo gittare in Tevere questa vostra figliuola, vi si abbatté un gentil'huomo spagnuolo chiamato don Diegho di Cartaginea, il quale, mosso a molta pietà, la campò*[38] *da' lanzi, come che egli si facessi. Menatola seco a Napoli, la diede per figliuola a questa madonna Gostanza, la quale, volendo ritrovare il padre, venne qua, come voi sapete.*

CORNELIO: *Et come ha ritrovato questa cosa Valerio mio?*

38. La salvò.

Act Five

LUCIO: Yes, sir!

DOCTOR CORNELIO: And what is he doing here?

LUCIO: I had started to tell you, but either you did not understand me, or you did not want to listen to me.

DOCTOR CORNELIO: Speak, speak, for now I will listen to you closely because you are saying things that I like.

LUCIO: He has found out that that girl who lives here is your daughter and his sister.

DOCTOR CORNELIO: Cammilla of Captain Musacchio?

LUCIO: What do you mean "of Captain Musacchio"? I'm telling you that she is your daughter.

DOCTOR CORNELIO: How can that be? I didn't have a daughter by that name. I had one whose name was Lucretia,[23] who, as I have told you many times, was killed by the German soldiers when she was three, together with her mother.

LUCIO: This is that Lucrezia who you thought was dead.

DOCTOR CORNELIO: You are amazing me. And how is it that she is here now?

LUCIO: I'll tell you. When the German soldiers, out of contempt for you for running away, had killed your wife, they went to throw your daughter into the Tiber, and they ran into a Spanish gentleman named Don Diego di Cartagena, who, moved by great pity, rescued her from the German soldiers, as if he were doing it for himself. He took her with him to Naples, gave her as a daughter to this Madam Gostanza, who, in her effort to locate the father, came here, as you know.

DOCTOR CORNELIO: And how did my Valerio learn of this?

---

23. Because the Roman matron Lucretia was considered a paragon of female chastity for committing suicide after having been raped by the son of the Etruscan tyrant, many Renaissance parents gave her name to their daughters. Lucrezia was the name of the wife in *Mandragola*.

LUCIO: *Statemi ascoltare. Pure hora ce lo diceva egli in casa Valerio, vostro figliuolo. Dopo il naufragio d'Algieri capitò a Cartaginea et qui ammalato fu riscevuto et cortesemente alloggiato da questo gentil'huomo. Dove più mesi dimorando, una volta a sorte d'un ragionamento in un altro travalicando, come accade, venne a conoscere che quella piccola puttina ch'el gentil'huomo haveva comprata da' lanzi era la sua sorella. Onde, ritornando in Italia desideroso di ritrovarla, fu accompagnato dal gentil'huomo fino a Napoli, il quale, et esso ancora, era desiderosissimo di usare seco questa ultima cortesia, oltre che per altre sue faccende doveva ritornare a Napoli, non la trovorono per essere madonna Ghostanza venuta qua. Sì che, giunti a Roma, domandando di lei, l'hanno trovata a punto et noi hanno ripieno di eterna allegrezza.*

CORNELIO: *Messer Lucio, tutto mi piace, ma io vorrei più manifesti contrasegni per credere che la sia la mia figliuola.*

LUCIO: *Non vi dich' io, che ci sono le scritture ancora.*

CORNELIO: *Le scripture, come?*

LUCIO: *Quando la venne alle mani di questo gentil'huomo l'havea un breve al collo, che gliene doveste fare voi, o la vostra donna, contro a' bachi,[39] il quale ha tenuto questa madonna Ghostanza appresso di sé con grandissima cura. Et al presente, havendolo aperto, vi ha trovato il nome suo, il vostro et della moglie vostra, con certe altre parole divote appropriate a decto male.*

CORNELIO: *Hora mi ricordo donde hebbi cotesto breve et chi me lo fece, il padre guardiano di Araceli,[40] che usava, oltr' al nome de' bambini, mettervi su quelli ancora del padre et della madre. Certo, ella è la mia figliuola, non ne sono punto dubbioso.*

39. Vermi.
40. La chiesa di Santa Maria in Aracoeli, sul colle del Campidoglio.

LUCIO: Listen to this. Your son Valerio was telling us about this just now in this home. After the shipwreck in Algiers, he ended up in Cartagena and there, while he was ill, he was received and courteously given lodgings by this gentleman. He remained there several months, and bit by bit, sometimes by chance in a discussion and other times by working at it, as it happens, he came to know that the little girl that the gentleman had purchased from the German soldiers was his sister. Therefore, on his return to Italy he wanted to find her. He was accompanied as far as Naples by the gentleman, who very much wished to provide him with this last courtesy because he had to return to Naples on business, but Madam Gostanza had left Naples to come here. Therefore, once they arrived in Rome, he asked after her. They found her, and they filled us with eternal happiness.

DOCTOR CORNELIO: Signor Lucio, all of this pleases me, but I would like more obvious proofs if I am to believe that she is my daughter.

LUCIO: Didn't I tell you that there are still documents.

DOCTOR CORNELIO: What do you mean, documents?

LUCIO: When she came into the hands of this gentleman, she had a pouch attached to her neck, which you or your wife must have made as protection from worms,[24] which Madam Gostanza kept with her, taking great care of it. And just now, I opened it, and I found her name, yours, and your wife's, with certain other devout words appropriate to this ill fortune.

DOCTOR CORNELIO: Now I remember where I got the certificate that is in the pouch and who made it for me. It was the priest in charge of the church of Aracoeli,[25] who, in addition to the name of the child, was in the habit of including the names of the father and mother. She certainly is my daughter. I no longer have any doubts.

24. The Italian, *bachi,* refers to the kind of worms that produce silk.
25. The church of St. Maria in Aracoeli on the Capitoline Hill.

LUCIO: *Oh, ringratiato sia Dio.*

CORNELIO: *Oh, Signore Dio, vedi a che rischio io son ito, di tor una mia figliuola per moglie! Hora veggio che tutto è advenuto et seguito di voluntà di Dio. Ma io non vo' più badare, voglio andare a vedergli, li mia figliuoli, i quali amendua tenevo per morti.*

LUCIO: *Voi havete mille ragioni, ma ascoltate, prima che vi partiate un'altra me accade dirvi, che forse non vi sarà meno cara.*

CORNELIO: *Sì, bene, ma che volete voi dirmi?*

LUCIO: *Che voi non solamente troverrete il figliuolo et la figliuola, ma il genero ancora.*

CORNELIO: *Come il genero?*

LUCIO: *Il genero, sì, quando ve ne contentiate. Et questo è Mario, mio figliuolo, el quale, sendone stato innamorato più mesi, da Valerio vostro gliè stata data molto volentieri et con quella dote medesima che da Fabio, suo cognato, gli deve essere renduta. Et io, quando a voi così piaccia, ho ratificato il parentado.*

CORNELIO: *Come non mi può egli piacere quando e' piace al mio figliuolo et a voi, mio amicissimo, ne son contento et buon prò ne faccia.*

LUCIO: *Bene ci venga. Hora non ci resta altro, se non che si perdoni a Gismondo Castrucci che, per fare servitio a Mario mio figliuolo, acciò ne seguisse questa buona opera, vi serrò nel fondaco del fratello.*

CORNELIO: *Fu dunque Gismondo Castrucci quel che mi serrò nel fondaco.*

LUCIO: *Voi havete inteso et, come vi ho detto, non per offendere voi ma per servire l'amico. Del che vedete quanto bene n'è poi risultato.*

CORNELIO: *Tanto mi è grato questo, che non solo gli perdono, ma lo voglio per buon figliuolo. Et ditegliene quando lo vedete et*

Lucio: Oh, God be praised.

Doctor Cornelio: Oh, Lord God, see what a risk I ran of taking my daughter as my wife! Now I see that everything happened according to the will of God. But I no longer want to think about it, I want to go see them, my children, both of whom I thought were dead.

Lucio: You have a thousand reasons for doing so, but listen, before you leave, I have to give you another piece of news that perhaps you will hold less dear.

Doctor Cornelio: Yes, all right, but what do you want to tell me?

Lucio: That you will find not only a son and a daughter but a son-in-law as well.

Doctor Cornelio: What do you mean a son-in-law?

Lucio: A son-in-law, yes, if you please. And this is Mario, my son, who, having been in love with her for several months, was given her as his wife by your Valerio very willingly and with the same dowry that Fabio, his brother-in-law, was to have given him. And I, hoping that this would please you, ratified the family agreement.

Doctor Cornelio: How can this fail to please me when it pleases my son and you, my very dear friend? I am happy about it, and may it do me good.

Lucio: This is welcome news. Now there is nothing left to do except to pardon Gismondo Castrucci who, to help Mario my son be able to complete this good work, locked you in his brother's warehouse.

Doctor Cornelio: So Gismondo Castrucci is the one who locked me in the warehouse.

Lucio: That is what you heard and, as I told you, it was not to offend you but to help his friend. And you can see how much good came out of that.

Doctor Cornelio: I welcome this so much that not only do I pardon him, but I want him for my good son. And

così ancora a Lottieri, suo fratello, al quale mi scuserete se io l'ingiurai di parole alquanto, benché egli mordessi non poco me.

LUCIO: *Così mi piace et che ogni cosa si dimentichi et che tutti siamo buoni fratelli.*

CORNELIO: *Così è l'animo mio et tanto a l'uno et a l'altro direte da parte mia.*

LUCIO: *Ma più non è da indugiare, voi andrete a vedere le vostre cose ritrovate et io andrò a raguagliare la mia donna di questo. Di poi, ci troverremo insieme, perché io intendo che tutta questa notte si spenda in far festa et allegrezza.*

CORNELIO: *Io vo, a Dio.*

SCENA ULTIMA

Gualcina, Mario, Gismondo, Lottieri, et Guicciardo

GUALCINA: *Io guardo et ascolto diligentemente ogni cosa, né, però, vegho, né odo cosa alchuna onde io possa coniecturare del successo del mio patrone. Misero lui, se la maladetta fortuna ha seguitato di nemicarlo poi che io mi son partito, così come haveva incominciato nella presenza mia. Ma chi è questo che esce fuori di là entro? Per Dio, che gliè Mario, mio patrone. Oh, me beato, poi che io lo veggio vivo et intiero.*

MARIO: *Chi vive di me più lieto oggi al mondo et più contento!*

GUALCINA: *Ringratiato sia Dio, che allegrezza fia questa mai, la quale tanto più mi deve essere cara quanto più di noiose disaventure la veggio nata.*

MARIO: *Oh, come desidero io di vedere et raguagliare il mio Gismondo, il quale assai tempo di me che non habbia inteso cosa che assai lo molesti. Almeno vedess' io il Gualcina, con il quale mi potessi rallegrare della mia gioia.*

GUALCINA: *Padrone, eccomi. Feci per lo meglio che io vi lasciassi in quel modo et mi fuggissi, acciò che di fuori vi potessi mandare qualche soccorso, non feci io bene a spignervi vostro patre?*

MARIO: *Non accade scuse di questo, poiché io non ricerco simili adiuti da servo alcuno et all' hora maximamente che fa di*

tell him when you see him, and Lottieri his brother too, and make my excuses for having insulted him with certain words, although he took some big bites out of me, too.

LUCIO: This is how I like it, that everything is forgotten, and we are all good brothers.

DOCTOR CORNELIO: That is my disposition, and tell this to both on my behalf.

LUCIO: But we should not linger any longer. You go and see those that have returned to you, and I will go and inform my wife of this. Then we'll spend some time together, because I intend that we pass this entire night in festivities and good cheer.

DOCTOR CORNELIO: I am going. God be with you.

FINAL SCENE

Gualcina, Mario, Gismondo, Lottieri, and Guicciardo

GUALCINA: I watch and listen to everything diligently, and yet I neither see nor hear a single thing allowing me to figure out what has happened to my master. Poor guy, if damned fortune continued to be his enemy after I left as it had begun to be while I was still there. But who is that who is coming out of the house? By God, it's Mario, my master. Oh, lucky me, because I see him alive and whole.

MARIO: Who living in the world is more happy and content than I am today?

GUALCINA: May God be praised. What happiness can this be, made all the dearer to me by the tediousness of the misadventures from which I saw it born.

MARIO: Oh, how I want to see and compare notes with my Gismondo, who has not heard from me for a long time about something that bothers him so much. If only I could see Gualcina, with whom I could celebrate my joy.

GUALCINA: Master, here I am. I did the right thing when I left you that way and fled, so that when I got outside I could

bisogno di cuore et d'armi. Gualcina, la cosa è ita meglio che noi non pensavamo, anzi talmente che meglio non si poteva desiderare.

GUALCINA: *Et come, padrone mio? Fatemi tosto partecipe di tanto bene.*

MARIO: *La Cammilla si è trovata essere figliuola del medico et da Valerio, suo fratello, che uno era di quelli che qua intrarono armati, et da suo patre di poi, maestro Cornelio, m'è stata data et conceduta per moglie.*

GUALCINA: *Oh, te beato et noi tutti contenti et felici.*

MARIO: *Sono uscito fuori a posta con questi panni, che dentro mi sono stati prestati, per ritrovare l'amico mio, sì per raguagliarlo del tutto et sì ancora per intendere qualche cosa del fatto suo, come sia gito di poi. Harestilo veduto o inteso nulla di lui?*

GUALCINA: *Né udito, né veduto cosa del mondo. Ma vedilo, vedilo a punto, che di là ne viene tutto frettoloso.*

MARIO: *Ben venga il mio caro Gismondo. Rallegrati per conto mio, che ben ne puoi havere giusta cagione.*

GISMONDO: *Prima che hora mi son rallegrato et ho inteso con mio sommo piacere et diletto il tutto.*

MARIO: *Et quando et da chi?*

GISMONDO: *Pure hora da messer Lucio, tuo patre, il quale per aggiunta mi ha data ferma speranza di contentare et me ancora, dove era il più misero et il più infelice huomo che fusse al mondo.*

MARIO: *Ma che odo io, non hai tu appresso la tua Aurelia?*

GISMONDO: *Ohimè, tu non sai li affanni mia che in breve hora mi sono sopra giunti gravissimi et dolorosissimi.*

send some help. Didn't I do a good thing by pressing your father?

MARIO: There is no need to look for excuses, because I do not ask any servant for this kind of help, at most for the needs of the heart and of arms. Gualcina, the thing went better than we thought, in fact as well as anyone could want.

GUALCINA: What do you mean, master? Share this good news with me.

MARIO: Cammilla has been found to be the daughter of the doctor and by Valerio, her brother — who was one of those who entered the house armed — and then by her father Doctor Cornelio, she was given to me as my wife.

GUALCINA: Oh, lucky you, and we are content and happy.

MARIO: I came out of the house on purpose wearing these clothes, which were lent to me inside, so I could find my friend and greet him and fill him in on everything and then learn something about his affairs, how things went afterward. Have you seen him or heard anything of him?

GUALCINA: Neither heard nor seen anything at all. But look, here he is, here he really is, he is coming from over there in a hurry.

MARIO: Welcome, my dear Gismondo. Be cheerful on my account because there is a righteous reason.

GISMONDO: I already am cheered because I heard everything to my greatest pleasure and delight.

MARIO: When and from whom?

GISMONDO: Just now from Signor Lucio, your father, who in addition gave me the firm hope that he would yet be able to change me from the most miserable and unhappy man on earth to a contented one.

MARIO: But what am I hearing? Don't you have near you your Aurelia?

GISMONDO: Oh me, you don't know the very grave and painful troubles that have piled on me in a short time.

MARIO: *Oh, Dio, che cosa è?*

GISMONDO: *Messer Guicciardo, vero padre di lei et Lottieri, mio fratello, hanno discoperta tutta la frode et miseramente me l'hanno tolta.*

MARIO: *É adunque in Roma messer Guicciardo Gualandi?*

GISMONDO: *Sì, dico, et ogni cosa è stata per andare in rovina, ma io ho ferma speranza che ogni cosa sia di corto per assettarsi con sommo mio diletto. Ma, oh Mario, eccoli qua l'uno et l'altro. Salutaglili et priega Lottieri, mio fratello, che mi perdoni et me aiuti. Va' tosto alla volta sua, va' animosamente, non manchare.*

LOTTIERI: *Quanto a me, essendo le cose ite come sono andate et da stornare non si possono, non mi poteva accadere cosa più grata di questo vostro nuovo parentado.*

GUICCIARDO: *Et a me similmente, che mi pare allogarla a persona che l'ama assai, nobile et da bene.*

MARIO: *Messer Lottieri et voi messer Guicciardo, Dio vi salvi. L'amore et la giovinezza hanno fatto procedere a Gismondo, vostro fratello, più oltre che non si convenia. Pure egli vi è fratello di sangue et in honore et in reverenza desidera d'esservi buon figliuolo et voi vi prega siate contenti di fargli dare per moglie la figliuola costì di messer Guicciardo.*

LOTTIERI: *Mario, non più! Con messer Lucio, tuo padre, pure hora habbiamo ragionato a bastanza et ambodue ne siamo contenti et hora semo inviati là dentro, dove egli ci ha detto che noi lo dobbiamo aspettare.*

GISMONDO: *Fratello, assai vi ringratio, imponetemi che altro peso più vi aggrada, ma, di gratia, poi che nella maggiore mi havete contento, non mi dineghate la minore ancora. Et questo è che voi, senza indugio alchuno, operiate che il Zingaro, che poco innanzi fu preso per mio fallo et mio errore, sia lasciato libero et sicuro.*

MARIO: Oh, God, what is the matter?

GISMONDO: Signor Guicciardo, her true father, and Lottieri, my brother, have discovered all of the fraud and unhappily they have taken her from me.

MARIO: So is Signor Guicciardo Gualandi in Rome?

GISMONDO: Yes, I say, and everything was about to be ruined, but I have the firm hope that everything will shortly be resolved to my great delight. But, oh Mario, here come both of them. Greet them and beg Lottieri, my brother, to pardon me and help me. Go to him now, go with spirit, don't fail me.

LOTTIERI: As far as I'm concerned, given that things have gone as they have and cannot go back to the way they were, nothing could have befallen me that would make me happier than this new family relation.

GUICCIARDO: And the same to me, because it seems to me that I am placing her with a person who loves her very much and who is noble and respectable.

MARIO: Signor Lottieri and you, Signor Guicciardo, God save you. Love and youth pushed your brother Gismondo farther than he should have gone. Yet he is a brother by blood and in honor and in reverence desires to be a good son to you and begs you to agree to give him as his wife the daughter of Signor Guicciardo here.

LOTTIERI: Mario, say no more! We had a rather long discussion just now with Signor Lucio, your father, and both of us are happy about it, and now we are heading inside, where he told us that we are to wait for him.

GISMONDO: Brother, I thank you greatly. Impose on me whatever other weight you like but please, given that you have granted my wishes for the most part, don't deny me this small part. And this is that you, without further delay, do what it takes so that Gypsy, who a little earlier was arrested for something that was my fault and my error, may be set free and be safe.

LOTTIERI: *Di questo niente non dubitare, che e' gli si è dato di già ordine a tutto et penso che oramai ne sia fuori, perciò che ad instanzia mia solamente era guardato. Andiamo tutti allegramente in casa, dove attenderemo messer Lucio, che la vera luce ne ha arrecato delle tenebre nostre. In questo mentre, goderenci et rallegrerenci insieme.*

LICENZA

GUALCINA: *Brigata, non aspettate altramente che messer Lucio ritorni, perché hora mai si fa notte, egli desidera di venire senza che altri lo vegha. Voi spettatori, lodatene o biasimate come a voi pare, che tutto si piglierà a buona parte. Noi, con i nostri Accademici, faremo festa et allegrezza, con animo di trattenervi altra volta più commodamente, per hora bastavi il buon volere et lo havere incominciato. Fatevi con Dio et allegratevi.*

Il fine del *Furto*

—ɯ—

LOTTIERI: Have no fears about this, because all the necessary orders have already been given and I think that he is out by now, because at my insistence he was only put under watch. Let us all go happily home, where we shall await Signor Lucio, who brought the true light to our darkness. In the meanwhile, let us enjoy one another and celebrate together.

FAREWELL

GUALCINA: Troupe, you should not wait with us for Lucio's return, because by now night has fallen, and he does not want his arrival to be seen by others. You spectators, praise or criticize as you see fit, and everything will be taken in good spirit. We, together with the members of our Academy, will celebrate happily and will keep in mind providing you with entertainment in the future in greater comfort. For now may it be enough for you that we have good will and that we have begun. Go with God and be of good cheer.

The end of The Theft

—m—

NOTES TO THE EDITIONS OF THE *INTERMEDIO* MUSIC

ALEXANDER DEAN

All five of the *intermedi* have been transcribed from a single source:

> Francesco Corteccia, *Libro primo de madriali* [sic] *a quatro voci di Francesco Corteccia Maestro di Cappella dello illustrissimo et eccellentissimo Duca Cosimo de Medici Duca Secondo di Firenze. Con l'aggiunta d'alcuni madriali novamente fatti per la comedia di Furto* (Venice: Antonio Gardano, 1547). Copy consulted: Biblioteca del Conservatorio Luigi Cherubini, Florence.

The voices are set in score order (CATB) and labeled according to the source partbooks. The transcriptions use the original note values, with modern note shapes, beaming, and barlines. The cantus appears in treble clef in all but "O come nulla vale," for which the edition substitutes treble clef for the C2 clef of the source. Transposing treble clefs have been used for C4 clefs (altus) and C3 clefs (tenor). Accidentals on the staff apply throughout the bar according to modern practice. Accidentals have been added editorially in square brackets as necessary to accommodate the modern barlines. Inflections assumed to be added in performance *(musica ficta)* are given editorially above the staff and apply only to the notes they appear over. In addition, editorial alterations have been made to the following source readings: in no. 2, "Quanto sia dolce voglia," m. 29, altus, note 3 is f sharp; in no. 3, "Non le parol'o l'herbe," m. 2, altus, note 4 is dotted eighth.

—ꕥ—

Select Bibliography

Sources

Sources can be found in the Textual Note at p. xxvii.

Studies

Critical writing in English about D'Ambra and his play is extremely limited. The following list does not pretend to be exhaustive but supplies at least a set of materials for further consultation, many, by definition, in Italian.

Andrews, Richard. "D'Ambra, Francesco." In *The Oxford Companion to Italian Literature.* Oxford: Oxford University Press, 2002. https://www.oxfordreference.com/view/10.1093/acref/9780198183327.001.0001/acref-9780198183327-e-982.

———. "*Gl'Ingannati* as a Text for Performance." *Italian Studies* 37 (1982): 26–48.

———. *Scripts and Scenarios: The Performance of Comedy in Renaissance Italy.* Cambridge: Cambridge University Press, 1993.

Angelini, Franca. "*Vecchio e nuovo: i prologhi.*" In *Letteratura italiana* 6, 77–84. Turin: Einaudi, 1986.

Antolini, Bianca Maria. "Corteccia, Francesco." *DBI* 29.

Attolini, Giovanni. *Teatro e spattacolo nel Rinascimento.* Bari: Editori Laterza, 1988.

Apollonio, Mario, and Fabrizio Fiaschini. *Storia del teatro italiano.* Milan: Biblioteca universale Rizzoli, 2003.

Bargagli, Girolamo. *Dialogo de' giuochi che nelle vegghie sanesi si usano di fare.* Edited by Patrizia D'Incalci Ermini. Siena: Accademia Senese degli Intronati, 1982.

Blumenthal, Arthur R. *Theater Art of the Medici.* Hanover, NH: University Press of New England, 1980.

Bonora, Ettore. *Ritratti letterari del cinquecento.* Milan: La Goliardica, 1964.

Bramanti, Vanni. "Ritratto di Ugolino Martelli (1519–1592)." *Schede umanistiche* 2 (1999): 1–49.

———. *Uomini e libri del cinquecento fiorentino.* Manziana (Rome): Vecchiarelli, 2017.

Brand, Peter. "Disguise and Recognition in Renaissance Comedy." *Journal of Anglo-Italian Studies* 1 (1991): 16–32.

Bristol, Michael. "The Festive Agon: The Politics of Carnival." *Carnival and Theater: Plebian Culture and the Structure of Authority in Renaissance England.* New York: Routledge, 1985, 199–213.

Bouwsma, William. "Renaissance Theater and the Crisis of the Self." Chap. 9 in *The Waning of the Renaissance 1550–1640.* New Haven: Yale University Press, 2000.

Canguilhem, Philippe. "La cappella fiorentina e il duca Cosimo Primo." In *Cappelle musicali fra corte, stato e chiesa nell'Italia del Rinascimento: Atti del Convegno internazionale, Camaiore, 21–23 ottobre 2005.* Edited by Franco Piperno, Gabriella Biagi Ravenni, and Andrea Chegai, Historiae Musicae Cultores 108, 231–44. Florence: Leo S. Olschki, 2007.

Carrara, Eliana. *Prima e dopo Vasari: Celebrazioni, programmi e apparati effimeri nella Firenze dei Medici.* Pisa: ETS, 2020.

Celse-Blanc, Mireille. "Du travesti a la folie simulée, ou les jeux du masque dans la comédie siennoise." *Visages de la folie (1500–1650).* Ed. Augustin Redondo and André Rochon. Paris: Publications de la Sorbonne, 1981, 45–54.

Chambers, David, and François Quiviger. *Italian Academies of the Sixteenth Century.* London: Warburg Institute, 1995.

Ciasca, Raffaele. *L'Arte dei Medici e speziali nella storia e nel commercio fiorentino dal secolo XII al XV.* Florence: Olschki, 1927.

Civai, Alessandra. *Dipinti e sculture in casa Martelli: Storia di una collezione patrizia fiorentina dal quattrocento all'ottocento.* Florence: Opus Libri, 1990.

Clubb, Louise George. "Theatregrams." *Comparative Critical Approaches to Renaissance Comedy.* Ed. Donald Beecher and Massimo Ciavolella. Ottawa: Dovehouse Editions Canada, 1986, 15–33.

———. *Italian Drama in Shakespeare's Time.* New Haven: Yale University Press, 1989.

Cummings, Anthony M. *The Maecenas and the Madrigalist: Patrons, Patronage, and the Origins of the Italian Madrigal.* Memoirs of the American Philosophical Society 253. Philadelphia: American Philosophical Society, 2004.

————. *MS Florence, Biblioteca Nazionale Centrale, Magl. XIX, 164–167.* Royal Musical Association Monographs 15. Aldershot, Hants: Ashgate Publishing Limited, 2006.

————. "Music for Medici Festivals: Some Additional Works Recovered." *Musica Disciplina* 56 (2011): 275–334.

————. *Music in Golden-Age Florence, 1250–1750: From the Priorate of the Guilds to the End of the Medici Grand Duchy.* Chicago: University of Chicago Press, 2023.

————. "Musical References in Brucioli's *Dialogi* and Their Classical and Medieval Antecedents." *Journal of the History of Ideas* 71, 2 (April 2010): 181–85.

————. "On the Testimony of Fragments (or, Alessandro Striggio the Elder and the Genesis of the Genere Concitato)." *Studi musicali* 4, n.s. 1 (2013): 39–60.

————. *The Politicized Muse: Music for Medici Festivals, 1512–1537.* Princeton, NJ: Princeton University Press, 1992.

D'Accone, Frank A. "Corteccia, Francesco," *GMO.*

————, ed. *Music of the Florentine Renaissance* 8. Neuhausen-Stuttgart: American Institute of Musicology, 1981.

De Benedetti, Emilio. *La vita e le opere di Francesco d'Ambra.* Florence: La Rassegna Nazionale, 1899.

Dionisotti, Carlo. "Annibal Caro e il Rinascimento." *Cultura e scuola* 5.18 (1966): 26–35.

————. *"Mutazione" e "riscontro" nel teatro di Machiavelli e altri saggi sulla commedia del cinquecento.* Rome: Bulzoni, 1972.

Fabbri, Mario. "La vita e l'ignota opera-prima di Francesco Corteccia, Musicista italiano del Rinascimento." *Chigiana* 22, n.s. 2 (1965): 185–217.

————, Elvira Garbero Zorzi, and Annamaria Petrioli Tofani. *Il Luogo Teatrale a Firenze: Brunelleschi, Vasari, Buontalenti, 31 Maggio–31 Ottobre 1975.* Milan: Electa, 1975.

Ferroni, Giulio. *Il testo e la scena: Saggi sul teatro del cinquecento.* Rome: Bulzoni, 1980.

Fido, Franco. "*La scena del principe a Firenze: commedie di Francesco d'Ambra.*" In Patrizi, *Sylva*, 261–80.

Fubini, M. *Studi sulla letteratura del Rinascimento.* Florence: La Nuova Italia, 1948.

Gareffi, Andrea. *La scrittura e la festa: Teatro, festa e letteratura nella Firenze del Rinascimiento.* Bologna: Il Mulino, 1991.

Ghirardi, Sabina. "La ricerca di una lingua 'viva' e 'vera' per il romanzo. I notabilia manzoniani al *Furto* di Francesco d'Ambra." *Annali Manzoniani,* 3rd series, no. 1 (2018): 92–115.

Greco, Aulo. *L'istituzioni del teatro comico nel Rinascimento.* Naples: Liguori, 1976.

Haar, James. "The Florentine Madrigal, 1540–60." In *Music in Renaissance Cities and Courts: Studies in Honor of Lewis Lockwood.* Edited by Anthony M. Cumming and Jessie Ann Owens, 141–51. Warren, MI: Harmonie Park Press, 1997.

Herrick, Marvin T. *Italian Comedy of the Renaissance.* Urbana: University of Illinois Press, 1960.

Lasca, and Carlo Verzone, ed. *Rime burlesche edite e inedite.* [Hillsborough]: Lulu, 2015.

Lepri, Nicoletta. *Le Feste Medicee del 1565–1566: Riuso dell'antico e nuova tradizione figurativa.* Vol. 1. Vicchio di Mugello: LoGisma Editore, 2017.

Lorch, M. de Panizza. *Il teatro italiano del Rinascimento.* Milan: Edizioni di Comunità, 1980.

Mamone, Sara. *Il teatro nella Firenze medicea.* Milan: Mursia, 1981.

Mango, Achille. *La commedia in lingua del cinquecento.* Florence: Lerici, 1966.

Manzoni, Alessandro. *Scritti linguistici inedita.* Edited by Antonio Stella and Maurizio Vitale. Milan: Centro di Studi manzoniani, 2000.

Maylender, Michele. *Storie delle accademie d'Italia.* 5 vols. Bologna: Lincino Capelli, 1926, 3:355.

———, and S. E. Luigi Rava. *Storia Delle Accademie d'Italia.* Vol. 3, Finti-Lydii Lapidi. Bologna: A. Forni, 2002.

Ojeda Calvo, Maria del Valle. "Un ejemplo de la fortuna europea de Francesco d'Ambra. Los enredos de Martín, compuesta por

Cepeda." In *Filologia e critica nella modernità letteraria, Studi in onore di Renzo Cremante."* Edited by Andrea Battistini, Arnaldo Bruni, and Irene Romera Pintor, 11–31. Bologna: Clueb, 2012.

Patrizi, Giorgio, ed. *Sylva: Studi in onore di Nino Borsellino.* Rome: Bulzoni, 2002.

Phillips, Kristin Kathleen. "Changing Planes: Perspectives in Italian Renaissance Literature." Ph.D. diss., UCLA, 1999.

Pietropaolo, Domenico. "The Stage in the Text: A Theatrical Stratification of Italian Renaissance Comedy." In *Comparative Critical Approaches to Renaissance Comedy.* Edited byDonald Beecher and Massimo Ciavolella, 35–51. Ottawa: Dovehouse Editions, 1986.

Pirrotta, Nino. "Corteccia, Francesco." In *Enciclopedia dello spettacolo* 3, col. 1531–32. Rome: Le Maschere, 1956.

———, and Elena Povoledo. *Music and Theatre from Poliziano to Monteverdi.* Translated by Karen Eales. Cambridge Studies in Music. Cambridge: Cambridge University Press, 1982.

Plaisance, Michel. *Florence. Fêtes, spectacle et politique à l'époque de la Renaissance.* Manziana (Rome): Vecchiarelli, 2008.

———. "La politique culturelle de Cosme Ier et le fêtes annuelle a Florence, 1541–1550." In *Les fêtes de la Renaissance.* Edited by Jean Jacquot and Elie Konigson, 3, 133–52. Paris: Centre national de la recherche scientifique, 1975.

———. "Une première affirmation de la politique culturelle de Côme Ier: la transformation de l'Académie des 'Humidi' en Académie Florentine (1540–1542)." In *Les écrivains et le pouvoir en Italie à l'époque de la renaissance.* Edited by André Rochon, 361–438. Paris: Université de la Sorbonne nouvelle, 1973.

Radcliff-Umstead, Douglas. *The Birth of Modern Comedy in Renaissance Italy.* Chicago: University of Chicago Press, 1969.

Riposio, Donatella. *Nova Comedia v'appresento: Il prologo nella commedia del cinquecento.* Turin: Tirrenia stampatori, 1989.

Romei, Danilo, Michel Plaisance, Franco Pignatti, Francesco Berni, Anton Francesco Grazzini, Giovanni Maria Cecchi, and Francesco Beccuti. *Ludi Esegetici.* Manziana (Rome): Vecchiarelli, 2005.

Ronconi, Alessandro. "Prologhi 'plautini' e prologhi 'terenziani' nella commedia italiana del '500." In *Il teatro classico italiano nel*

cinquecento: Atti del convegno, Roma, 9–12 febbraio 1969, 197–214. Rome: Accademia nazionale dei Lincei, 1971.

Salingar, Leo. *Shakespeare and the Traditions of Comedy*. New York: Cambridge University Press, 1974.

Sapegno, Natalino. *Compendio di storia della letteratura italiana.* Florence: La Nuova Italia, 1963–65.

Scrivano, Riccardo. *Cinquecento minore*. Bologna: Zanichelli, 1966.

Stäuble, Antonio. "Tipologie dei prologhi nelle commedie del cinquecento." In *Lettere italiane* 63 (2011): 5–34.

Vestri, Veronica, and Eliana Carrara. *Prima e dopo Vasari: Celebrazioni, programmi e apparati effimeri nella Firenze dei Medici*. Pisa: ETS, 2020.

Yates, Frances Amelia. *Renaissance and Reform: The Italian Contribution*. London: Routledge & Kegan Paul, 1983.

—〰—

This Book Was Completed on 16 December 2024
At Italica Press, New York & Bristol.
It Is Set in Adobe Garamond
And Printed on
Acid-Free
Paper.

—〰—